Discovering English Churches

Discovering English Churches

A beginner's guide to the story
of the Parish Church from before the
Conquest to the Gothic Revival

Richard Foster

British Broadcasting Corporation

This book accompanies the BBC Television series
'Discovering English Churches', first broadcast on BBC2 from
17 October 1979 and repeated on BBC1 from 7 June 1981

Series presented by Donald Sinden and produced
by Richard Foster

Published to accompany a series of programmes
prepared in consultation with the
BBC Continuing Education Advisory Council

The drawings in this book are by
Brian Delf

This book is set in 11 on 12 point Monophoto Garamond
Printed in England by Jolly and Barber Limited, Rugby
and bound by Webb and Sons Limited, London N12

First published 1981
Published by the British Broadcasting Corporation
35 Marylebone High Street, London W1M 4AA

ISBN 0 563 16466 2

Contents

Acknowledgements

I would like to begin by expressing my gratitude to the clergy and parish councils of the churches up and down the country who helped in the production both of the 'Discovering English Churches' television series and of this book, in particular to the Very Reverend Peter Moore, Dean of St Albans, for casting a churchman's eye over these pages. I am greatly indebted to Peter Burman, Donald Findlay and David Williams of the Council for Places of Worship for providing research facilities and much erudite advice, and to the authors, too many to mention by name, whose works were consulted there.

My thanks are also due to designer Angela Reeves, and picture researcher Judy Moore, for turning the manuscript into a book; to Alan Heath, to whom I owe the original inspiration for the television series; and above all to my friend and colleague, Irene Clarke, for much encouragement and practical support throughout the project.

Richard Foster
Twickenham, 1980

Introduction

A parish church is rather like an old man's bicycle that has had three new wheels, two sets of handlebars, the pump stolen and replaced, and the frame repainted so many times that no one can count the colours – yet to its owner, it is still the same bicycle he bought all those years ago, a trusted friend and an object of great affection. So it is with our churches. As fashions and needs moved with the times, successive generations removed, replaced, restyled and restored. The parts changed, but the church remained. The community held on so tenaciously to its spiritual focus that many of our churches stand today on ground that has been regarded as holy or magic for thousands of years.

Stop at any country church on a sunny weekend and you are unlikely to be the only one there. Wandering along the aisles, peering up at the stained glass and browsing among the monuments, are people who would probably never dream of attending a church for regular worship. Yet here they are, drawn to an unfamiliar church, surely not by the smell of furniture polish and musty books, but by the appeal of the past and the need for a little peaceful silence in a noisy modern world.

There are over 16,000 parish churches in England, well over half of them dating from medieval times. Each of them is unique, a product of its own particular history. But each also shares in the tide of events that shaped this country and its people. For the visitor it is a free museum and art gallery. The everyday life of common folk, the adventures of kings and great families, the politics of Church and State, the skilled hand of the craftsman, the ravages of war and plague, and the rise and fall of commercial prosperity, are as clearly written in the stones of the parish church as are the beliefs it was built to enshrine. All we have to do is learn to read its language, allow ourselves some imagination, and be prepared for a little detective work. This book is intended to offer the church-browser a few clues and open some lines of investigation.

1: Through a Glass Darkly

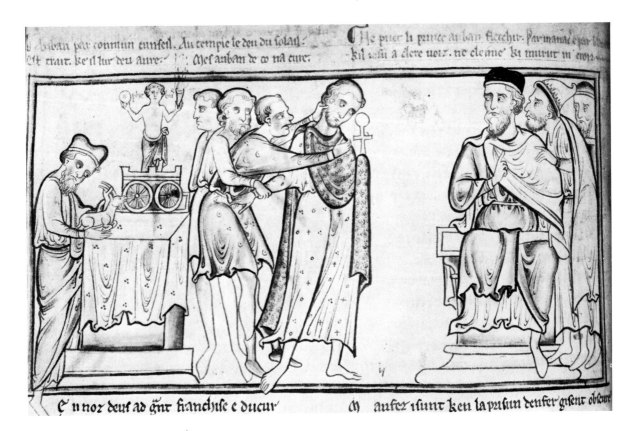

Cu noz teuf ab gur franchife e ducur | Cl autez ifunt ken la prifun tenfer grfent obfcur

St Alban refuses to worship at a
pagan altar. From a medieval
manuscript telling the story of
his martyrdom.

As long as any merchant could remember, a trade route had linked the
market places of Antioch, Tarsus, Athens and Constantinople with
the misty western regions of the British Isles. Such trade routes were
arteries of civilisation carrying new ideas and beliefs around the
ancient world. During the second century, following this route and
by-passing the Roman-dominated land mass of Europe, the traders'
ships brought a new and dangerous import to Britain – Christianity.
Dangerous because Roman rule embraced most of the known world,
and the worship of Jupiter and his pantheon was the official religion
of the Empire. Though normally tolerant of the religions native to
the lands it occupied, Rome saw a potential threat in the monotheism
of Christianity, and the new religion was suppressed in waves of
vicious and widespread persecution. But in Britain the Roman occupation was only really effective in the south and east; in the western
regions, beyond the reach of Rome, the Christian faith gained a
foothold that was to be vitally important in the rise of Christianity.

A century later the new religion had already infiltrated Roman-
occupied territory despite its persecution. A pagan Roman soldier in
the city of Verulamium gave shelter to a fugitive Christian priest.
Won over by the priest's continual prayers and piety, the soldier
became converted to Christianity. When the hide-out was discovered
by the Roman authorities, soldiers were sent to bring the priest before the magistrate. But the convert disguised himself in the priest's
cloak and went in his stead. The magistrate was not deceived, and
when the soldier refused to renounce his new faith he was sentenced
to death. His execution gave Britain her first martyr – St Alban.

Previous page
*Christianity was brought back to
England by Celtic monks from
Ireland – from the 'Discovering
English Churches' television series.*

A fragment of wall plaster scratched with a secret word square, from a third-century Roman villa.

Living in constant fear of persecution, the Christian community could have no churches or overt symbols of their faith, and the Christian ritual had to be a clandestine affair celebrated in private homes. But the rooms used for worship may have had secret symbols. A villa in Cirencester probably built at the end of the third century and excavated in 1868 had this cryptic inscription scratched into its wall plaster:

```
R    O    T    A    S

O    P    E    R    A

T    E    N    E    T

A    R    E    P    O

S    A    T    O    R
```

The square is a multiple palindrome in Latin reading the same in four ways. A similar word-square was later found in the ruined city of Pompeii, inscribed maybe two hundred years earlier. If *rotas opera tenet arepo sator* has any complete meaning, it is probably *the sower guides the plough wheels carefully* – a slogan hardly likely to provoke the wrath of the Roman authorities. To all appearances it was a rather clever word-square with a trivial message. But to the Christians it was a talisman with a hidden meaning, and one that remained hidden until sixty years after the discovery of the square. Not until the 1920s was it realised with amazement and some disbelief that the letters could be rearranged to form a cross spelling *Paternoster*, the Latin name for the Lord's Prayer, in each direction and flanked by two 'A's and two 'O's representing *alpha* and *omega*, 'the beginning' and 'the end'.

```
                          A
                          +
                          P
                          A
                          T
                          E
                          R
A  +  P  A  T  E  R  N  O  S  T  E  R  +  O
                          O
                          S
                          T
                          E
                          R
                          +
                          O
```

A gold coin bearing the head of Constantine the Great, the first Roman Emperor to be converted to Christianity.

There can be no doubt that an effective, well-organised network of Christian converts already existed beneath the surface of Roman society well before 312 when the 'Peace of the Church', a religious truce declared by Emperor Constantine, brought an end to persecution. With this new-found freedom the Church rapidly organised itself into an ecclesiastical model of the Roman administration, with

bishops governing territorial sees based on the Roman *civitates*. The subsequent conversion of the Emperor himself transformed the underground religion of a persecuted minority into the official religion of the Empire.

The first 'churches' were probably house-chapels, rooms set aside specifically for worship in the villas of the well-to-do. Now that Christianity was respectable, these rooms could be decorated with overt Christian symbols. The sacred monogram, the *Chi-Rho*, appears on the wall of a room in an early fourth-century villa at Lullingstone in Kent alongside representations of the owner's family at prayer. A door that opens directly to the outside suggests that the house-chapel was used by fellow Christians from the community as well as the residents of the villa.

Although Britain was now formally Christian, in fact the worship of Christ was just one among several religions. Outside the Romano-British élite of the towns the old Celtic religion, firmly rooted in earth-mother and fertility cults, was still more relevant and potent for the countryman – the *paganus* as the Romans called him, giving us our word 'pagan'. And there were other newcomers besides the Romans. An infiltration of Germanic peoples had already begun, though on a small scale compared with what was to come, and they too had their own gods – Woden and his warlike family.

Even within Romano-British society religious belief was very mixed. While the upper room at the Lullingstone villa was being used for Christian worship, a room downstairs was set aside for pagan rituals. At one extreme there were pious Christian families, and at the other there was the Roman army still remaining tenaciously loyal to the cult of Mithras, despite being forced into occasional recognition of Christ. A cautious path between the new Christianity and the old Roman pantheon was probably the road most people took. The ambiguity surrounding conversion to Christianity is illustrated by the mosaic floor of a fourth-century villa unearthed in a field near St Mary Hinton, Dorset, in 1963. Two roundels form the focal points of the

Two roundels, from a fourth-century mosaic floor, illustrate the ambiguity that surrounded conversion in Roman Britain. Left, *the earliest known British representation of Christ;* right, *Bellerophon of pagan mythology slaying the Chimaera*.

design. In one, the *Chi-Rho* appears behind the head of a man with pomegranates, Roman emblems of eternal life, on each side – without doubt a representation of Christ, and probably the earliest as yet discovered in Britain. The second roundel illustrates the pagan story of Bellerophon slaying a two-headed monster, the Chimaera. Are we standing in a pagan household or a Christian one? Has the designer used the representation of Christ as just another decorative god-motif, or are we looking at the floor of a house-chapel in which the story of Bellerophon was intended as an allegory of Christ's triumph over death or evil? Whatever our interpretation now, at a time when the persecution of Christians was still just within living memory, the ambiguity was doubtless a prudent one for the owner of the villa.

Within a hundred years of the last stone being set into the St Mary Hinton floor, the power of Rome began to crumble, and its legions were recalled from this distant outpost to defend the very heart of the Empire. The Romano-British left behind elected their own local 'governors' and tried to maintain the structure of the former adminis-tration. The house-chapel at Lullingstone continued to be used for Christian worship even though the villa's wealthy owners, harried perhaps by the threat of Germanic invasions, had followed the legions back to Rome and left the villa to fall into ruin. Without proper military support the attempt to carry on proved futile. Across the North Sea they came – Angles, Saxons and Jutes. The invaders flooded in, and the veneer of Britain's *Pax Romana* peeled away.

The newcomers were warlike tribes with a social structure and values quite different from those of the classical Mediterranean world. They built their settlements in the countryside well away from the Romano-British towns which were abandoned to decay:

> 'Snapped rooftrees, towers fallen,
> the work of the Giants, the stonesmiths,
> mouldereth.'

So sang an unknown Saxon poet describing *Aquae Sulis*, the Roman city of Bath. Such ruins were regarded with awe and suspicion, haunts of the angry ghosts of their vanquished inhabitants. But it was more than superstition that kept the conquering tribes away from the old cities. The new settlers had no use for the niceties of a pseudo-Roman society or for the piety and humility taught by its religion. Their deities were fierce warrior gods thundering across the sky and hungry earth-goddesses demanding satisfaction by sacrifice to ensure the return of spring and a fruitful harvest. Physical courage and unswerving loyalty were the virtues their tribal society needed and their religion preached. It had much in common with the earth-mother and fertility cults of the old Celtic religion that still held sway in many parts of Britain; it had little in common with the spirit of Christianity. As new territorial boundaries formed and reformed, and tides of refugees fled from one homestead to another, Christianity was beaten back. But it survived, just. In the remoter corners of the land, the distant north and west, Christianity held its ground despite the turmoil that swept the rest of the country.

No doubt the young Patricius and his Romanised British parents were only one of thousands of families split up by the anarchy of these times. Patricius, better known to us as St Patrick, was abducted from his home by a band of Irish pirates and sold into slavery in Ireland. After a few years he managed to escape on a ship to the Continent. There, probably in France, he received training in Christian theology and was consecrated a bishop. In 432 Patrick returned to Ireland to organise the Christianity he had already found there. Christianity had become synonymous with the Roman Empire, and Patrick sought to make Ireland a part of both Roman Christianity and civilisation. But the tide of history was against him. The collapse of the Roman Empire continued with France and Italy falling like Britain into the hands of the barbarians, thereby isolating Ireland from Mediterranean influence. Separated now from the mainstream of the Continental Church, the ghost of the falling Roman Empire, Christianity in Ireland developed along independent lines to form what is generally called the Celtic Church. Ireland was largely untouched by pagan invaders until the ninth century, and the intervening four hundred years provided the opportunity for the richly imaginative artistic and literary life of Irish Christianity to flourish. The Celtic Church was essentially monastic, each monastery linked to a particular tribe and governed by an abbot who acknowledged no ecclesiastical superior. Though these communities were autonomous and often remote establishments, they had become sophisticated centres of learning and provided bases from which groups of missionary monks set out to convert the Picts of Scotland and the Angles of northern England.

On the mainland of Britain social change was afoot. The temporary homesteads from which warring tribes had fought for every acre of land were fast becoming permanent townships where several different family groups lived together peaceably under the protection of a lord or thegn. The tribe-based form of society was giving way to a more organised hierarchical structure, foreshadowing the feudal system of England after the Norman Conquest. Now a man owed

Top
The invading Angles and Saxons brought their own fierce warrior gods with them. In this eighth-century manuscript the god Hermod rides to Hell to rescue another god, Baldur, who had been sacrificed and was finally restored to Heaven.

Above
St Patrick who organised Christianity in Ireland, while England reverted to paganism.

Above
*The waves of the Atlantic crash around
the Great Skellig Rock which provides
a dramatic and typically isolated setting for one of Ireland's ancient Celtic
monasteries.*

Right
*Part of a page from the Book of
Kells, a product of the rich artistic
and literary life of Irish Christianity.*

The Saxon cross in the churchyard of St Lawrence, Eyam, Derbyshire.

allegiance not to his clan, but to his thegn. In turn the thegn acknowledged fealty to one of the kings of the seven kingdoms into which the land had become roughly divided. The division of territories between the thegns contributed much to what was later to become our system of parishes. Many parishes today have boundaries which were first marked out during these Saxon centuries. Within his own domain the thegn took over the military, judicial and economic functions which until then had been the responsibility of the clan and which would later be performed by the State. This stabilisation and structuring of society did much to prepare the ground for the return of the Christian faith, which, in its relative coherence, would provide a spiritual dimension to the new-found social stability.

And so from Ireland the roving missionaries came, welcomed by some thegns, spurned by others. As they travelled across the countryside the monks set up simple wooden crosses to mark the meeting places where the faithful could gather to hear the Word, and the newly-converted to receive baptism. The 'Life of St Willibald' tells us that on the estates of great and good men 'they were wont to have, not a church, but the standard of the Holy Cross . . . lifted up on high'. Where the Christian community grew stronger, its strength was symbolised by the erection of stone crosses. Some of these Saxon crosses have survived, and good examples can be seen at Gosforth, Bewcastle and Irton in Cumbria, Ruthwell in Dumfriesshire, Eyam and Bakewell in Derbyshire, and Abercorn in West Lothian. Fragments of ancient crosses are fairly common and can often be found tucked away in some corner of the church labelled 'Saxon stone work'. Some fragments were even built into the church by medieval builders who possibly saw them as no more than convenient blocks of stone, as at Middleton in Yorkshire where four crosses were built into the tower of the church. The early crosses were beautifully carved with geometric patterns that echo the link with Ireland, and panels illustrating Christian themes through near-pagan eyes.

The old religion had been embodied in the standing stones and stone circles of antiquity that traced their forgotten geometry across the face of Britain, and it seems appropriate that the southward progress of conversion should have been marked by these crosses, the standing stones of the new religion. A stone circle or burial mound was often chosen as the site for a meeting cross. To the missionaries this represented the triumph of Christian over pagan, conveniently supplanting the old religion yet retaining the ground which local people already respected as being 'holy'. The Celtic word for 'holy ground' is *ciric* – pronounced 'chirich' – the root of our word 'church'. The ground itself was more important than the church which stood on it; not until as late as the tenth century was the word used for the actual building. Though religion changed, the holy place, the *ciric*, usually stayed the same; many of our churches stand today on ground that has been thought of as magic since the very earliest times. A circular churchyard is often a clue to such an ancient site. Fimber Church in Yorkshire is built on a Bronze Age barrow. In Buckinghamshire the parish church of Edlesborough and its circular churchyard rise above the surrounding fields on a mound which the place-name suggests was raised as the barrow of Eadwulf; and at

Above
Lonely and majestic – Castlerigg Stone Circle, a pre-Celtic ring thirty metres (one hundred feet) across, near Keswick, Cumbria.

Right
A striking example of the artistic link between the geometric designs carved on Saxon crosses and the interlace patterns of Irish manuscript illumination. Right, *a fragment of a cross shaft at Abercorn Church, West Lothian;* far right, *part of a page from the Psalter of St Gall.*

Pagan and Christian side by side at Rudston, Humberside. Many churches were built on ground already regarded as 'holy' or 'magic'. This, the tallest monolith in Britain, was known as a Rood Stone in early Christian times and gave the village its name.

Rudston, Humberside, the parish church shares its churchyard with the tallest standing stone in Britain, a monolith nearly eight metres (over twenty five feet) high.

In front of the meeting cross a portable altar was sometimes set up for the celebration of the Christian ritual – a practice that was to be much frowned upon in later years. Such an altar of the seventh century is preserved at Durham Cathedral. Where services were held with some regularity, the monks built a wooden, chapel-like shelter to protect the altar and the sacrament from the elements. The people soon followed suit by building a rough shelter for themselves, and it has been suggested that this may be one of the origins of the medieval custom by which the clergy were responsible for the building and repair of the chancel, the part of the church housing the altar, and the laity were responsible for the nave, the part of the church in which the congregation stood.

When a thegn embraced the new religion himself, he built a church for his own use and that of his people. The thegns lived in barn-like wooden halls and the new churches were generally built as additions to the existing complex of buildings, as a contemporary illustration of a nobleman's house shows. Being ship-builders, the

Above
The medieval tithe barn at Bradford-on-Avon, Wiltshire, gives an impression of the great wooden halls in which the Anglo-Saxon thegns lived.

Right
An Anglo-Saxon drawing of a nobleman's house showing the church, on the right, as part of the complex of domestic buildings.

St Augustine, whose mission from Rome arrived in 597.

Anglo-Saxons were skilled in timber construction, and living in a countryside that was still thickly forested, they usually built their new churches of wood. The customary use of wood as the construction material for all buildings is shown in the Saxon word for 'building' – *getimbrian* – which implies a timber structure. In fact a church built of stone was so rare that when St Ninian built one at Whithorn in Galloway 'it was commonly known as Candida Casa, the White House', according to Bede's eighth-century history of the English Church, 'because he built the church of stone which was unusual among the Britons'. Of these wooden Saxon churches, none has survived. They were too easily destroyed at the hands of pagan raiders, by the slow decay of time and by the ability of later generations to build bigger and better. But we can get some idea of what these early churches may have been like from the wooden nave of the church at Greensted in Essex. The walls are made of half tree trunks set upright with their flat surfaces facing inwards. Though they may have been built as late as the early eleventh century, these rough walls give us as close a glimpse as we can get of the wooden halls to which the first Saxon church-goers came to worship.

The reconversion of England was under way – though it was to be achieved not by the Irish monks alone, but by a two-pronged attack. In Rome little was known of the survival of Christianity in these islands, and Pope Gregory the Great, inspired according to legend by the sight of fair-haired English children being sold in a slave market, determined to send a mission to Britain to convert the pagan 'Angles into angels'. The task was entrusted to a party of forty monks led by St Augustine and later provided from Rome with 'all things necessary for the worship of the church, namely sacred vessels, altar linen, ornaments, priestly vestments, and relics of the holy apostles and martyrs'. More important for the history of church building, Augustine brought with him skilled stonemasons, familiar with Roman building traditions, from the Continent.

Augustine seems to have been a little nervous about his mission. In Brittany on the last leg of his journey he heard such terrifying stories of the ferocious British, that he sent word back to Rome that the pagans were untamable, and prepared to turn back. Pope Gregory however refused to abandon the mission and urged Augustine onwards. In 597 Augustine and his party finally landed at Thanet on the Kent coast where Ethelbert, King of Kent and the most powerful English monarch at the time, had agreed to accept the emissary of Rome. After his gloomy apprehensions it must have been a surprise to Augustine to be so well received. He was to learn that the King's wife, Bertha, was already a Christian and even had her own church in Canterbury, the capital of Kent, which the missionaries were to be permitted to use.

It had been Augustine's intention to proceed north and establish a base in London from which to convert the rest of the land. Unfortunately, London remained obstinate in its paganism, refusing to accept his overtures. So he settled for the more hospitable Canterbury as the spiritual base of his new Church in England.

Flexibility was the key to the remarkable survival power of paganism. Pagan temples were always hospitable places for a new,

One of the 'pantheon' of Christian saints – St Apollonia, whose intercessions were said to cure toothache, from the medieval chancel screen at St Michael's, Barton Turf, Norfolk.

would-be deity. By its very nature, monotheism excludes and denies all rivals, but a religion based on a pantheon of gods can always find room for one more, or adapt an old god to fit a new model. When the Romans had arrived in the first century bringing Jupiter and his family with them, the immortal immigrants found the native deities to be friendly. The two pantheons were similar in many ways. It was not hard for Jupiter or Jove, father-god and sky thunderer, to become equated with Thunor, the local thunder-god – an association that was ratified when the Roman calendar was adopted in Britain and the fifth day of the week, *Jovis dies* in Latin, became called *Thunres dæg*, our modern Thursday. After the Anglo-Saxon takeover the gods changed their names again, but their personalities remained much the same.

Pope Gregory was well aware that the process of conversion would have to be one of such absorption and transformation. In a message to Augustine he advised that the pagan temples should not be pulled down, but that the idols in them be destroyed and 'holy water sprinkled in the temples, altars built, and relics set there. Let them become temples of the true God. So the people will have no need to change their places of concourse. And where of old they were wont to sacrifice oxen to demons, in this matter also there should be some substitution of solemnity: on the day of the saint to whom the church is dedicated, or the feasts of the holy martyrs whose relics have been set there, let them slay their beasts, no longer as a sacrifice to the devil, but for a social meal in honour of Him whom they now worship.' And so the feasts of the pagans became the festivals of the Church, and the memory of their origins faded into obscurity.

Christianity overcame the handicap of monotheism by setting up its own 'pantheon', a pantheon not of gods, but of saints. A pagan charm became a Christian prayer by adding a few words of Latin, to the laity the mystic language of the Church, and replacing the name of the heathen deity with that of Christ or one of His saints. Some of the saints were recruited from the early fathers of the Church, others were transmuted from pagan originals. A sufferer from toothache for example would invoke the blessing of St Apollonia for relief. She is usually represented holding a tooth in a pair of long forceps. Teeth are often seen as emblems of immortality by primitive peoples, and her long forceps are similar to a pair found in Delphi at the Temple of Apollo where they probably had some ritual use. St Apollonia's feast day, 9 February, falls within two days of the old Roman feast of Apollo, which would certainly have been observed in Britain and which was called the Apollonia. So looking at the saint as she appears in medieval rood screens and windows, perhaps we see the echo of a pagan feast that the early Christian Church considered too popular to be abolished in a hurry.

Not all the personalities of pagan folklore found Christian counterparts, but some managed to leave their mark on our churches just the same. For instance, a very common decorative motif takes the form of a human face peering through a mask of leaves which often spring from the corners of his mouth. This image is found carved on capitals, corbels, bosses and most frequently on misericords, the underside of tip-up seats in the choir stalls that provided a place for much of the

Echoes of pagan ritual:

Left to right
A giant built of wickerwork in which the ancient Britons are said to have burned a live human victim – the Green Man – to ensure the fertility of the land (recreated for the film 'The Wicker Man').

The Green Man carved on the doorway of St Mary and St David's, Kilpeck, Hereford and Worcester.

The Green Man on a misericord at Holy Trinity, Coventry.

The Green Man in his guise as the Garland King during a traditional Derbyshire ceremony.

'underground' imagery of our medieval churches. This tree-man appears both in naturalistic and very stylised forms. The foliage surrounding him varies, but significantly the most common is that of the oak, the holy tree of the Druids. Significant because his origin lies not in the stories of the Bible, but in the worship of trees and in pagan fertility rituals. As part of the midsummer rites the spirit of the tree was personified by the Green Man, a youth dressed in foliage who was led in procession through the fields to ensure the fertility of the land. Originally he may even have been sacrificed to provide the Earth Goddess with a sturdy young mate – in his 'Gallic Wars' Julius Caesar describes Druid rituals in which human victims were burned alive in giant images woven of wickerwork and covered with foliage. With the coming of Christianity the potency of the Green Man was sapped, and the ritual itself echoed down the centuries until it became merely a traditional ceremony of obscure significance, like that at Castleton in Derbyshire. There, in his guise as the Garland King, the Green Man still rides through the village covered from head to foot in a cage of leaves and flowers. Even so he rides not to the fields, but to the parish church where his floral cage is hoisted to the top of the tower. Though robbed of his significance, the popularity of the image of the Green Man was undiminished. There is scarcely a medieval church in England in which his presence cannot be found in some nook or cranny, and even some Edwardian suburban houses show his face in its leafy mask peering down at us.

If it seems strange that the Church should have readily adopted the image of the Green Man despite his dubious history, it is even more surprising that the Earth Goddess herself should appear in our churches. From the earliest times the English pagans had paid homage to the idol of a female figure with enormous genitals, which

The Earth Goddess, in her embodiment as 'sheela-na-gig', carved on a corbel at St Mary and St David's, Kilpeck.

represented the Earth Goddess and is called, in Anglicised Gaelic, *sheela-na-gig*. Today eighteen of these sheelas are known in England, and all but one of them are to be found in Christian churches. So it is clear that the old gods did not die overnight; some were absorbed into the new religion and others allowed for some time to coexist with it. As Pope Gregory had told Augustine, 'The Holy Church chastises some things through zeal, and tolerates some through meekness, and connives at some things through discretion, so that she may often, by this forbearance and connivance, suppress the evil which she disapproves.' A violent conversion would have been unwise and unnecessary since many parallels could be found between the old religion and the new. Having incorporated heathen customs into its practice, the Church could then set about the obliteration of their original significance with time and the monopoly of the written word on its side.

With conversion progressing on two fronts – the Irish missionaries of the Celtic Church from the north and west, and the Roman mission of Augustine from the south-east – the country became ostensibly Christian within the space of three-quarters of a century. But though the two Churches brought the same message, it came in different forms. The Celtic Church had grown up virtually isolated from the influence of Continental Christianity, and many of its practices now diverged from those of the Roman Church. The Celtic monks did not use the round tonsure on the crown, but shaved their heads from ear to ear, possibly as the Druid priests had done. They dedicated each of their churches in the name of the monk who had founded it, rather than an established Christian saint. There were differences too in the ministry of baptism. Even the celebration of Easter, the most important festival in the Christian calendar, fell on different dates. Underlying these disagreements was a contrast in temperament and structure, the Celtic Church defending its independence, and the Roman Church proud of its cosmopolitan hierarchy.

While the two Churches had worked in different territories there had been little friction, but as each gained ground, rivalry grew up between them. Eventually a choice had to be made. At the time, the *bretwalda*, the Lord of the Britons, was Oswiu, King of Northumbria, and in 664 he summoned the famous Synod of Whitby to resolve the dispute. The fundamental question was the acceptance or rejection of the supremacy of Rome, a question that was to repeat itself in English history. Oswiu himself opened the debate saying that those who awaited one kingdom in Heaven and served one God should have one rule of life. The one rule, it was finally decided, was to be that of Rome. For Northumbria at least the question was settled, and those bishops of the Celtic Church who could not bring themselves to fall in line with the royal judgement sought exile in other regions where their form of the Church still held sway. But it was not long before the rule of Rome came to embrace the whole of the British Isles.

There had been more at stake than the choice between two forms of worship; the acceptance of the Roman Church brought England back into the cultural mainstream of Europe and paved the way for the fusion of her three traditions – the Anglo-Saxon, the Celtic and the Roman – into an age bursting with literary and artistic vitality.

Left
The tenth-century crypt of
St Wystan's, Repton, Derbyshire.
Each of its columns is carved from a
single piece of stone.

Right
The blessing of the Church added a
new dimension to the notion of king-
ship; the coronation of Eadgar
from a modern stained glass window
in Bath Abbey.

The bishops of the Roman Church were less monastic in outlook than their Celtic counterparts, and fostered the growth of the non-monastic clergy who lived among and ministered to the laity. Bishops and thegns worked together to set up a system of parishes corresponding broadly to the division of the land between the thegns. Each parish was to have its own place of worship and an endowment of land or money to support a priest. In many ways the priest was still a private chaplain to the thegn who had provided the land or endowment for the church. The proximity of church to manor house in many of our villages bears witness to this relationship. Although a parish priest was directly under the authority of his bishop, the thegn reserved the right to choose him, a right that remained with the lord of the manor throughout medieval times.

Opting for Rome added an impetus to the already established move away from tribalism towards feudalism, a movement that led eventually to a racial and political unity under one king. The notion of kingship now gained an extra dimension. The blessing and support of the Church conferred on the Crown a certain sanctity and a claim to the loyalty of its subjects over and above the might of the sword. Since the Church held a monopoly on learning, the Crown's chief advisers were inevitably churchmen, and so in their hands lay much of the responsibility for the development of the economic and legal systems of the country. The Church of Rome, having based its structure on the administration of the Roman Empire, now, in its turn, provided the administrative model for the emerging English nation. The division between Church and State was a blurred one; the clergy had both ecclesiastical and civil faces. Through them until the end of the twelfth century, the Church was probably controlling a good half of the country's labour force and economic resources in education, the training of administrators, the development of farming methods and particularly in the building of churches and the many crafts that involved.

Above and right

Roman tiles, possibly from a nearby ruined villa, were used to create a decorative effect above doors and windows at All Saints, Brixworth, Northamptonshire. Built in the seventh century (belfry and spire added in the fourteenth), Brixworth is perhaps the most impressive of our Saxon churches.

The ascetic Celtic monks had been content to build even their cathedrals out of wood and rushes, but their successors built with the grandeur of Rome in their heads and preferred the permanence of stone where possible. The ruins of Roman cities and villas still stood in the English countryside, and they were to serve both as examples for the builders and sources of ready-hewn stone. At Over Denton in Cumbria the masons carried off an entire arch from a Roman fort on Hadrian's Wall to serve as a chancel arch in their church. Roman tiles are incorporated in the walls of the Church of All Saints, Brixworth in Northamptonshire, to achieve a decorative effect round doorways and windows. Since the churches harked back to the buildings of ancient Rome both in inspiration and style, this period of architecture is called the *Romanesque*, and is usually divided into *Pre-Conquest Romanesque* and *Norman Romanesque*.

The churches of the pre-Conquest Romanesque period were based on two models – the Roman *basilica plan* and the *Celtic plan*. It was from a compromise of these plans that the typical English parish church was to evolve.

The Roman basilica had served the functions of temple, exchange and lawcourt, and when the first churches came to be built these familiar and imposing public halls provided the obvious prototypes.

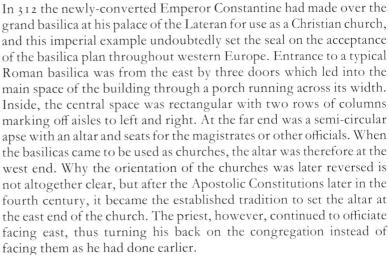

The polygonal Saxon apse of All Saints, Wing, Buckinghamshire, marred only by windows of a later date. The apse was the main distinguishing feature of the basilica plan favoured by the Continental Church.

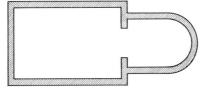

The basilica plan

In 312 the newly-converted Emperor Constantine had made over the grand basilica at his palace of the Lateran for use as a Christian church, and this imperial example undoubtedly set the seal on the acceptance of the basilica plan throughout western Europe. Entrance to a typical Roman basilica was from the east by three doors which led into the main space of the building through a porch running across its width. Inside, the central space was rectangular with two rows of columns marking off aisles to left and right. At the far end was a semi-circular apse with an altar and seats for the magistrates or other officials. When the basilicas came to be used as churches, the altar was therefore at the west end. Why the orientation of the churches was later reversed is not altogether clear, but after the Apostolic Constitutions later in the fourth century, it became the established tradition to set the altar at the east end of the church. The priest, however, continued to officiate facing east, thus turning his back on the congregation instead of facing them as he had done earlier.

The Continental *basilica plan* was, of course, the one favoured by Augustine and introduced by him to Britain, though it is likely that some of the pagan temples he was to reconsecrate here would already have been built in similar Roman fashion. As it appeared in English churches, the basilica plan consisted of two cells: a nave to house the

27

Above
A nineteenth-century drawing of St Mary's, Reculver, Kent, shows the demolition of the last example of a Saxon triple arch which usually separated nave and chancel in basilica plan churches.

Right
The Saxon church of St Lawrence, Bradford-on-Avon, Wiltshire, built in the eighth century with a square-ended chancel in the Celtic fashion.

Opposite
The dark, evocative interior of St Lawrence. A tall, narrow archway separates nave from chancel. Above it, new stonework shows where a Rood was once carved.

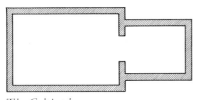

The Celtic plan

congregation, and a chancel in which stood the stone altar. The nave was rectangular with a west entrance and usually without side aisles; the chancel ended in a semi-circular or polygonal apse. The two parts of the church were separated by a screen of three arches supported by two columns. Unfortunately this dividing triple arch cannot now be seen; the last surviving example at St Mary's, Reculver in Kent, was demolished at the beginning of the last century.

True to form, the *Celtic plan* was more austere – in its simplest form an undivided rectangular cell, but more commonly two-celled. Both parts were rectangular, the chancel being smaller and narrower than the nave. A single narrow archway between the two virtually obscured the congregation's view of the altar. It has been suggested that the consecration of the sacrament, in the earliest days of the church, took place out of sight of the laity behind curtains drawn round the altar, and the narrowness of Saxon chancel arches may be an echo of that custom. Instead of a west door, the builders of Celtic plan churches seem to have preferred side entrances to north and south. Often porches were added which seem disproportionately large, as at St Lawrence, Bradford-on-Avon in Wiltshire, where the north porch is almost as big as the chancel itself. Various ideas have been put forward to explain its size, including the suggestion that women were excluded from the main body of the church and only allowed to hear the services from the porch. The most probable

The English preference for square-ended chancels revealed by excavations on the site of St Mary's, Winchester, Hampshire. The foundations show clearly how an early apsidal chancel was squared off when it was rebuilt on the rectangular Celtic plan.

explanation however is a less sexist and more practical one. The porch was used for much of the more secular side of church matters. Civil business was transacted there, disputes argued, bargains struck, and oaths witnessed by the priest. The door of the north porch at Bradford-on-Avon is set off-centre, which may have been to allow space for a small altar to be placed against the east wall. Part of the baptism service was held there and marriages were solemnised, not in the church itself, but in the porch. When, a few hundred years later, Chaucer was to write of his Wife of Bath 'husbands at church door she had five', he meant it quite literally.

The Saxon builders brought together the Celtic and basilica plans and developed an arrangement that was distinctively English. The Celtic Church may have been the loser at Whitby, but its influence on the architecture of the parish church largely overwhelmed that of the Roman Church. The English stubbornly preferred their chancels to be square-ended, despite the repeated introduction of the apse by the Romans, and later the Normans. Side entrances remained more popular than west doors, and the subsequent adoption of the west tower provided the most prominent and typical feature of the English parish church.

Although many Saxon churches, like St Lawrence at Bradford-on-Avon, had no towers, where pre-Conquest masonry is to be found it is most likely to be in the tower. Well over seventy Saxon towers are still standing. Towers had been built for bells as early as the seventh century. According to his biographer, St Wilfrid built a bell tower at his church in Hexham, Northumberland, which was founded in 674. Most of the early towers were probably independent structures of timber. The stone towers that survive are of a later date, and the large number to be found on or near the east coast may suggest that they also had a defensive purpose. From the end of the eighth century Viking raids became almost a feature of everyday life in these eastern regions. Their raids were fast and savage. Churches were reduced to blazing shells and their blackened stonework smashed down. A pillaging Dane captured by the villagers could expect an equally violent fate. There is a legend that those caught were flayed alive and their skins nailed to the church door. In fact, analysis of particles of skin found under the iron-work on doors of three Essex churches confirmed that the skin was not only human but also from fair-haired victims. In these troubled times the church tower could have provided a place of refuge and a store for the village's weapons. A common feature was a room for the priest with a small window looking down into the nave from the west wall of the church.

The tops of the Saxon towers we see today have usually been refinished in a later style, as at All Saints, Earls Barton in Northamptonshire, where the most splendid pre-Conquest tower in the country is topped with an incongruous battlemented parapet. Continental examples and the evidence of contemporary illuminated manuscripts suggest that a tower was originally finished with a pyramid-shaped wooden roof or blunt four-sided spire, like that of the church of St Mary the Virgin at Sompting in West Sussex. Many of the Saxon towers in East Anglia are round, which may again be evidence of a defensive purpose, but probably has more to do with the lack of local

Above
The Saxon tower of All Saints, Earls Barton, Northamptonshire, famous for its decorative pilaster strips and long and short work. The incongruous battlemented parapet was added later.

Right
Saxon towers were originally topped with pyramid-shaped timber roofs like this one at St Mary's, Sompting, West Sussex.

Far right
The tower of St Peter's, Foncett St Peter, Norfolk. Round towers were common in areas where good building stone was not available to make the quoins at the corners of a square tower.

Top
Long and short work, a characteristic of Saxon building which provides extra strength at the corners of rubble-built walls, from All Saints, Earls Barton.

Above
A typical, round-headed Saxon window with baluster shafts, from the tower of All Saints, Earls Barton.

stone of dense enough texture to make strong *quoins* for the corners of a square tower. It was not until after the Conquest when Caen stone was imported from Brittany that the masons of East Anglia had freestone good enough to demonstrate the abilities brought to fruition in their lovely 'wool churches' of the fifteenth century.

With good stone in short supply, the walls of most pre-Conquest churches were built of rough rubble incorporating any material conveniently to hand. *Herringboning* is a method of building up a rubble wall which is typical of this period. Rows of stones are laid diagonally, each row leaning alternately to left and right to produce a characteristic zigzag effect. Since the walls were only made of rubble, they needed to be sturdily built and were usually almost a metre (three feet) thick. To achieve the extra strength needed at the corners of a building, the Saxons used large vertical stone slabs set alternately with horizontal slabs which penetrated and gripped the walling. This *long and short work*, as it is called, went out of fashion soon after the arrival of the Normans, and so its presence in a church is often a sign of pre-Conquest building. A plaster made of hair and straw mixed with sand and lime was used inside and out to provide the rough walls with a smoother surface. The cut stone round doorways and windows was left unplastered and usually given a coat of lime-wash. The plain walls were often decorated on the outside with thin flat stone battens called *pilaster strips* (or *lesenes*) after the pilasters of classical architecture. The pilaster strips served no structural purpose and were purely for decorative effect, in some places, like Earls Barton (see page 31), weaving a geometric network, in others simply dividing a wall into bays.

The use of the narrow pilaster strips underlines a general vertical emphasis in pre-Conquest architecture which recalls its debt to the techniques of timber construction. There had been a natural conservative tendency to translate the familiar proportions and designs of woodwork into stone. The nave of St Lawrence, Bradford-on-Avon, for instance, is almost twice as high as it is wide, giving the whole structure a vertical emphasis which is also apparent in the tall, narrow doorways and arches. Windows too show the influence of timber building techniques. They often occur in pairs or even larger groups, with adjacent lights separated by a short shaft shaped like a lathe-turned wooden baluster. The shaft is not fitted flush with the surface of the wall but set back in the centre of its thickness. Window heads are sometimes triangular, formed by two stone slabs leant together, once again in imitation of timber construction. There are also round-headed windows in the Roman fashion, but instead of being made up of separate wedge-shaped *voussoirs*, they are often cut from one piece of stone. The windows were very small and often set high up in the walls. The masonry round them was usually cut back at an angle to let in more light. It must still have been very dark inside the church, but the priest doubtless knew his Latin offices by heart and the congregation would have been incapable of reading even in broad daylight.

Today the plain interiors of these pre-Conquest churches seem to us austere and primitive, making it hard to imagine the grandeur of the church amidst a village of little better than wooden huts, or the

One of two flying angels, all that survives of the Saxon Rood at St Lawrence's, Bradford-on-Avon, Wiltshire. The quality of its design and execution exemplifies the sophistication of late Saxon carving.

wonder it must have struck in the hearts of men and women whose lives depended so precariously on scraping a living from the land. To correct our impression we must put back the carving and colour that time has almost completely destroyed. Mouldings and sculpture were picked out in coloured distemper. The plastered walls were painted with patterns and pictures, the most popular being the Last Judgement and St Christopher. By far the most important representation appeared above the chancel arch. There was painted or carved the *Rood* – the figure of Christ on the Cross usually flanked by the Virgin Mary to the left and St John the Evangelist to the right. This focal point of the church takes its name from the Anglo-Saxon word for the Cross itself. At the church of St Swithin, Headbourne Worthy in Hampshire, the battered outline of a carved Saxon Rood can still be seen, despite the mutilations of iconoclasts of a later age. But the original nave is now a vestry, and the Rood, obscured by iron tie-bars and bare electric light bulbs dangling on long flexes, presents a sorry sight. At St Lawrence, Bradford-on-Avon, we are left with a happier if less complete impression. All that remains there of the Rood is a pair of carved angels flying with napkins to catch the drops of blood from Christ's hands. Judging by these splendid carvings the whole Rood must have been magnificent.

The return of Roman Christianity to Britain acted as a catalyst, bringing about a fusion between the equilibrium of classical antiquity and the dynamism of the pagan world. From this fusion the cosmology of the medieval world was to emerge. Christian imagery became charged with pagan intensity and vigour, a vigour well illustrated by the strident verse of the Saxon poem 'Dream of the Rood'. This poem first appears in runic form, cut into the Saxon cross at Ruthwell. It closely parallels an earlier poem written in honour of Baldur, a pagan god who had much in common with Christ. In the poem, the Cross itself describes the scene of the Crucifixion. The picture it draws is not that of the Lamb going meekly to sacrifice, but the heroic warrior, the thegn's man, eagerly meeting his fate with honour. Let us end our glimpse through a glass darkly by bringing together the Christ of the 'Dream of the Rood' with His image as a Saxon craftsman carved it for the little church at Daglingworth in Gloucestershire:

Almighty God ungirded Him,
    eager to mount the gallows,
unafraid in the sight of many:
    He would set free mankind.

I shook when His arms embraced me
    but I durst not bow to ground,
stoop to Earth's surface.
    Stand fast I must.

I was reared up, a rood.
    I raised up the great King,
liege lord of the heavens,
    dared not lean from the true.

How they mocked at us both!
    I was all moist with blood
sprung from the Man's side
    after He sent forth His soul.

2: After the Conquest

Fighting knights from a painted frieze said to represent the 'Psychomachia', the allegorical battle of the Virtues and Vices, at All Saints', Claverley, Salop.

Previous page
A medieval illustration of the Norman succession to the English throne, showing William the Conqueror top left.

With the advent of the millennium it was widely believed that the last trumpet would sound and the world come swiftly to its end. On the contrary, the year AD 1000 passed with no such calamity and ushered in a century of regenerated vitality. 'It was as though the very world had shaken herself and cast off her old age, and was now clothing herself in a white robe of new churches', wrote the eleventh-century chronicler, Raoul Glaber. Doubtless Anglo-Saxon England would have been content to remain on the periphery of this expansive mood in Europe had it not been for the decisive events of 1066. Continental influence had already been felt quite strongly at the court of Edward the Confessor, but with the successful conquest of England by William, Duke of Normandy, the spring tide of Norman energies broke against the country's shores, turning the trickle of Continental culture into a flood.

At a national level England mustered no resistance to its new Norman masters. The country was still a patchwork of geographical areas, a mosaic of races lacking any national identity. It was an assortment of parts that had yet to be forged into a whole – and that was the job the Normans meant to do. Their power of organisation and tireless energy left no corner of England untouched. As the territories of the Anglo-Saxon thegns and earls were seized one by one, the Conqueror granted them to his barons. A strict, land-based feudalism was imposed everywhere, replacing the existing hierarchies that had grown up in forms that differed from region to region. The basic unit of territory was now the *Manor*. Manors were grouped into *Hundreds*, and Hundreds into *Shires* or *Counties*. William rewarded his barons' loyalty by granting them possession of manors, but he was careful to scatter each baron's land widely throughout the country. This judicial distribution effectively prevented the barons from building up their lands into large principalities whose power might

A 'crocodile head' from St Mary and St David's, Kilpeck, Hereford and Worcester. One of the many carved ornaments at the church which show that Scandinavian influence was still felt in the more remote corners of the country despite persecution by the Conqueror.

.then have challenged that of the Crown, as had already happened on the feudal mainland of Europe.

New men from Normandy were put in charge over native Englishmen in all walks of life. Though only 25,000 Normans at most could have settled here during the first twenty years after the Conquest, such was their impact that the Anglo-Saxon population rapidly became second-class citizens under the rule of an aristocracy who did not even speak their language. The language of Court and culture was French; the language of Church and learning was Latin. Written Anglo-Saxon all but disappeared, and the spoken language was seen as the despised and barbarous tongue of an ignorant peasantry. Not until the middle of the fourteenth century did French give way to English in courts of law. Much of our vocabulary of warfare, politics, justice, religion, cookery and art derives from the French of this time and records in language the areas of life to which the Normans made their greatest contributions. But the benefits of the Conqueror's regime had their price, and, of course, it was the conquered who had to pay. As the new lords of the manor claimed their rents and dues, the standard of living for the Anglo-Saxon dropped sharply. As the feudal structure tightened its grip, his burden of civil and military obligations grew heavier. The native population, downgraded economically and culturally, resented their new masters. Risings were frequent despite the tight military rule made manifest in the network of hastily built castles that spread across the country.

The risings were put down with swift force and little mercy. When two northern earls, Edwin and Morcar, rebelled for a second time, William ravaged their lands with scorched-earth ferocity. Man and beast were slaughtered alike, and from York to Durham no house was left standing. The smoking countryside lay neglected and depopulated for some sixteen years – an awesome warning to the rest of England that the Normans meant business. The churches were destroyed with the villages, so few of North Yorkshire's churches date from before the twelfth century.

The north, especially Yorkshire, had been heavily populated by Danish settlers, and the strong influence of Scandinavian society and culture had long served to divide it politically from the rest of England. William's 'harrying of the north', however, drastically reduced the numbers of these settlers and so paved the way to a more unified England. Many of those who escaped the sword fled west or sold themselves into slavery in Scotland, beyond the reach of the Normans. The resistance of Scandinavian society was broken, and north and south were brought closer together under the common yoke of feudalism. But the influence of Scandinavian design lingered on in the pockets of the countryside to which they fled. In the 'crocodile heads' that decorate the west end of the twelfth-century church of St Mary and St David at Kilpeck, Hereford and Worcester, we see perhaps an echo of the fearsome figureheads that guided Viking long boats across the North Sea.

Nearly all our cathedrals and parish churches were established during the century that followed the Norman Conquest. Most were rebuilt by succeeding generations, but a great number survive, in part or whole, as evidence of the successful conquest and the ambition and

The first years of Norman rule were devoted to building the great cathedrals and castles that were the outward show of establishment power. Durham Cathedral, towering over the River Wear, is one the most outstanding Romanesque churches in Europe, an impressive monument to the ambition and organisational abilities of England's new masters.

energy of the men who had achieved it. Almost within a generation of the 'harrying of the north' the Cathedral and Castle of Durham rose imperiously above the waters of the Wear – a remarkable achievement in a region that had been poor enough even before the Conqueror's terrible vengeance. William ordered the castle to be built on his way back from a foray against Malcolm of Scotland. He saw the area as a buffer state vital to defence against the Scots, and therefore needing strong local government. In these exceptional circumstances the bishopric of Durham was elevated to a palatinate, a virtual kingdom where the palatine bishop enjoyed every secular power that did not trespass on that of the Crown itself. The imposing architecture of Cathedral and Castle witnessed the twin powers of Church and State.

Masons and labourers at work, from a medieval illuminated manuscript. The exploitation of labour under the feudal system, which was imposed throughout the country, enabled the Normans to organise building on an unprecedented scale.

The reorganisation of the Church was as extensive as that of the State. Even before William set sail for Hastings, he had managed to convince Rome that the invasion was to be something of a crusade. Rome was keen to enforce celibacy on the clergy here and to persuade the English Church to toe the official line more closely, so William was granted the Papal banner and blessing on his venture. The Normans believed that they had come to a country whose religious life was poorly developed and badly organised. They were dismayed to find that the Anglo-Saxons had built their cathedrals, not in major towns, but in the remote countryside, a custom which the early historian William of Malmesbury ascribed to the influence of the Celtic missionaries who had 'preferred to bury themselves ingloriously in marshes than to dwell in lofty cities'. To the Normans, cathedrals were important administrative centres that needed to be close to the flux of everyday life not hidden away from it. So in 1075 the Council of London decreed that dioceses should be organised from towns instead of insignificant villages. Only ten of the pre-Conquest cathedrals retained their former status. Almost half the bishops had already been replaced by William's men, and those that were left were to be succeeded by Normans. By 1080 Wulfstan of Worcester was the only Anglo-Saxon bishop remaining in office. In the monasteries the story was much the same; many of the abbots kept their positions, but their successors were not to be Anglo-Saxons. This influx of foreign clergy brought a much needed new life to the Church. The standards of learning and religious devotion were raised, and the efficiency and number of ecclesiastical houses increased.

The need for new cathedrals and monastic churches launched a programme of building on a scale unprecedented in England and matched only by the urban expansion produced by the Industrial Revolution some eight hundred years later. The architecture of this period, roughly the century that followed the Conquest, is described as *Norman Romanesque* to distinguish it from the earlier Romanesque style of the Anglo-Saxon builders. Both are called Romanesque since their forms were derived ultimately from the architecture of ancient Rome, but what was a distant echo in pre-Conquest work, was, in the work of the Normans, a more direct inheritance through the classical buildings of Roman Gaul. From them the Normans had acquired the semicircular arch, the barrel vault and the division of piers into base, shaft and capital.

France, like the rest of Europe, was already well provided with churches and monasteries, so scope for development of the Norman Romanesque style was becoming limited in its native land. The Conquest of England, however, provided the church builders with almost virgin territory, and under its new rulers the country was thrust into the vanguard of architectural experiment. The Normans thought big, and the ability to co-ordinate and channel economic and technical resources made it possible to realise their ambitions. The feudal system imposed throughout the country provided the means to raise the large sums of money needed for the new building programme, and the use of the feudal *corvée*, a forced-labour arrangement, allowed manpower to be assembled and directed where and when it was required. Most of the important Romanesque buildings of Nor-

The skill of the Norman builders did not always match their ambition – the Priory Church of St Peter at Dunstable, Bedfordshire, shown in this nineteenth-century engraving, originally had two west towers, but both collapsed during one stormy night.

man England, both ecclesiastical and secular, were larger than their counterparts in Europe. The great hall built at Westminster between 1097 and 1099 by the Conqueror's son, William Rufus, was the largest room in Europe for more than a century, rivalling in scale the basilica that Emperor Constantine had made over to the Christians in 312 and comparable to many of the buildings of ancient Rome. The naves of the new cathedrals and monastic churches reached unheard-of lengths; their towers rose, imposing and monumental, above the wooden huts and thatched roofs of the townsfolk. 'We labour to heap up stones,' lamented Wulfstan, the last Anglo-Saxon bishop, 'but we neglect the care of souls.' He agreed reluctantly to the building of a new cathedral at Worcester, but despised what seemed to him to be an unhealthy materialism: 'We, poor wretches, destroy the work of our forefathers, only to get praise to ourselves. That happy age of holy men knew not how to build stately churches: under any roof they offered themselves as living temples to God.'

Pre-Conquest churches had not all been crude wooden huts – there had been stone churches too, with carving and sculpture that compared more than favourably with that of the Normans. But they were few in number and modest in intention. By comparison the Norman buildings were to be daringly ambitious. Ambition, however, was not always matched by technology, and a great number of proud towers came tumbling down. The church of the Augustinian Priory at Dunstable in Bedfordshire was badly damaged by the collapse of both its west towers during one stormy night. And though the clergy might have found it expedient to blame the thunderbolt vengeance of the Almighty, the real culprit was the scant knowledge of structural stability. The stability of Norman architecture depended on its own inert mass rather than the dynamic balance of thrust and counter-thrust that was to enable the builders of later centuries to reach greater heights. The impression of mass and solidity that characterises Norman Romanesque is to some extent an illusion. The thick walls and pillars that seem to be built of huge blocks of masonry were, in fact, built of rubble and faced with relatively thin slabs of stone. This skin of masonry is called *ashlar*. Where wealth or convenience afforded, the Norman masons preferred to use the Caen stone of Normandy since they were already familiar with its qualities and handling. The stone was imported in large amounts, often ready-shaped at the quarries according to plans sent out from England. Since roads were very poor, it was actually quicker and cheaper to transport French stone by sea than to haul English stone any great distance overland. Even when a native stone was favoured, like that quarried at Barnack in Northamptonshire which became so popular that supplies were virtually exhausted by the end of the fifteenth century, transport to the building site was still by water for as much of the journey as possible. Since haulage over long distances could cost more than the stone itself, much skill went into planning routes by sea and river to minimise expense. Most of the actual construction work was still carried out by native masons under varying degrees of supervision by Norman master masons. So the ability and technical resources of the labour force were very variable, and badly jointed ashlar or the disintegration of a poorly bonded rubble core was often the cause of

The north transept of Winchester
Cathedral, built before the death of
William the Conqueror, typifies the
massive scale and robust severity of
the early Norman Romanesque style.

the later collapse of many Norman structures. The perfection of the
lime-burning process which greatly improved the quality of mortar,
and the production of accurately cut ashlar were to be key technical
improvements during this period.

Before the turn of the twelfth century, little attention was paid to
the parish church since the Normans' initial priorities were with the
great cathedrals and castles that were the outward show of establish-

Left

When their initial preoccupation with the great cathedrals was over the Normans turned their attentions to the parish churches. At St Andrew's, South Lopham, Norfolk, an unusually tall new tower was added to the existing Saxon church. The battlemented parapet was added in the fifteenth century.

Right

Saxon churches everywhere were extended or rebuilt. Some, like St Lawrence, Bradford-on-Avon, Wiltshire, were abandoned when grand new parish churches were built. Part of a nineteenth-century engraving of Bradford-on-Avon shows the old Saxon church, to the right, lost among a huddle of buildings. The blind arcading of the chancel is all that was visible to provide a clue to the existence of the church. Compare this with the restored church shown on page 28.

ment power. But during the next half-century the building programme was extended to the parish. Almost all the old pre-Conquest timber churches were rebuilt in stone, and many new ones were raised in villages that had never before boasted a church of their own. Existing stone churches were enlarged where possible, or abandoned to more worldly uses. When a grand new parish church was built at Bradford-on-Avon in Wiltshire, the Saxon church there first became a charnel house, and then was put to such a variety of secular uses over the years that all recollection of its existence as a church was forgotten. Not until the middle of the last century, by which time it was part school, part private cottage and part factory shed, was the church rediscovered, restored and reconsecrated.

Relations between the villagers and their new masters were not always easy. The lords of the manor were well aware of being a ruling minority and sought to make their position as secure as possible by fortification of their homes and by rigid control of local affairs. As much of the civil administration and day-to-day business of the village centred on the parish church, the local lord of the manor liked to keep the building under a watchful eye. So castle and church are often found side by side, repeating in miniature the pattern set by the Conqueror at Durham. Since the lord of the manor usually provided the grant of land on which the church stood and met a large part of the building costs, it was not unreasonable that it should be built to suit his convenience. The new churches played a large part in establishing what were to become the great families of medieval England. Heraldry became an important element in the decoration of churches, not only recording the piety and generosity of the benefactor, but also affirming his hereditary right to estate and privilege. There is evidence that the pedigree of a noble family was sometimes displayed in the church rather like a secular version of the Tree of Jesse which set out Christ's lineage. A fragment of a stained-glass window at Thaxted Church in

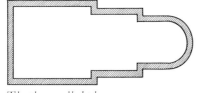

The three-celled plan

Essex depicts an armoured knight holding his shield and standing on the curling branch of what could have been such a family tree. The arms on his shield are said to be those of the Mortimers, though the glass is now weathered beyond recognition.

The plan of the parish church was influenced by the more elaborate ritual and pageantry that the Continental Church brought to public worship. The parish church needed not only to accommodate the growing size of the congregation, but also to provide the laity with a better view of the proceedings so they could fully appreciate the 'theatre' of religion. To this end, the narrow chancel arch that had almost completely separated chancel from nave was opened out, and, though the old two-celled plan continued to be used for many churches, for others a three-celled plan was adopted with *nave*, *choir* and *sanctuary*. The church of St Mary and St David at Kilpeck provides a typical example of this new plan. Here the sanctuary ends in a vaulted apse, the form always favoured on the Continent and now reintroduced by the Normans. At Stewkley in Buckinghamshire the church of St Michael and All Angels provides a common variation on the same three-celled arrangement. Here the sanctuary is square-

Above
The tower of St Bartholomew's,
Fingest, Buckinghamshire, with
its unusual double saddleback roof.

Opposite
The stern grandeur of the Norman
Romanesque style typified by one
of the most ambitious of Norman
parish churches, St Michael and St
Mary's, Melbourne, Derbyshire.
This imposing church was raised in
the middle of the twelfth century on
the cruciform plan with an aisled
nave. It was built for the first Bishop
of Carlisle, a new diocese created by
the re-organisation of the Church
after the Conquest.

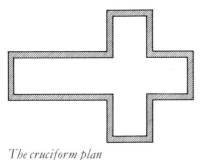

The cruciform plan

ended, and a central or *axial* tower is raised above the choir. Despite the Continental preference for the apse, the majority of churches were still built with a square east end, perhaps because it provided the village craftsmen with fewer technical problems. The greater number of apsidal churches to be found in the south-east of the country may indicate the areas into which the Normans brought their own masons.

In some more important churches the simple two- or three-celled plan was abandoned in favour of the less common *cruciform* plan. Square, projecting *transepts* were added to north and south between the nave and the chancel to form the shape of a cross. Nineteenth-century romantics took the cruciform plan to be a deliberate representation of the Cross of Christ, and even maintained that the slight misalignment found between chancel and nave was sometimes a subtle symbolic reference to the droop of Christ's head on the Cross as it was invariably shown in medieval paintings. It is a picturesque theory, but one that can be discounted since the misalignment is often so small as to be undetectable and is also found in churches that are not cruciform in plan. As we shall see later, such geometric inconsistencies are more likely to be due to the fact that chancel and nave were often rebuilt independently. In adopting the cruciform plan the master mason was primarily concerned not with symbolism but with space and structure. Above the *crossing*, where the arms of the cross intersected, a central tower was raised on four great arches supported by four massive piers.

Norman towers were usually squat and sturdy, rather short in comparison with their width, and square or rectangular in plan. Central and axial towers conformed to the proportions of the crossing or choir above which they were raised. In East Anglia, however, handicapped by the lack of good building stone to make strong corners or *quoins*, the masons continued to build round towers. Often a small turret carried a spiral staircase up an outside corner of a tower. The towers, unlike their Anglo-Saxon forerunners, were not originally designed for bells, though later in the period belfries were added to the tops of existing towers. Tower roofs were either of the blunt pyramid kind that had been common before the Conquest (see page 30), or a type of gabled roof called a *saddleback*. At Fingest in Buckinghamshire the church of St Bartholomew has the unusual feature of a double saddleback, which was reconstructed in the seventeenth century.

Throughout the twelfth century the population continued to expand and where finances permitted the naves of churches were extended to provide more accommodation for their growing congregations. This was usually done by adding *aisles*, about half the width of the nave, on one or both sides. Aisles not only enlarged the floor space of the church, they also enhanced the potential for ritual, making effective processional walkways and furnishing places for statues and side altars dedicated to patron saints. On the rare occasions when the Norman masons married the cruciform plan with the aisled nave, they undoubtedly achieved the most imposing of their parish churches, as the majestic church of St Michael and St Mary at Melbourne in Derbyshire demonstrates. The addition of aisles brought to the parish church the most striking feature of

Round and compound piers alternate in the northern nave arcade of St Mary's, Kirkby Lonsdale, Cumbria.

Norman Romanesque architecture that had already ennobled the greater churches of England – the stately *arcade* of semicircular arches carried on massive *piers*. Following the tradition of classical architecture, each pier had three main structural parts: *base, shaft* and *capital*. The shaft was the main part of the pier. Some early examples were square or rectangular in section, often with slender columns grafted on to the flat faces or cut into the corner angles to make them *compound* shafts. Late in the period, octagonal shafts made their appearance, but generally Norman piers took the massive cylindrical form so well illustrated at Melbourne.

The bases of the piers were usually square and plain with chamfered edges and a simple roll moulding round the foot of the shaft. Occasionally a small leaf-shaped carving, or sometimes an *angle spur*, decorated the projecting corner of the base.

Capitals were of three main types. The basic pattern was set by the *cushion capital* which was shaped like a cube with the four lower corners rounded off so that it was circular in section where it met the shaft and became square above. The *scalloped capital* was of a similar shape, but the rounded part was cut with vertical fluting to give the characteristic scalloped effect. The *volute capital* formed another variation in which four leaves sprang from round the neck, curled over under the corners of the square part and ended in scroll-like volutes. In later Norman work the leaf carving of volute capitals became quite elaborate, recalling their distant ancestors, the Corinthian capitals of classical architecture. The four flat faces of the cushion capital presented the sculptor with tempting surfaces that were hard to resist. They were often vigorously carved with religious scenes, animals, amusing faces or pure geometric patterns. The topmost part of the capital was the *abacus*, a square flat slab of stone with its under-edge bevelled or chamfered. From the abacus sprang the characteristic semicircular arch.

Norman arches were almost always semicircular, the few exceptions being those that were 'stilted up' into a horseshoe shape. Originally they were plain and square in section as though they had been cut straight through the wall with a pastry cutter, but later the roundness of the arches was emphasised by concentric recessed bands of stone, called *orders*. The linear effect they created was sometimes carried on down the supporting piers by slender shafts. Before long the simple mouldings of the arch became another target for the exuberant sculptor who enriched them with *billet*, *nailhead*, *lozenge*, *cable*, *beakhead* and the ubiquitous *chevron* – bold geometric mouldings that produced a rich texture of light and shade. In the beginning these mouldings were chopped out with an axe and many of the designs must have had their origin in wood carving. During the second half of the twelfth century the chisel was to come into use and make possible sharper detail and deeper undercutting. Now that the original colouring has disappeared from these churches, much of the charm of

a Norman interior comes from the contrast between its stark walls and the densely patterned borders created by these mouldings.

Since the church was in daily use, when aisles were added the masons worked in such a way as to cause the minimum of disturbance. The north aisle was usually the first to be built. There were two reasons for this. Firstly, a superstitious belief that evil and ignorance of the Gospel emanated from the north produced a strong prejudice against burial on the dark, north side of the church, leaving the land there relatively free of graves and so more convenient for new building. Secondly, the main entrance to the church was usually the south door, so work on that side was bound to be more disruptive. The first stage was to build the outside wall of the aisle parallel to the existing nave wall and to bridge the space between with a sloping roof. The nave wall was then knocked through at regular intervals and the piers of the new arcade built in the gaps. With the upper wall now supported by the piers, further breaches were made roughly following the intended arcs of the arches. The old masonry was left underneath to act as arch-centerings while the *voussoirs*, the wedge-shaped stones that made up the arch, were set in place. The arcade thus completed, the redundant walling was simply knocked away and the new aisle opened into the church. It is, therefore, in the walling above the nave arcades that the oldest stonework in a church is often to be found. In due course a south aisle was usually built to match that to the north, but there are many churches where only the north aisle was added.

Aisles effectively solved the problem of space, but the problem of lighting was made more difficult. Glass was very expensive so Norman windows were still quite small, often little more than slits, and as the nave became wider, so it became darker. This difficulty was overcome in later times by piercing the wall above each arcade with a row of windows to form a *clerestory*. In Norman architecture, however, clerestories were very rare except in the great monasteries and cathedrals, so most parish churches remained mysteriously gloomy. As in pre-Conquest building, the masonry around the windows was cut back to make the most of what light there was, and their rounded tops were often carved with decorative mouldings. The sharpness of daylight makes the geometric patterns particularly striking here, and the carving was sometimes extended down the sides of the window to create the beautiful effect that can be seen framing the east window of St John the Evangelist's Church at Elkstone in Gloucestershire, built around 1180. Some of the grander parish churches sported circular windows, usually as a feature of the west front. At Barfreston in Kent the church of St Nicholas has a circular window with a kind of miniature arcade radiating from the centre to form a *wheel window*. These wheel windows were the forerunners of the famous Gothic rose windows which became very fashionable on the Continent but found little favour here. Though much Norman architecture survives up and down the country, there are few original windows to be seen. The need for more light in the nave and the appeal of stained glass meant that most Norman windows were replaced by the larger versions of later centuries. Those that have survived are mostly to be found in towers.

Outside, windows were often set under an arch supported by
shafts with capitals. Sometimes an empty or *blind* arch was added to
each side of the window to form a short ornamental arcade. A simple
idea, but in the hands of the eager masons and sculptors it was
developed and embellished with such ingenuity that it became
perhaps the most distinctive contribution of the Normans to the
exterior decoration of the church. Semicircular arches seem to leap
along the broad bands of arcading, a large arch spanning two smaller
ones, one arch interlacing with another, open or blind by turns. This
elaborate decoration was usually reserved for the tower or the west
front of the church.

Above
A carved corbel from St Mary and St David's, Kilpeck, Hereford and Worcester. The corbels support a corbel table, a Norman innovation which gave extra support to the eaves of the roof.

Above right
Norman doorways, like this one at St George's, Heckingham, Norfolk, usually formed a shallow tunnel of concentric bands of mouldings and recessed shafts.

Elsewhere the walls seemed rather plain, lacking the big windows that were yet to come. Here and there simple *buttresses* divided the walls into bays and gave some sense of surface relief. They were not yet buttresses in the strict structural sense in that they did not provide support in places that took particular stress; the wall still supported itself by virtue of its own thickness. They were really just sturdier versions of the pilaster strips of pre-Conquest building.

A structural, and sometimes very decorative, exterior feature introduced by the Norman builders was the *corbel table*, a horizontal projecting band of stone running beneath the eaves which gave extra support to the roof (see page 106). The corbel table derives its name and its strength from the series of supporting stone blocks, called *corbels*, which were bonded into the wall. These corbels provided the ever-ready sculptor with yet another excuse to display his art and sometimes his sense of humour. Returning again to Kilpeck we see the result in just one small church – some ninety corbels carved as grotesque heads, animals, scenes from contemporary life and mythical figures of pagan folk-lore, some of them so 'indecent' that they were discreetly removed during Victorian times. Only two of the corbels are obvious Christian images; both of them represent the *Agnus Dei*, the Lamb of God. They are both found in significant places, one over the east window, and the other above the south door.

*The variety of design and crafts-
manship of Norman tympana
reveal the cultural diversity of
twelfth-century England.*

Top
St Nicholas', Barfreston, Kent.

Above
*St John the Evangelist's, Elkstone,
Gloucestershire.*

The south door had symbolic importance. Being the main entrance to the church it represented the doorway to Christian life and was often the most elaborately decorated part of the exterior of a small church. The recessed orders of the arch above the doorway were often carried down to the ground as a series of shafts, each with its own carved capital, creating a shallow tunnel of concentric bands of pattern around the door. The focus of many Norman doorways was the *tympanum*, the semicircular panel between the flat top of the door and the arch above it. Its carving was usually the *tour de force* of the church exterior. The frivolity indulged elsewhere was abandoned here, and the carving often carries a serious, almost ritualistic touch. Formalised religious scenes, Christ in Majesty, and the Tree of Life were favourite subjects. Tympana show a great diversity in style and standard of craftsmanship, and in them we see something of the

Top
*St Giles', Water
Stratford, Buckinghamshire.*

Above
*St Stephen's, Moreton
Valence, Gloucestershire.*

cultural melting pot of twelfth century England. In some we catch the
sophisticated measure of the cosmopolitan ruling class, in others the
easy hand and lively eye of an individual craftsman expressing his
own beliefs and joys. At the church of St Nicholas at Barfreston in
Kent, and St John the Evangelist at Elkstone in Gloucestershire, the
tympana, showing Christ in Majesty and Christ giving the Benediction,
have an almost classical sense of solidity and composure, recalling the
contemporary churches of southern France. By contrast, the tympanum
of St Giles' Church at Water Stratford in Buckinghamshire expresses
the power of divine majesty by strength of line rather than suggestion
of solid form – as we noted before, a characteristic of Scandinavian
influence in Anglo-Saxon art. The same vigorous linear quality is
seen in the carving of St Michael and the Dragon on the tympanum of
St Stephen's at Moreton Valence in Gloucestershire. This emphasis

An interior view that must have been typical of the many small Norman churches built after the Conquest. This is St Michael and All Angels', Stewkley, Buckinghamshire, built on the three-celled plan with nave, choir and a vaulted sanctuary beyond.

on the linear is unlikely to represent the survival of pre-Conquest traditions of carving; more probably it was transmitted through Anglo-Saxon manuscripts preserved in monastic libraries. The Normans had admired and encouraged the artistry of the Anglo-Saxon manuscript illustrators, and their work must have provided an obvious source of reference and inspiration for the carving of these religious scenes. Line and mass are the two main visual elements at the sculptor's disposal, and it was the balance and interplay of the two that distinguished the best of Norman design in England. But an underlying preference for line was to survive in the artistic soul of the country, and two centuries later it reasserted itself in the uniquely English style of Gothic architecture, Perpendicular.

As the south door represented the doorway to Christian life so, inside the church, the chancel arch, standing between the nave and the chancel, symbolised the passing from life here on Earth to life hereafter. Accordingly it was richly decorated with the characteristic range of Norman mouldings, and sometimes the wall above it was painted with a *Doom*, the scene of the Last Judgement. Such was the quality of these carved chancel arches and doorways that they were often retained when the rest of the church was rebuilt in a more 'up-to-date' style.

The more elaborate ritual favoured by the new clergy required the chancel to be larger and better equipped than in pre-Conquest churches. The altar in Anglo-Saxon times had often been made of wood, and was still sometimes known as Christ's or God's Board in the early Middle Ages. In 1076 however, William the Conqueror's Primate, Archbishop Lanfranc, decreed that all altars should be made of stone, and stone altars were the rule from that time until the sixteenth century when the wooden Communion Table replaced the stone altar. The single slab of stone that formed the main part of the altar, the *mensa*, was incised with a small cross in the centre and at each corner. These five crosses marked the places anointed with holy oil during the consecration of the altar and symbolised the Five Wounds of Christ. The original consecration crosses can still be seen on the twelfth century altar in the church of St Mary de Haura at New Shoreham in West Sussex.

The chancel was now usually equipped with a *piscina*, a kind of small sink with a hole through which the holy water used by the priest to wash his hands during Mass could drain away undefiled into sanctified ground. The piscina had been introduced as early as the ninth century, but then it was seldom more than a drainhole in the floor to the east of the altar. In the Norman period *pillar piscinas* were fairly popular, taking the form of a small basin supported on a stone shaft through which the water drained away. More usually though, the piscina was set in an arched recess in the south wall beside the altar. The recess was often incorporated into a new permanent feature of the chancel, the *sedilia*.

The sedilia were a row of recessed stone seats, usually three, occupied during certain parts of the Mass by the officiating priest, the deacon and the sub-deacon. They were sometimes arranged like three steps, and it may be that their occupants were seated according to rank, with the celebrant taking the highest place nearest the altar. The

Above

*A splendid example of an 'Ayles-
bury' font from Holy Trinity,
Bledlow, Buckinghamshire.*

Below

*The font at St Mary Magdalene's
Eardisley, Hereford and Worcester,
vigorously carved with two men fighting with spear and sword. On the
other side, Christ rescues Adam from
Hell. The carving belongs to a local
school of sculpture that produced some
of the finest Romanesque work surviving in England.*

Not all fonts were made of stone. This lead font from St Augustine's, Brookland, Kent, shows the signs of the zodiac and the labours of the months.

three seats were surmounted by an arcade of three round arches, usually decoratively carved, which was extended by a fourth arch when the sedilia and piscina were incorporated in one unit. In poorer churches the clergy had to make do with simple wooden seats, and it may be that sedilia built of wood had been used in earlier times, but, if they were, no trace of them now remains. Woodwork of any sort from this period has long since disappeared, and the only form of church furniture surviving in quantity is the font.

Fonts were comparatively large since baptism was still by immersion. They were usually made of stone and the bowl lined with lead. Early Norman fonts were simple circular tubs, decorated to varying degree with carved patterns; later fonts were rather like large square sinks, supported by a thick central shaft and four smaller ones at the corners. In the Hereford and Worcester area there is a particularly interesting group of fonts whose rich and imaginative carving provides some of the best examples of Romanesque sculpture in England. Each is shaped rather like a squat wine glass, a large round bowl supported on a short thick stem. Also bowl-shaped are another group of fonts called 'Aylesbury' fonts since they are all to be found in that area of the Chiltern Hills, and may be the work of one unknown craftsman. Unlike the Hereford and Worcester group, these fonts have no figure carving. The bowl is fluted and usually a cable moulding runs around the rim; the pedestal takes the form of an inverted scalloped capital. Not all fonts were of stone, some were made of lead. Some thirty examples of lead fonts are still to be seen. The most elaborate is that in the church of St Augustine at Brookland in Kent, which shows the twelve signs of the zodiac and the labours of the months grouped under arcading. Also worthy of mention are the seven surviving fonts carved from the dark marble of the Tournai quarries in Belgium. These large, handsome fonts were square-bowled and decorated with a style of figure work that suggests they may have been imported ready-made from Belgium. Their carving shows scenes from the life of St Nicholas, the Creation and the Fall, and a selection of grotesque monsters. The artistic quality of many Norman fonts no doubt contributed as much to their survival as the sanctity of their purpose, and a very large number of them are still to be found in our churches.

Baptism, the daily offices, the solemn rites of marriage and the burial of the dead – the round of life for the ordinary parish priest continued relatively undisturbed by the revolution of the Conquest. The new 'barons' of the church had had their own way in some things, but not in all. It had been hoped to extend the celibacy of the cloister to the non-monastic clergy, but even the attempts of the influential Archbishop Lanfranc of Canterbury, himself a former monk of the French Abbey of Le Bec, had failed, and in general the parish priest remained a married man. In the 'Life of Wulfric of Haselbury' the story is told of the vicar of Ashwell who was required to give an undertaking that he would pay a fine of thirty marks if he again associated with his mistress – but his married status was never called into question. The parish priests were only one section of the non-monastic clergy; it was a fact of life that to achieve their positions the majority of professional and educated men, including the 'civil

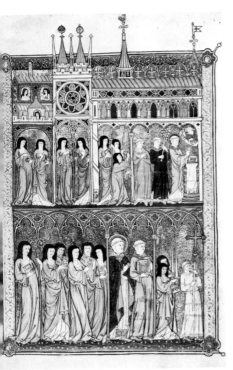

A medieval illustration of life in a nunnery. Throughout the twelfth and thirteenth centuries religious houses grew in number, wealth and influence.

service' through whom the country was administered, had taken at least minor holy orders. To have denied wives and legitimate children to this the intellectual class of society would have been unwise for the future, even if it had been practicable at the time. Where the wind of change was felt by the parish priest, it was most likely to be in his financial standing, particularly if his church was one of the many to be appropriated by the increasingly powerful monasteries.

Monastic life had already been firmly established in England long before the coming of the Normans of course, but the Conquest, treading on the heels of a monastic revival on the Continent, opened up new territory for expansion and colonisation by the European monasteries. The founding of Battle Abbey on the very spot where King Harold had fallen was the first step in the establishment of a network of new monasteries throughout the country. By the middle of the next century there were almost five hundred monasteries in England, many of them daughter houses of French monasteries.

The community who lived in a monastery was bound by vows of poverty, chastity and obedience. Their religious and everyday lives were governed by the accepted Rule of their Order. The largest and most influential of the Orders were the Benedictine, the Cluniac and the Cistercian Orders. The building in which the monks lived might be an *abbey* or a *priory* depending on the Order to which it belonged and the status of the house. Smaller houses were sometimes affiliated to larger establishments and known as *cells*. The head of a monastery was an *abbot*, and his second in charge was the *prior*. By a peculiarly English tradition, a bishop's see was usually established in a monastic church, which thus became a cathedral as well. The Normans continued this practice after the Conquest, organising eight of their new dioceses around cathedral-monasteries. In these cases the bishop was the nominal abbot while the prior became the working head of the monastery. Though its members were bound by individual vows of poverty, the monastery as an institution sometimes grew very rich, and its abbot or prior became correspondingly powerful. Undoubtedly some of this wealth was created by the industrious hands and technical innovation of the monks themselves, but much of it came from the appropriation of the rectorial tithes of parish churches.

The proliferation of monasteries depended on endowments by secular benefactors, and many a Norman baron assuaged a guilty conscience by endowing a monastic house with a gift of land from his newly acquired estates. The land was not necessarily intended for building; its primary purpose was to provide the religious house with an income through rents and dues. This gift of land included any church that happened to be standing there and the tithes due to it. Some churches even became owned by foreign monasteries. This practice of granting parish churches to religious houses, or indeed to any other institution since they were sometimes later granted to colleges, is called *appropriation*. Monastic appropriation of parish churches became very common; two fifths of the county of Wiltshire was owned by religious houses or high-ranking clergy during the eleventh century, and by the time of the Dissolution of the monasteries, a third of the parishes of Surrey had been appropriated. The monastery usually also received the advowson, the right of presen-

The expansion of religious establishments depended on endowments, usually of land, by lay benefactors. In this stained glass window from Malvern Priory, Hereford and Worcester, William the Conqueror grants a charter to Aldwyn, the first Prior of Malvern.

tation to the benefice. In effect the monastic appropriator became the rector of the church. So with the appropriation of a church the major part of its endowment, including the tithe of crops and stock, went to the monastery to which it had been granted, leaving the parish priest with only the lesser tithe and the altar offerings. The situation was open to much abuse, and the flow of resources was often one way, with the monastery getting rich at the expense of the parish church. As rector it was the duty of the appropriating monastery to provide a priest for the church and pay his stipend. This priest performed the various parochial duties as a substitute for the rector and so was called a *vicar* from the Latin word *vicarius* meaning 'substitute'. But, though they received the better part of the tithes, the monasteries often tried to save themselves the expense of paying a stipend by appointing one of their own monks for the cure of souls in the parish instead of a vicar. It was the responsibility of the bishops to see that vicars were appointed to their churches. But even when a monastery did fulfil its rectorial obligations, the stipend paid to the vicar was generally little enough, and the parish priest had no guarantee of a decent living until the Lateran Council of 1215 instituted *vicarages* which were to be held freehold by the parish priest. Eventually the priest was also provided with his own house by the Church, and the proportion of vicarages to rectories today gives us some measure of the extent of monastic appropriation.

In its role as rector of an appropriated church, the monastery was also responsible for maintaining the chancel in good repair and bearing the cost of building a new one if necessary. Provision of furnishings and fittings for the chancel was, however, the responsibility of the parishioners, as was the maintenance of the nave. The ambitions of the local people for their church were not always shared by the often distant monastery to whom the church had been granted. At Melton Mowbray in Leicestershire, for instance, the nave of St Mary's was to be rebuilt at the turn of the fourteenth century in grand fashion by the parishioners. After some fifty years the work was well in hand, and it fell to the monastic appropriator, a Cluniac monastery many miles away in Lewes, West Sussex, to build the chancel. But it seems the priory was unwilling to part with more than the minimum of cash since the chancel they provided was less than half the size of one of the church's transepts, disproportionately small and mean-looking. Perhaps it was all they could afford – many monasteries remained poor and were loathe to spend what little they had on distant churches they never used. Once again the bishops did their best to see that the monastic appropriators fulfilled their rectorial obligations, but it was no easy task. In 1388, the Bishop of Winchester delivered an ultimatum to Merton Priory: 'Since at each of our Visitations it was discovered and shown that the chancel of the church at Effingham in our diocese, appropriated to your monastery, is well known to be in a state of great and obvious ruin as to its roof, walls and windows, as also the grave complaint of the parishioners has of late informed us that no one for a long time has been able to, nor can now celebrate Divine service in the said chancel . . . we therefore order and command you that before the Feast of St Michael next coming you cause the same chancel of the church of Effingham to be repaired as it requires in decent fashion; otherwise when that term has expired, we will cause the said chancel to be repaired at your expense from issues of the church.' It would appear that some monastic appropriators were more interested in the collection of their tithes than in the cure of the souls whose labour produced them. But not all monasteries were such bad 'landlords'. Some churches had the good fortune to be appropriated by wealthy institutions, and the fine chancel of St Mary the Virgin at Adderbury in Oxfordshire testifies to the generous fulfilment of rectorial duties by monastic appropriators on some occasions.

Though it may not have seemed so to the man in the street, the monasteries were in fact playing a major role in the economic development of the country. They were the chief innovators of agricultural techniques. Arable land was made more productive, waste land was turned to cultivation, and the introduction of sheep-runs laid the foundation of the international wool trade that was to bring prestige and wealth to medieval England. With the tenure of land went the responsibility for building roads and bridges, a duty that almost acquired the status of holy work. The Cistercians in particular effected much of the clearing away of the forest that kept villages apart. Improved communications between villages meant that surpluses produced by the better farming methods could be more easily moved from one place to another. The self-sufficiency of the pre-Conquest village gave way to broader economic horizons.

Until the middle of the eleventh century, England had been only tenuously attached to Europe, for in culture and society she had been closer to Scandinavia. With the Norman Conquest, that link had been severed and the country was swept into the mainstream of feudal France. In the next century, under the Angevin kings, the dual kingdom of England and Normandy-Aquitaine was forged, and this island, no longer perched on the edge of the world, became an inextricable part of Europe. International trade increased, and where trade led, culture followed. With French and Latin as their passports, the English nobles and clergy could travel freely between the castles and abbeys of the Continent. And even the humblest villager, perhaps seeing his church's tithes go to some distant foreign abbey, could hardly be unaware that he was now part of a wider world.

3: A Wider World

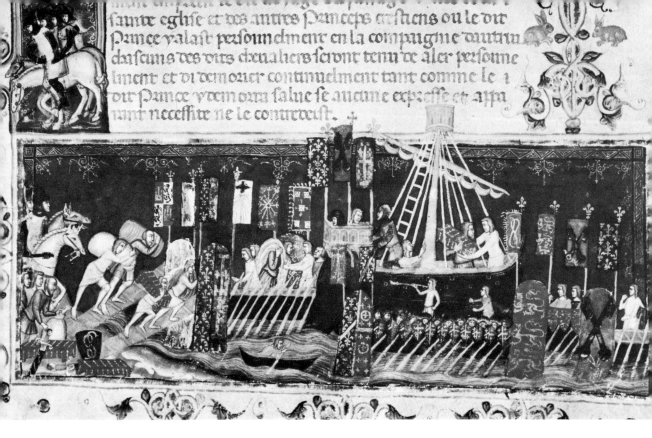

A French medieval manuscript illustration of crusaders preparing to set sail for the Holy Land.

The wider world to which England now belonged was called Christendom, the only collective name by which Europe knew itself and one that summed up the social, cultural and spiritual beliefs that were the foundation of the medieval world. Christendom was a powerful but elusive kingdom that existed more in spirit than in territorial reality, a kingdom of like minds which men of many countries were prepared to lay down their lives to defend. Christendom was not a political unity as the Roman Empire had been, it was a cultural unity, forged by Roman Christianity and the universal feudal system, and governed by princes of Church and State hand in hand. The influence of classical Greece and Rome had weakened and the focus of western civilisation shifted away from the Mediterranean towards the north and west, closer to England. Europe began, as it were, to think for herself and to develop a culture that was properly European, with France and Italy leading the way in artistic matters, and the feudal states of Germany and France setting the political pace.

It would have been surprising if such far-reaching changes had not been mirrored in the architecture of the times, and indeed they were. During the second half of the twelfth century a break was made with the Romanesque style that had held sway for centuries, and Europe moved towards an architectural style of her very own. The new style differed so radically from the classical tradition that, five hundred years later, Sir Christopher Wren could disdainfully refer to it as *Gothic*, meaning 'barbarian'. Its most characteristic feature was the introduction of the pointed arch. A modest change it may seem, but it was one that was to be of critical importance both aesthetically and structurally.

Previous page
Pilgrims set out to see something of the wider world (from a medieval manuscript).

Of course the new Gothic style did not replace the Romanesque overnight. The architecture of the years between 1160 and 1200 shows features of both styles and is usually called the *Transitional* period. The term Transitional is a little misleading in that it implies an intermediate style between Romanesque and Gothic, and suggests that the Gothic style in some way grew out of the Romanesque, which it did not. In fact the Transitional period is characterised by a continuing reliance on the established building principles of inert stability punctuated by bursts of experiment with forms of construction based on the dynamic balance of thrust and counter-thrust. The Gothic style was a completely new departure, and the seeds of its inspiration lay beyond the boundaries of Christendom itself.

The decline of classical influence in Europe coincided with a growing contact with the Islamic culture of the East, a contact largely brought about by the Crusades. Until the end of the eleventh century Christendom had played a defensive role against the Saracens, but the wave of self-confidence that was sweeping Europe turned the tables, and Christendom became the aggressor. In 1095 Pope Urban II instigated the first official Crusade for the recapture of Jerusalem, and the following year the assembled Crusaders marched east. Two years later the port of Antioch fell to the Christians after the miraculous intervention of St George who appeared on horseback armed with a lance and struck down many of the infidels. The scene is illustrated in a carving over the door of the church of St George at Fordington in Dorset. The following year, 1099, this First Crusade reached a successful climax with the recapture of Jerusalem and the Holy Sepulchre after a siege of six weeks.

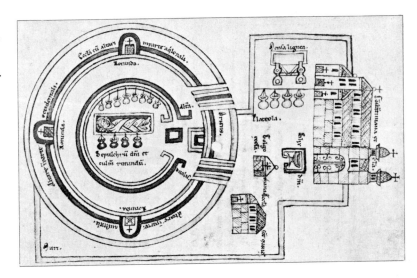

A medieval plan of the church of the Holy Sepulchre in Jerusalem, showing the circular church recaptured by the Crusaders, and surrounding buildings.

In Jerusalem, Constantine, the first Christian Emperor, had originally built a basilica with a semicircular apse over the supposed tomb of Christ. But the building had been destroyed by the Persians in the seventh century, and when it was rebuilt by the Christians, they simply completed the circle of the apse, forming the circular Church of the Holy Sepulchre that the Crusaders now recaptured. The Holy Sepulchre became the inspiration for round churches built all over Europe. In England five are still to be seen: Holy Sepulchre, Cambridge; St Sepulchre, Northampton; the Temple Church in London; Little Maplestead Church in Essex; and the Chapel of Ludlow Castle in Salop. St Sepulchre in Northampton was founded by Earl Simon de Senlis at the turn of the twelfth century possibly as a gesture of gratitude for his own safe return from the First Crusade.

The homecoming Crusaders brought back with them new ideas and new skills. They had had their eyes and their minds opened to a culture richer and more sophisticated than their own. They had seen sumptuously coloured buildings with graceful pointed arches, ingenious mechanical devices, and precious stones and metal intricately wrought by highly skilled craftsmen. They returned full of astonishing stories of distant lands and determined that something of that culture should be theirs. It was no mere coincidence that the years of the Crusades saw a sudden improvement in building technology in Europe. From the chain of castles the Crusaders had built to defend Christendom they had learned much for themselves about fortification and structural design; from captured Saracen engineers they probably learned more. Thick rubble walls were replaced by walls of finely jointed ashlar, thinner but stronger. The blocks of ashlar were larger than before, providing even more strength. Most Norman buildings had been constructed of relatively small blocks of stone, their size limited by the weight that could be carried by a man or raised by primitive lifting tackle. The use of larger blocks of stone indicates a dramatic improvement in the efficiency of lifting machinery, stimulated perhaps by the introduction of Saracen machinery captured by the victorious Crusaders, or at least by the application of the Eastern principles of mechanics they had picked up. It is even

Above
After the success of the Crusades, pointed arches, the structural basis of the Gothic style, first began to appear in the great monastic churches of Europe, as here in the majestic ruin of the Cistercian abbey at Rievaulx, North Yorkshire.

Above right
Holy Sepulchre, Cambridge, one of several round churches built by the homecoming Crusaders in imitation of the circular church of the Holy Sepulchre in Jerusalem.

possible that Eastern engineers were brought back as prisoners to work in Europe. Neath Abbey in West Glamorgan is said to have been built by a certain 'Lalys' who may have been just such a prisoner.

Through this contact with the world beyond Christendom and increasing experimentation with building technology at home, the pointed arch made its appearance in European architecture. Where it was first used in the West must inevitably be a matter of conjecture, though it is generally acknowledged that Autun Cathedral in France, built between 1120 and 1132, provides the earliest example of a building employing pointed arches as a major feature of its design. In England the transverse arches of the nave vault at Durham Cathedral are pointed and may have been built as early as 1104, just five years after the successful conclusion of the First Crusade.

During this Transitional period the pointed arch appeared in buildings that were otherwise quite Romanesque in character and structure. Though the effect of the pointed arch on the visual aspect of architecture was to be profound, its introduction was primarily for structural rather than aesthetic reasons. This is evident from the fact that where both semicircular and pointed arches are used in one building, it is the pointed arches which support the greater loads, the

Above
The cellarium of Fountains Abbey, North Yorkshire, where the lay brothers ate. This remarkable building is 100 metres long (over 300 feet) and has a ribbed vault with semicircular diagonal ribs and pointed transverse ribs so that the vault rises to a uniform height along the centre.

central tower of a cruciform church for instance, while the semicircular form is retained for secondary and decorative arches. The semicircular arch had a weak spot at the top. There the voussoirs that made up the arch were subject to less mutual compression and so were more likely to be pushed out of place by the weight the arch supported. The pointed arch eliminated this weakness; in effect it acted as two parts of an arch leaned together, each half supporting the other. This inherent strength was one of two factors which contributed to the successful introduction of the pointed arch. The second was the solution it offered to the problem of stone vaulting.

Though few parish churches boasted stone vaulting, it is worth considering the development of vaulting in the greater churches, since they were seedbeds of innovation where a new style was growing which the smaller churches were to adopt with an enthusiasm that was tempered only by their means. The problems of stone vaulting had never been really effectively solved by the Romanesque builders. Their first attempt had been the *barrel vault*, a semicircular tunnel of masonry built over a wooden framework, called *centering*, which was removed once the mortar between the blocks of stone had set. Barrel vaulting could only be used to span a short space and so was mainly confined to small low areas. A further development was the *groined vault*, formed by the intersection at right angles of two barrel vaults, the *groins* being the lines of intersection. Towards the end of the Romanesque period this continuous, solid approach had been superseded by the *ribbed vault*, a rather different approach to the problem.

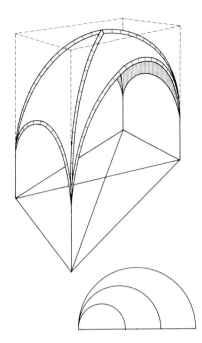

Until the Gothic era vaulting was limited by the rigid geometry of the semicircular arch. Arches along the sides and diagonals of a rectangle inevitably rose to three different heights and made vaulting awkward.

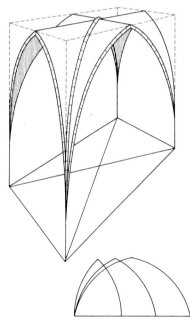

The pointed arch was more flexible. By making the point of each arch more, or less, acute it was possible to build a vault rising to a uniform height throughout.

The ribbed vault was built in two stages. First a framework was constructed of six arches supported on four piers or springers, four arches joining adjacent piers and two crossing the frame diagonally. The spaces between the arches were then filled in with small blocks of masonry, the *webbing*. This represented a major step forward from the narrow barrel and groined vaults, but further progress was hampered by the rigid geometry of the semicircular arch. A semicircular arch must always rise to a height equal to half the distance it spans, so the arches that crossed the vault diagonally always rose higher than the side arches, since the diagonals of a square are inevitably longer than its sides. To equalise the heights, the lower arches could be 'stilted' up, or the diagonal ones made to spring from points lower on the piers than the side arches, but either solution produced a rather inelegant result. When the area to be vaulted was rectangular rather than square, the problem was made even worse with the three unequal spans producing arches rising to three different heights and leaving the Romanesque builders quite bewildered.

The introduction of the pointed arch solved these problems at a stroke. A pointed arch can be made to rise to any height, irrespective of the distance it spans, by making it more or less pointed. By pointing all the arches of a vaulted area to varying degrees, the vault could be built to a uniform height throughout. Thus vaulting was freed from the geometrical confines of the semicircular arch and rose higher and wider than could have been dreamt of before. By the end of the twelfth century this quiet revolution in vault construction had permeated the structural design of the whole church.

Once again the agent of change was the pointed arch. The structural purpose of an arch was to conduct the thrust of the load it carried down through the supporting masonry of the piers, or walls and buttresses, to the ground. The line of thrust depended on both the shape and loading of the arch. The shape of the semicircular arch meant that the horizontal component of the line of thrust was comparatively large, and tended to push walls or piers outwards. The supporting masonry had, therefore, to be very thick, otherwise the thrust from the arch could not be accommodated and the structure became unstable. A pointed arch carrying the same weight resolved a larger proportion of its thrust into the vertical component and so conducted it more directly to the ground. This allowed the supporting masonry to be made thinner since there was less horizontal thrust to be accommodated. Accurately placed and designed buttresses were used to provide additional support at strategic points on the outside of the wall dictated by the lines of thrust. A new and revolutionary attitude towards architectural structure was made possible. Instead of the block-by-block building of the Romanesque period, in which ill-defined thrusts were hopefully dissipated by the sheer mass of masonry, a skeletal system of construction was evolving in which thrusts were guided along the self-supporting 'bones' of the structure. Walls were reduced to screens of masonry that filled in between the 'bones' provided by the arcades and buttresses.

Relieved of much of their structural role, the walls of the succeeding Gothic period were able to rise higher and become thinner still. It was possible to make windows larger and larger until the walls

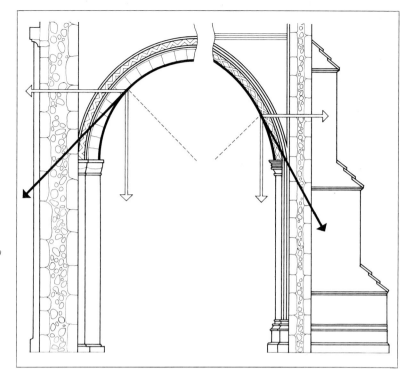

A very simplified explanation of the structural superiority of the pointed arch. The semicircular arch (left) resolves a large proportion of the weight it carries into an outward horizontal thrust, while the pointed arch (right) resolves a greater proportion vertically. To resist the outward thrust of the arch and achieve stability, the supporting masonry for a semicircular arch must, therefore, be thicker than that for a pointed arch. Although in this example the masonry that supports the pointed arch is only half the thickness of that supporting the semicircular arch, with the help of a well-placed buttress, it can be seen to accommodate the thrust of the weight carried by the arch much more efficiently.

themselves seemed to be translucent screens of stone tracery and painted glass. The stern, massive grandeur of the Romanesque style was transcended by the force of soaring line and aspiring energy into a new and sublime architecture. From classical architecture Romanesque had inherited breadth and horizontality, symmetry and static balance; these qualities reflected the climate and predictability of the Mediterranean world where men thanked the benevolent gods for what they knew they would receive. By contrast, the new Gothic architecture was to be characterised by dynamic balance and a restless assertion of verticality that defied gravity; it reflected the more fearful and forceful world of the unsettled north where hostile gods had to be propitiated for their favours. The Gothic style was to dominate ecclesiastical building for centuries, but without the introduction of the Eastern pointed arch it would not have been possible. It is a telling demonstration of the cultural unity of Christendom that such a dramatic change could be achieved throughout Europe in the space of some sixty years.

The backbone of Christendom was provided by the monasteries, and the Cistercians in particular must be credited as a major force in the Transitional flux towards the Gothic style. The Cistercians were a new Order, born of the wave of confidence and self-examination that had accompanied the early Crusades. Until then monastic life had been dominated by the Benedictine Order. Since their foundation in the eighth century by Benedict of Aniane, the Benedictines had had a chequered career of alternating decline and revival. A principle of the Order was that the proper use of art was for the highest service, that is, in praise of God. Piety was expressed in splendour. The Benedictine monks called upon the services of the most skilled craftsmen and

the wealthiest benefactors to build vast churches, elaborately decorated with colourful wall paintings and rich carving, and furnished with precious plate, jewelled shrines, sumptuous hangings and vestments of rare Eastern textiles. The workshops of the great monasteries were the studios of the leading artists of the day and schools for young apprentices. Despite its ups and downs and the rival groups that broke away, the Benedictines remained the most important Order. Under their auspices the cathedrals of Canterbury, Peterborough, St Albans, Durham, Ely, Winchester and Norwich were raised, as were the great abbeys of Malmesbury, Sherborne, Pershore and Tewkesbury. The Cluniac Order, which separated from the Benedictines nearly a hundred years after the death of Benedict, differed in its administrative structure from its parent Order but maintained the tradition of splendour in ceremony and surroundings.

This magnificence of the Benedictine and Cluniac monasteries provoked a reaction in favour of austerity and simplicity that gave rise to the Cistercian Order at the beginning of the twelfth century. The walls of the Cistercians' churches were to be colourless, the windows of plain glass and even the altars were to be painted in just one colour. Vestments were to be of the simplest kind and the everyday habit made of plain undyed wool. There was to be no representation anywhere of the human figure other than that of Christ on the Cross. Architecture was to be adequate and dignified in design rather than ostentatious; ornament and elaborate mouldings were to be shunned. Thus the masons' attention was concentrated on proportion and structural design rather than superficial decoration, and the new monasteries of the Cistercians provided fertile ground for the development of techniques of construction based on the pointed arch. Their great abbeys of Fountains, Kirkstall, Abbey Dore, Rievaulx and Tintern provided influential models for the builders of parish churches, and it is due in part to the restraining influence of the Cistercians that the thirteenth century parish church acquired the dignified beauty of the early Gothic style.

Naturally the parish church lagged behind the innovatory monastic churches, and its architecture shows the movement from Romanesque towards Gothic in a more spasmodic way. Pointed arches are found as early as the twelfth century in some churches, like Bredon in Hereford and Worcester, and Walsoken in Norfolk, but as late as the thirteenth century other churches, St Mary's at Shrewsbury in Salop for instance, still employed the old semicircular arches. During this Transitional period the masons seemed quite happy to combine Romanesque and Gothic features quite haphazardly – there seems to be no logical reason why the central tower of St Mary's Church at Broadwater in West Sussex, for instance, should have a semicircular arch supporting its east side and a pointed arch for the west. In the same county the churches of St Nicholas at Old Shoreham and St Mary de Haura in New Shoreham show a text book range of architectural features from Norman Romanesque through to full Gothic.

As well as in the tentative use of the pointed arch, the transitional nature of the second half of the twelfth century shows itself in some minor features like the carving of ornament. The introduction of the chisel now provided the sculptor with more flexibility than afforded

A monk of the first monastic Order, the Benedictines (above) *and a monk of the austere Cistercian Order* (below) *founded in the twelfth century.*

71

by the axe. The edges of the arch orders could be finely chamfered to give a more delicate effect of light and shade than in earlier work. Conversely, mouldings could be more deeply undercut to produce bolder relief with sharper contrasts. The zigzags of the chevron moulding sometimes became very pronounced. At Burpham Church in West Sussex the chevron moulding round one of its arches acquired such a spiky appearance that it became known locally as the 'Crown of Thorns'. The deeply undercut chevron was probably the forerunner of the *dogtooth* ornament that was to be so characteristic of early Gothic decoration.

The carving of capitals changed too. The crudely carved scenes and grotesque animals that had decorated cushion capitals were abandoned; the heavy scalloped capital gave way to more delicately carved variations; and the pseudo-Corinthian volute capitals evolved into the *stiff-leaf* capitals that were another of the hallmarks of early Gothic work.

The shafts of piers no longer needed to be so massive and, in place of the huge cylinders of masonry that characterised Norman churches, the builders of the Transitional period began to use more slender columns and octagonal piers. Sometimes, as in the church of St Nicholas at Castle Hedingham in Essex, columns and octagonal piers are used alternately in an arcade, subtly introducing a pleasing note of variety. The plain, square bases of the piers became more sophisticated, the carved corner leaf, which had appeared earlier, being used more commonly.

By the second half of the twelfth century the sculptor's axe had been replaced by the chisel which enabled him to achieve more delicate results as this elegant group of capitals from All Saints', Faringdon, Oxfordshire, shows.

By the turn of the thirteenth century the Romanesque style had been ousted by the new Gothic style. The point of no return had probably been the rebuilding of the choir of Canterbury Cathedral in a completely Gothic manner by the French mason, William de Sens. The hesitation of the Transitional period was now over, and ecclesiastical architecture embarked on a journey of over three centuries during which time the religious beliefs and determined ingenuity of the medieval mind found eloquent expression in the grandest, most sublime churches to be seen in Christendom.

All over Europe the great churches raised to cover the shrines of martyrs and to house the relics of saints became focal points for a growing army of pilgrims. The corporate spirit of Christendom and better communications extended the mobility of the clergy and nobility to the rising middle class and the less well off. Many ordinary people joined pilgrimages to unfamiliar parts of the country and even overseas. Medical science was rudimentary, and for many of the lame and sick touching the relic of some holy martyr offered the only hope of cure. At Whitchurch Canonicorum church in Dorset, the lead reliquary containing the body of the church's patron saint, St Candida, is still to be seen. It is set in a stone tomb-chest with holes in the sides through which the pilgrims could touch the actual reliquary. For the healthy, a pilgrimage might be undertaken seriously as part of a penance, but perhaps more often it was simply a pious excuse to have a good time and see something of the new wide world.

Whatever their reasons for going, the pilgrims doubtlessly came back, as the Crusaders had done before them, with new ideas and expectations. Their own parish church may have seemed rather dull and old fashioned, and a desire was stimulated to achieve locally something of the magnificence they had seen on their travels. Increasingly the means to fulfil their ambitions became available. The rising fortunes of the middle classes provided a ready supply of wealthy benefactors, and the masons, no longer parochial builders but designers belonging to an elite pan-European society, acquired the aesthetic judgement and technical skill with which to meet the aspirations of their patrons.

4: The Church Builders

Although Gothic remained the accepted style of architecture for over three hundred years, retrospective study of its origins and development was largely ignored until the close of the eighteenth century. The new thinkers of the post-Reformation centuries preferred to turn their eyes back to the distant glow of the classical Golden Age. The first serious attempt to collate research and stimulate popular interest in Gothic architecture was Thomas Rickman's 'Attempt to Discriminate the Styles of English Architecture', published in 1817. Though he disliked the disparaging overtones of the term 'Gothic', Rickman kept it and subdivided the style into three periods: *Early English*, spanning the thirteenth century; *Decorated*, covering the first half of the fourteenth century; and *Perpendicular*, from the middle of the fourteenth century to the first part of the sixteenth. Until quite recently it was still the custom to follow Thomas Rickman's original subdivision of the Gothic era despite his somewhat misleading terminology. For instance, no chauvinistic claim can be made for an exclusively English origin of the Early English style. These, however, are the terms used in the printed guides found in many churches and in most literature on the subject, so, treading with some caution in the footsteps of tradition, the Victorian names are retained here. Most misleading is the implication that there were three clearly defined styles confined to three precise periods of time. In practice, Gothic architecture has many moods, determined as much by scale and materials, skill and money, as by date. The church builders in one corner of the country might sometimes have used a style that had long fallen out of fashion elsewhere. Rickman's periods overlap considerably; styles are often mixed and sometimes transitional. So with these reservations in mind, how is the architectural history of more than three centuries to be divided into manageable parts?

The most dramatic of dividing lines is provided by the Black Death, and since the story of the parish church is the story of its people, it is also the most appropriate. The Black Death swept through Europe, decimating men, women and children in its path, and reached England in 1348. Over a third of the population was wiped out. Church building came to a standstill for a generation or more as skilled craftsmen fell victim to the plague. The practical impact on architecture was mirrored by a halting of the spirit, which some see expressed in the more mechanical feel of the late Gothic style, Perpendicular. But let's look first at the development of the Gothic parish church during the century and a half before the Black Death, Rickman's Early English and Decorated periods.

The twelfth century had seen a flurry of ecclesiastical activity and a boom in church building, so that by the middle of the thirteenth century the parish system was well established, and each community had at its heart its own parish church. Church building from now on had a different character. Few new churches were needed; it was largely a matter of rebuilding existing ones, in part or whole, either out of structural necessity or for reasons of taste. Many of the Norman parish churches had been built in a hurry, often by workmen of dubious ability, and much of their masonry was already unsound. Heavy Norman towers in particular had a disconcerting habit of tottering on inadequate piers and, if they fell, they took a good deal of the church with them. Fire was a constant hazard throughout medieval times. The earlier churches had been thatched, or roofed with wooden shingles, and once fire took hold there was little the parishioners could do to prevent the flames from spreading.

Pride and fashion as well as necessity provided a stimulus to rebuilding. Life was getting better. Socially the Anglo-Norman fusion was complete and an 'English' identity had emerged. Growing flocks of sheep grazed on widening pastures as the wool trade reached its zenith, pouring wealth into the monasteries and, increasingly as time went on, into the secular hands of the wool merchants. The standard of living was improving, as yet unchecked by the economic setback of the Black Death and the debilitating effects of the Hundred Years' War which followed Edward III's claim to the French throne in 1337. Increasing prosperity of parish or manor was reflected in the partial or complete rebuilding of many churches in grander fashion. The parish church was still, in a sense, private property. It 'belonged' to the lord of the Manor, or to a religious institution who provided it for the use of the parish and, as we have seen, was responsible for the fabric of the chancel. Like other property, it could change hands, and the rebuilding of a chancel bigger and better was often the result of a church coming 'under new management'. The parishioners did their bit too, vying with their neighbours to replace adequate but old-fashioned naves with impressive new ones. Often they were far larger than the congregation required, an expression not of need, but of civic pride.

This change in the nature of parish church building was made possible by, and in turn fuelled, a change in the church builders themselves. The Gothic style had been born in the workshops of the great religious houses, and the skilled craftsmen and designers were

The building of St Albans Abbey from a thirteenth-century manuscript of the 'Lives of the two Offas'. To the left of the illustration, the patron confers with the master mason who carries compasses and a set square; to the right, masons work stone blocks and set them in position using a plumb-line level.

still to be found there during the first years of this period. The building of parish churches had been on a different scale altogether, mainly the work of casual labour with, perhaps, a few important features like windows and doorways specially commissioned from a trained craftsman. But during the thirteenth century there was to be a shift of emphasis from the monastery and religious patronage towards the parish church and more secular patronage. Various factors contributed to this shift. More of the profits of the flourishing wool trade finding their way into the pockets of the private wool merchants and lower landed gentry diverted wealth from the monasteries to the parishes; the popularity of the Friars preaching in the growing towns undermined the authority of the insular and sometimes high-handed religious establishments; and in 1279 the Statute of Mortmain, by making it an offence to grant land to a religious house without licence from the king, effectively checked the expansion of monasteries and brought endowment under strict royal supervision, thus taking the first step on the road to Reformation. The trained craftsmen leaving the monastic workshops had skills for sale, and the parishes increasingly had the cash to pay for them. All that had to be done was to bring the two together, and the architectural lessons learned in the great churches were brought to the parish.

Who then were the men behind the building of a Gothic church? Were there architects, engineers, contractors and financiers as there are today? In effect, though not in name, there were. Let's start with the initiator of the building project and call him the *patron*.

The patron could come from one of several walks of life. He could be a high-ranking member of the clergy possibly representing some religious institution, a nobleman, a rich merchant, or, perhaps most commonly, the churchwardens acting on behalf of the parish. The patron was responsible for deciding the scale and general form of the building. His subsequent involvement in the actual design of the church varied. A member of the aristocracy or a high churchman, being cultured and well-travelled, would probably have a developed interest in architecture and would have been capable of making an

informed, even talented, contribution to the design. On the other hand, the churchwardens as patron played a humbler role. Drawing upon local models, they would stipulate that the tower, say, be like that of one village church and the windows like those of another.

A wealthy or influential patron often left his mark on the church in the form of his coat of arms or, more enigmatically, as a *rebus*. The rebus was a visual pun on a name. At the church of St Bartholomew-the-Great, at Smithfield in London, for instance, the oriel window bears the rebus of Prior Bolton. It shows the *bolt* of a cross bow piercing a barrel, the old name for which was a *tun*, hence Bolt-ton. Such word games and riddles had a great appeal to the medieval mind.

Once building was under way, the patron's function was mainly administrative: assembling the necessary manpower, materials and machinery for each stage of construction and making sure that the money was there to pay for them. His job was not an easy one. When the church was being rebuilt in grander fashion because the parish or manor had come upon good times, money was no problem, but often enough rebuilding was made necessary by some disaster and the patron had to organise the building funds in a hurry. With the disaster fresh in people's minds money came in readily, but a church, or even just part of one, could take a long time to rebuild, and the problem lay in maintaining the flow of money once the initial wave of piety had subsided. Societies and fraternities were set up to keep the fund fed with small but regular donations. The church's holy relics might be sent around the country to stimulate interest in the rebuilding and to raise more money. And if the patron was influential enough, the rich could be bribed to part with their cash by persuading the Pope to grant indulgences to all who contributed to the work. The patron made careful estimates, but as today, many buildings turned out to be more expensive than was originally anticipated. It seems that the parishioners helped to keep costs down by joining in the less skilled labouring themselves. During the building of a new church tower at Totnes in Devon the villagers helped hew stone at the quarry and lent their horses to cart the stone to the building site. Records elsewhere

79

The flying buttresses of Rheims Cathedral, one of the sophisticated drawings from the notebook of Villard de Honnecourt, a French master mason of the mid-thirteenth century.

show that fines were imposed on those who avoided their allotted days' work for the church.

While the patron was taking care of the financial and administrative side of the project, the man responsible for the actual design of the church and its execution was the *master mason*. Today we would call him the architect – a man who could conceive the complex structure of a Gothic church, as a whole and in detail, and bring it into being by communicating his vision to the craftsmen and labourers working under him. The master mason was also the equivalent of our modern structural engineer. In old records he is sometimes referred to as the 'machinator' or the 'ingeniator', though the second term was more commonly applied to those involved in military building. The functions of architect and engineer were united in the master mason and remained so until the Renaissance when the break with the, by then, traditional Gothic style and the coming of the gentleman architect split the two roles. Unlike the later architect, the medieval master mason had worked his way up through the building trade and was familiar, through his own personal experience, with all the techniques and practices that he supervised at each stage of the construction of a building.

The more successful of these architect-engineers lived well and were able to dictate their own terms of employment. As part of the contract the patron was often required to provide a house to accommodate the master mason and his family. The master mason might also expect to receive a new robe each year and a pair of gloves, the special mention of which in many documents suggests that gloves held some importance as a status symbol. Some master masons achieved positions of note not only within their craft but in society as well. In fact the skill of the master mason was so well respected that God Himself could be portrayed as the Divine Architect of the Universe, holding the world in his compasses, the emblems, together with the set square, of the mason. But their success sometimes caused resentment: Nicolas de Biard, a Dominican preacher, complained that 'the master masons hold measuring rod and gloves in their hands and say to others: "cut here", and do not work themselves; nonetheless they receive the greater fees . . . Some work with words only.' It seems that this intellectual, with his formal education, was particularly affronted that a man should rise through his trade to a position where he could 'work with words only'.

Communication, however, was an important element of the master mason's job, and on a building of any substantial scale it was vital. Where many masons were employed on a large church, working drawings must have been needed to co-ordinate their efforts. In England, unfortunately, very few technical drawings of this time have survived. On the Continent, however, there are sophisticated architectural drawings, from as early as the first half of the thirteenth century, which reveal the depth of knowledge and breadth of interest of the master masons. The best known are the surviving thirty-three pages of the notebook of one Villard de Honnecourt.

Villard was born in the village of Honnecourt near Cambrai in northern France and was a practising master mason during the second quarter of the thirteenth century. He must have been a fairly success-

ful man because we know that he was invited to work as far afield as Hungary. On his travels he drew buildings that appealed to him, either for technical or aesthetic reasons. Some of the drawings, like the south west tower of Laon Cathedral, which Villard greatly admired, are recognisable as the buildings that still stand today. And it was not only architecture that interested him. His notebook also contains sketches of animals, among them a lion which he states proudly to have been drawn from life, and several mechanical devices, including a crossbow 'which never misses' and the earliest known representation of a water-powered saw. A particularly interesting diagram shows an angel designed to rotate by primitive clockwork so as to follow the path of the sun across the sky – foreshadowing the invention of the mechanical clock before the close of the thirteenth century.

Villard's collection of drawings was made primarily for his own personal use, a notebook that provided a record of ideas and inspiration for his own designs. But later he turned it into a kind of text book for teaching up-and-coming masons by adding explanatory notes to the drawings and an introduction: 'Villard de Honnecourt greets you and entreats all who will use the devices found in this book to pray for his soul and remember him. For in this book is to be found sound advice on the qualities of masonry and the uses of carpentry. You will also find firm guidance on the drawing of figures after the lessons taught by the art of geometry.' A modest introduction it may seem for such an astonishing book, but then we have no reason to consider Villard de Honnecourt as having been exceptional among master masons. After his death, further diagrams and notes were

A building scene from a medieval manuscript, showing the masons' lodge in the background.

added by two other masters, and the sketchbook seems to have remained in use until at least the end of the century. Doubtless there were many such collections in circulation, here as well as on the Continent, and Villard's claim to fame lies only in the chance survival of his particular sketchbook. There were probably men of both greater and lesser talents than Villard, but his sketchbook clearly dispels the image of the Gothic church builder as an illiterate craftsman, muddling his way through on a mixture of intuition and faith.

It is also clear that the men who worked under the master mason were there, not to express their religious devotion, but to earn their daily bread. The building trade, ecclesiastical and secular, was one of the major employers of labour and, as the records of York Minster show, this was no golden age of industrial relations. During one four-day period in 1345, the Master of Works there complained of men refusing to work and men unfit to work, absenteeism and quarrelling, defective workmanship and the suspicious disappearance of building materials. And in London a few years earlier, four carpenters roughed up a 'foreign' carpenter as an example to others who were prepared to work for less than the local going rate! It is only to be expected that the records should highlight the trouble-makers at the expense of the majority of builders who worked conscientiously enough. More like than not there was malpractice among employers too, but, since it was they who wrote the records, less is known of it.

It seems that the City of London was the only place where the demand for labour was constant enough for the masons to be able to form any kind of recognised professional association. Elsewhere the spasmodic nature of the building trade and the itinerant working life it forced upon masons discouraged them from forming local *guilds* like other craftsmen. These craft guilds could have a permanent membership working under a set of *ordinances* approved by the municipal authorities of their town. The ordinances were very moral and religious in tone, reflecting not so much the piety of the guild as the temper of the times. They covered practical and organisational matters and exerted control over wages. Unlike the Weavers, the Goldsmiths, the Haberdashers and the Hatters, the masons were unable to present such a united wage front, and pay was a matter of individual negotiation between mason and employer. Wages were, therefore, subject to great variation. The records of Caernarvon Castle, for instance, show that the fifty or so masons employed there during one year were paid at seventeen different rates. Rates of pay varied according to the rank and skill of the mason and also the time of year. In summer the customary working day was just over twelve hours, but during winter fewer hours of daylight and bad weather could reduce the day to eight hours or less. Accordingly the employers paid a summer rate and a lower, winter rate, and even in some places an intermediate rate for spring and autumn.

Despite their lack of any effective collective bargaining the masons seem to have done fairly well for themselves. On average, the least skilled labourer, hewing and carting stone, earned $1\frac{1}{2}$ pence, perhaps two pence, a day; at the other end of the scale, the master mason could expect between one and two shillings a day with his other privileges on top. Unlike the other masons he might also

A ceremonial 'tracing board' from a masonic lodge, painted with various emblems of the stone mason's craft which were adopted in the seventeenth century by the speculative Freemasons and charged with symbolic and religious significance.

receive his day's pay whether or not he actually worked on the building site. In between, the roughmasons, stone-cutters, free-masons and setters, were paid according to their grade. The free-masons, rated second only to the master masons and specialist carvers, were the highest paid of these, receiving around $4\frac{1}{2}$ pence each day. In these years before the Black Death prices and wages were relatively stable and a middle-income mason was earning about three times what he needed to spend on food. A single man could live quite comfortably. But with a family the budget became rather stretched, and most working masons seem to have needed to supplement their income by other means. Some had agricultural holdings which they left to the care of their wives and children when they were working away on a building site, or tended themselves when the building trade was slack. We know that some masons kept horses and carts which they rented out, others dealt in dressed or undressed stone, and some even owned small quarries. One John Walsyngham of Oxford appears to have been not only a mason but an innkeeper too!

The masons' working life revolved around the *lodge*. Though primarily a workshop, the masons also ate and sometimes slept there during their midday break. Building a lodge for the masons was the carpenters' first job on the site. It varied in size according to requirements. The lodge was always built of timber but could be anything from a lean-to shed to a complex of several rooms with lofts and an adjoining *trassour* or *traycing house*, the master mason's drawing office. Life in the lodge was run to rules enforced by the master mason, who could recommend fines or other disciplinary action for those who behaved badly or produced defective work. The lodge was the first port of call for the travelling mason when he arrived in town. There he made himself known to the master mason by exchanging a special greeting, perhaps a secret handshake, which confirmed his status. By custom, the master mason was obliged to provide the new-comer with two weeks' work and the hospitality of the lodge before directing him to where further employment might be found.

At this point it should be mentioned that the mysteries of modern speculative Freemasonry cannot be shown to have any direct link with the medieval mason's craft. The word 'mysteries' was used in medieval times to describe any art or craft and had no occult over-tones. Speculative Freemasonry seems to have begun quite independently during the seventeenth century, the earliest recorded 'initiation' being that of Elias Ashmole into a lodge at Warrington in 1646. The Freemasons adopted the craft rules and technical terms of the medieval masons and gave them symbolic meanings. For instance, the *lewis*, which was a kind of clamping device used to lift large blocks of stone, became not only a symbol of strength, but also the name given to a freemason's son whose duty it is to 'bear the heavy burden of the day . . . so as to render the close of their (his parents') days happy and comfortable.' Of course the masons, like the guilds, did have their trade secrets to protect their economic interests and maintain standards of workmanship. But their concerns were practical rather than occult: the solution of problems of construction in ways that were both structurally sound and aesthetically pleasing. This meant that the more skilled masons, as we have seen in the case

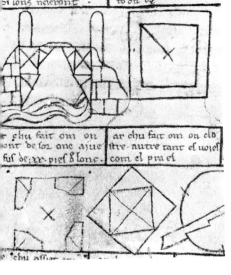

A detail from the pages of Villard de Honnecourt's notebook showing one of the masons' 'secrets' – the 'doubling of the square'.

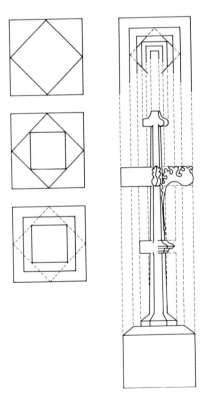

A very simplified adaptation of Roritzer's explanation of constructing a pinnacle by doubling the square.

of Villard de Honnecourt, had a working knowledge of geometry and, at a time when even the most elementary science smacked of magic, this undoubtedly served to clothe the craft with a certain esoteric aura.

Among the later additions to Villard de Honnecourt's notebook is an oblique reference to the most important of the masons' 'secrets': 'how to take the elevation from the plan' in the words of the rules of the German lodges set down in 1459. This was the method by which all the proportions of the elevation could be contained in and derived from the plan, using the geometrical properties of certain regular figures, in this case the square. One illustration in the notebook shows a square drawn within a square with its corners at the mid points of the larger square. In a nearby drawing the inner square is rotated through 45° to bring it parallel to the outer square. This 'doubling of the square' is a geometric operation that can be traced back to the writings of Plato in the fourth century BC. In the fifteenth century a book by Matthäus Roritzer shows how this general principle was applied to the specific task of constructing a *pinnacle*. A pinnacle is a stepped, cone- or pyramid-shaped piece of masonry that crowns a buttress, and was the outcome of increasingly sophisticated buttress design in Gothic architecture. Roritzer's drawings show how all the vertical proportions were derived from operations on the plan, a successive 'doubling of the square'. The aesthetically pleasing proportions of the pinnacle reflect, therefore, not the judgement of the mason's eye, but the intrinsic geometric properties of the square. Variations on the same method could be applied to other architectural features, and other regular figures, the triangle in particular, were used in similar ways. It must be stressed that the use of these regular figures was a practical means to a practical end. Although various geometric figures also acquired symbolic meanings, the triangle being equated with the Trinity for example, the methods were kept secret, not to guard some mystic truth, but to protect the masons' livelihood, and it has been suggested that the failure to survive of similar technical documents in England is due to deliberate destruction rather than accidental loss.

The arrival of the Black Death in the middle of the fourteenth century rocked the economic stability of the country. The shortage of labour meant that everyone was able to demand a higher wage. In an attempt to keep wage rises down, Edward III proclaimed a royal ordinance 'against the malice of servants who were idle and unwilling to serve after the pestilence without excessive wages.' Two years later Parliament, sitting for the first time after the Black Death, passed the first Statute of Labourers which confirmed the earlier ordinance and set maximum wages at pre-Black Death levels: 'Item, that carpenters, masons, tilers and other roofers of houses shall not take more for their day's work than the accustomed amount; that is to say, a master carpenter 3d and other 2d; a master mason of free-stone 4d and other masons 3d; and their servants (ie labourers) $1\frac{1}{2}$d. . . . .' Justices of Labour were appointed to enforce the Statute, and employers as well as workers who contravened the law were liable to fine or imprisonment. Despite successful prosecutions in the beginning, the Statute failed to contain rising wages, and stiffer penalties were introduced in later years, adding no doubt to the growing social tensions that were to come to a head in the Peasants' Revolt of 1381.

It is probably more than coincidence that the Articles of Masonry, also known as the Old Charges, date back to this period. Though they had been slow to form guilds like other craftsmen, the masons had already adopted a set of accepted 'customs' which were applied with relative uniformity throughout the country. It seems likely that this code of practice had evolved as early as the twelfth century during the boom period of monastic building when the masons' lodges at major ecclesiastical foundations became semi-permanent institutions and acquired established rules and regulations. The mobility of working masons also tended to lead to a unifying of practices since men from different parts of the country needed to be able to work side by side, affably and efficiently. In the face of the Statute of Labourers, the Articles of Masonry represent a timely formalisation of these customs.

The first Article deals, appropriately enough, with wages and stipulates that the mason should be paid the wages he deserves 'after the dearth of corn and victual in the country . . .', in other words that pay should be linked to the cost of living so that the mason's wage could keep pace with inflation. This, of course, was totally at odds with the government who, through the Statute of Labourers, were attempting to keep inflation down by keeping wages down – a conflict we still seem unable to resolve some six hundred years later! There is nothing in the Articles, however, to improve the working mason's security of employment. The master mason is urged to replace any mason that is 'imperfect or uncunning' as soon as possible, and it was apparently quite sufficient notice to inform a workman before noon that his services were not required the following day.

The Articles also deal with apprenticeship, and in some detail. The apprentice had to be without 'any maim for the which he may not truly work as him ought for to do' and could not be illegitimate or 'born in bond blood.' As in other trades, apprenticeship was to be for a minimum of seven years because 'such as been within less term may not perfectly come to his art.' As well as giving instruction in the craft, the master mason provided his apprentice with board and lodging and sometimes a little spending money. After seven years the apprentice could become a master mason in his own right, in theory. In practice, he served several more years as a journeyman, travelling from building site to building site, broadening his experience and gaining in expertise. There seems to have been a marked contrast between the ideal and the practical in all medieval trades and if only master masons had been allowed to take apprentices there would not have been enough trained masons to sustain the building industry. So there must have been other, perhaps less official, ways of learning the trade, and it is very likely that the quarry workshops provided alternative training grounds, especially for those boys content to set their sights lower than the top job of master mason. Masons might also have been recruited from the more experienced masons' labourers, their 'servants', and it would have been only natural for a father to teach his trade to his own son.

Before the building of a church began, the patron and the master mason agreed a contract which covered both the master mason's

Apprentices prove their skills in front of a guild official. Before a craftsman was awarded the status of a master, he had to make a 'master-piece' for the guild.

terms of employment and the basic design of the church. In 1442, the parishioners of Dunster in Somerset decided to build a tower on to their parish church, and a contract was drawn up between the churchwardens and John Marys, the mason. The contract stipulated that the tower was to be one hundred feet high. It was to have buttresses of the 'French' type (that is, a single buttress set at an angle to the corner rather than two buttresses set at 90° to each other) at three of its corners and a stair turret at the fourth. Certain of the windows were to be made to designs already commissioned from another mason, and the whole was to be crowned with battlements and pinnacles. For this John Marys was to be paid thirteen shillings and fourpence for each foot built, and twenty shillings for the pinnacles. The tower was to be completed within three years. For their part, the parishioners were to provide the necessary materials and a place for the mason to keep his tools. The provision of ropes, winches, arch centerings, etc, was their responsibility too, and they were also to lend a hand with moving the crane and carting any stones that were too heavy for two or three men to handle.

It was quite common for the churchwardens or patron to require the master mason to base his design for the new structure on an existing church nearby. In the building contract for Helmingham church in Suffolk, the mason Thomas Aldrych was to build a tower 'of the fashion of the steeple of Bramston.' And at Walberswick church, in the same county, the tower was to follow the general design of that at Tunstall, but with a west door and windows like those of Halesworth. Sometimes the mason submitted plans so that the patron could see just what he was getting for his money, and there is some evidence to suggest that the patron signed these preliminary drawings as evidence of his approval. From the contracts that have survived it would seem that responsibility for providing the stone for building usually lay with the patron, though the master mason might be expected to advise on selection and to check quality at the quarry.

Choice of stone was largely determined by location and finance. While the great monasteries could afford to send to some distant quarry for their stone, the parish churches could not. Unless they had the advantage of a very wealthy benefactor, their choice was limited to what was available locally. Some districts had fine building stone, some had inferior stone, and some had none at all. Since the mason had to tailor his designs to suit the qualities and shortcomings of the stone with which he was provided, this dependence on local materials was the major factor contributing to the stylistic variations in parochial church architecture. The prevalence of round towers in East Anglia, for instance, due to the lack of good building stone for the corners, has already been mentioned. Wherever possible, when a church was rebuilt or enlarged, money was saved by re-using the same stone. When Catterick church in North Yorkshire was rebuilt, Richard of Cracall, the mason, was required to demolish the old church and transport the stone to the new site. If there was insufficient stone to complete the work, he was to get additional stone from the quarry at his own cost.

Since haulage was such a vital consideration in budgeting for building stone, the most successful quarries were those close to the cheapest form of transport – water. The Purbeck and Portland quarries, for instance, were on the coast, and Barnack, Ketton and Tadcaster by navigable rivers. Barnack in Cambridgeshire, Ketton in Leicestershire, and Tadcaster in North Yorkshire are all on the geological belt of *oolitic limestone* which stretches north-east from Dorset to the Yorkshire coast, and which produced the best building stone in England. Limestone is a sedimentary rock, and oolitic limestone takes its name from the tiny, concentric spherical shells, called *ooids*, of which it is composed. These tightly-packed granules of calcium carbonate give the stone a dense texture that enables it to be cut freely in any direction, hence the medieval term *freestone*. At the southern end of this belt, quarries at Painswick in Gloucestershire, Chilmark, Box and Corsham in Wiltshire, Dundry in Avon, and Ham Hill and Doulting in Somerset, gave the West Country the warm, honey-coloured limestone from which its lovely 'wool' churches were built. By contrast, the even whiteness of Portland stone, which was not used extensively until after medieval times, produced a rather cold effect. A belt of *magnesium limestone*, so-called because the calcium in the molecular structure of the stone has been partly replaced by magnesium, runs north from Derbyshire to the coast of Northumberland. It provided the stone for many splendid churches in that area, including York Minster.

A poor relative of these fine limestones is a hard chalk called *clunch*. Clunch was ideal for detailed carving but the sculptor could only use it for interior work since it was too easily eroded by exposure to the elements. Deposits of *red sandstone* are found in a belt that runs north-west from Hereford and Worcester to south Lancashire. The softness of sandstone made it easy to dress, but it too weathered badly, and by the nineteenth century the exterior carving and window tracery of sandstone churches had all but worn away. Nonetheless, the deep, warm colour of the stone made it very popular and lends an attractive character to many Midland churches. In Kent, a local stone related to clunch, called *Kentish rag* or sometimes *ragstone*, was commonly used for walling, though it was too hard to be used where precise cutting or fine carving was required. *Granite*, found in Cornwall, is harder still and was not generally used before the fifteenth century. The intractability of this grey stone gave Cornish churches a rather uniform and austere appearance, an exception being St Mary Magdalene at Launceston where the masons carved the exterior with a wealth of ornament in total defiance of the stone itself.

In much of south east England and in East Anglia there was no building stone of any quality at all. In these areas the masons were faced with the choice of either importing good stone from a distance or making do with whatever other building materials were available locally. Due to the flourishing wool trade, East Anglia was comparatively prosperous, and the first, more expensive, alternative was sometimes open to the masons there. The stone they favoured was the *Caen* stone of Normandy, mentioned earlier, which could be floated across the Channel more economically than English stone could be carted across the countryside. Where they could not afford to import sufficient stone for the whole building, they used it only for the important parts of the structure, the quoins, windows and doors, and

Knapped flints set in a dressed stone create a jewel-like effect in this detail of the flushwork at St Mary's, Wool-pit, Suffolk.

got by with inferior material elsewhere. Necessity is the mother of invention, and in the eastern counties the mixing of imported free-stone with local *flint* produced a particularly beautiful technique of construction called *flushwork*. The flints were knapped, that is split open, to reveal a shiny black surface and then set in between contrasting panels or narrow strips of light-coloured freestone. The effect produced varied from simple chequer boarding, as at St Mary's, Luton in Bedfordshire, to the elaborate flushwork panelling seen at St Mary's, Coddenham in Suffolk. In earlier years particularly, flints were used unknapped to face rubble walling. They were set in place with rather a large amount of mortar and given a thick coat of plaster to achieve a fairly even surface.

In these stoneless districts the only other alternative building materials were timber and, later, brick. Timber was frequently used for porches and, especially in Essex, for towers and belfries. Sometimes the arcade that separated the nave from an aisle was built of wood too. At Selmeston Church in East Sussex, for example, the fourteenth-century nave arcade is carried by octagonal oak columns set on stone bases. By the end of the fifteenth century, the craft of brick-making had come across from Flanders, and brick was occasionally being used to repair, and later build, some churches, most notably in Essex again.

Mention must also be made of the use of *Purbeck marble* since it is a particular feature of Gothic architecture in its Early English style. This dark-coloured stone was first employed by William de Sens to provide a decorative contrast inside the choir of Canterbury Cathedral, and thereafter it became popular everywhere for slender, detached shafts set around piers and in wall arcading. It was also used for carved tombs and effigies. Shafts of Purbeck marble were supplied to the masons ready-dressed and polished, the shafts not being built up of drum-shaped blocks as columns were, but turned on a stone-lathe. The stone was quarried in Dorset and is not, strictly speaking, a marble at all but a *fossiliferous limestone* whose characteristic fossil is that of a water snail, *paluctina carinifera*, which can be seen quite clearly in the stone. The demand for the 'marble' was such that quarries of similar stone were opened up at Bethersden in Kent, Petworth in West Sussex and Frosterley in Durham.

By the time the supplies of stone started arriving at the building site, the carpenters had finished constructing the masons' lodge and turned their attention to assembling timber scaffolding and making ready the hoists and cranes. The ground had been cleared ready for the master mason to supervise the setting out of his plan for the new church. The first task was to mark out the church's main axis.

The longitudinal axis of a church always lay east–west, with the altar at the eastern end. Early on there had been a few rare exceptions to this rule, none of which has survived, where the length of the nave ran north–south. But since, even in these buildings, the altar remained in the east wall set in an apse, we may consider the 'devotional' axis to have still been east–west. Modern surveying of the orientation of medieval churches, however, reveals striking deviations from true east, both to north and to south. In Hereford and Worcester, for instance, orientations vary between 50° north of east (Llancillo Church) and 38° south (Abbey Dore Church). As yet there is no completely acceptable explanation for this fascinating phenomenon, but two theories are of interest.

According to the first theory, the church was not aligned to the true east, but to the position of the rising sun on the feast day of the saint to whom the church was to be dedicated. This idea was very popular with the Victorians, conjuring up a romantic scene in which clergy and masons gathered before dawn to drive a wooden stake into the earth where the high altar was to stand. Then, as the sun rose, greeted by the chanting of monks, the axis of the new church was marked out by driving in a second stake to line up with the first and the rising sun. It is certainly a charming image with pleasing links to pagan tradition, but there is no mention of the theory prior to the seventeenth century, and it does have a major practical drawback. In the English climate, the chance of a clear sunrise on many a saint's day must have been very slim, and the masons were hardly likely to pack up their tools and postpone building operations for twelve whole months in the hope of a clear morning the same time next year.

A second theory is that the churches were aligned to the east with the aid of a magnetic compass. At first sight this would seem to suggest that all churches should lie due east without any deviation at all. But in fact magnetic north is not fixed; it varies slightly from place to place and year to year, and over a span of centuries this geomagnetic variation could be considerable. The problem here is that the magnetic compass is not heard of in Europe until as late as the twelfth century, and then it is as a ship's compass consisting of a needle set in a piece of wood and floating in a bowl of water. There is much mystery

Holy Trinity, Bosham, West Sussex, shows the misalignment between nave and chancel which is commonly found in churches where the two parts were rebuilt independently.

surrounding the origin of the compass, however, and although it is generally assumed to have been of arabic invention, it is almost certain that a south-pointing compass was in use in China many centuries earlier. Is it possible that such a compass or lodestone was available early on in England? If accepted, the magnetic orientation theory would also explain the commonly found misalignment between nave and chancel, referred to previously. In this age of rebuilding, the chancel was often rebuilt independently of the nave. After demolition of the chancel, the chancel arch might be blocked up to protect the rest of the church from the elements. So the axis of the new chancel could not be sighted from the nave, but had to be set out on its own. If the new east–west axis was found using a magnetic compass, it would almost certainly be divergent from the original axis, and the misalignment would reflect the geomagnetic shifts of the intervening years.

Once the main axis of the church had been determined, the rest of the plan could be set out. Gothic churches are designed in repeating *bays*, a legacy perhaps of the timber tradition of building with posts and beams. Each bay consisted of an arch supported by two piers. Buttresses divided the external walls to match the internal divisions, and windows and doorways were set between them. The length of the bay, therefore, was the basic measurement upon which the other dimensions of the church depended.

In medieval times there was no universal standard of measurement, each village had its own. The standard of length was called the *rod* or *pole*, and later the *perch*. It varied from sixteen to twenty-four feet (five to seven and a half metres), and, according to tradition, was determined by stopping sixteen adult men on their way into church and making them stand with their right feet in line, one behind the other. A length of timber was cut to match and this became the standard pole for the village. The pole and its simple multiples and divisions provided the units in which the parish church plan was laid out. A cord cut to the length of the pole and folded twice, for instance, produced the medieval yard. The church had to be set out in these simple basic units because the builders had only roman numerals with which to work, and even the most elementary calculation could not be worked out without the help of counters or an abacus until the end of the sixteenth century when the arabic numerical system arrived by way of Spain. Until then the builders had to rely upon systems of proportion. A right-angled corner can be set out using a piece of rope knotted to divide its length in the ratio of $3:4:5$. When the rope is laid out to form a triangle with the knots as corners, the angle between the 3 and 4 sides is always $90°$. It is not known for certain when this method was first used, and early on the squaring of rectangular areas may have been by a trial-and-error matching of the diagonals. The importance to the mason of learning proportional systems of working is emphasised in Villard de Honnecourt's notebook. As well as the all important 'secret' of taking the elevation from the plan, he presents several examples of how small drawings may be 'scaled up' from the tracing board to full size on the sculptor's stone by resolving irregular shapes into underlying regular figures, which could be drawn up to any size by the rules of geometry.

When the main walls and piers of the church had been marked out, the foundations were dug by the masons' 'servants' and filled in with rubble tightly packed by a *pile-driver*. A small pile-driver would probably have been built by the carpenters on site, but if they were near a large town or major building centre, they may have been able to hire a bigger one, as contractors do today. It was unusual to level the ground before building. Instead the masons accommodated the natural rise and fall of the land by building up the lower parts of the wall until they reached an even level all round, a kind of plinth on which the church would sit.

At the quarry, the *hewers* chopped the stone out in great lumps and broke it down into workable pieces. The *roughmasons*, using heavy, double-headed hammer-axes, formed the stone into roughly squared blocks and then handed over to the *stone cutters* who produced precisely shaped blocks. The stone cutter worked with a broad chisel

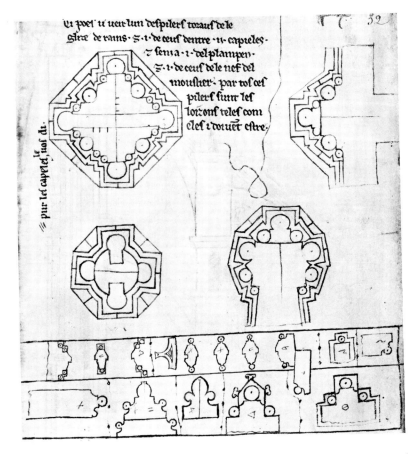

Another page from *Villard de Honnecourt's* notebook showing plans of piers and the templates or 'mouldes' from which the stones for them were cut to shape.

called a *bolster*. During the thirteenth century, masonry was dressed with great care using the bolster vertically, but by the turn of the fourteenth century the masons found they could work faster, though with less care, if they held the bolster diagonally. This change from vertical to diagonal tooling-marks gives a useful indication of the date of masonry. Each stone block had a *face*, the surface exposed in the completed wall; two *beds*, the bottom and top surfaces on which the stone and that above rested; and a *tail*, which was buried in the thickness of the wall. When a single block was needed to run right through the wall and show a squared face on both sides, it was called *perpeyn ashlar*.

A higher rank of stone cutter was responsible for shaping the circular drums for simple pillars and the curved voussoirs of the arches. More complicated pieces for vaulting, complex piers, tracery and pinnacles, were the handiwork of the *freemason*, and important decorative elements, like capitals, were often carved by the master mason's own hand.

The success of the church, structurally and visually, depended on the masons' ability to produce accurately shaped stones. The precise *profiles*, or sections, of the stones, and the jigsaw-like setting out of the worked pieces were drawn up by the master mason on *tracing boards* or sometimes on a specially made plaster floor-slab. The tracing floor from above the north porch of Wells Cathedral shows a confusion of incised lines among which the profiles of several architectural features

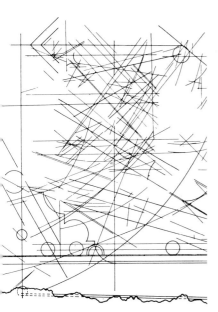

Among these lines scratched on part of the floor slab over the north porch of Wells Cathedral, the profiles of various architectural features, set out by the master mason, can be seen. From these profiles the masons cut their templates.

can be seen. At All Saints' Church, Leighton Buzzard in Bedford-shire, a number of drawings on one of the piers of the crossing appear to be the master mason's preliminary sketches for the tracery of the church's windows. Unfortunately the church was much altered during the fifteenth century, and the earlier windows were removed, so we are unable to compare them with the mason's drawings.

Using templates cut from oak boards or lead sheet, called 'mouldes' in contemporary records, the profiles drawn up by the master mason were transferred to the squared blocks of stone, which were then chiselled down to shape. It would seem that journeymen sometimes 'borrowed' these templates as they travelled the country since identical profiles can be found in the mouldings of arches and piers of quite unrelated churches. The mouldes were sometimes sent to the quarry so that stones could be worked there. This reduced the weight of stone to be carted and so saved money. Certain quarries had their own lodges which could supply some ready-made features like doorways or small windows with simple tracery. Famous master masons, like Henry Yeveley and later William Orchard, had their own workshops turning out complete prefabricated window kits for the convenience, if the patrons could afford it, of lesser masters.

Each mason, whatever his status, had his own *mason's mark* which he carved on the finished stone like a signature. The mark was not intended for show and was either carved on one of the beds or incised on the face of the stone where it would later be concealed by coats of limewash or wall painting. The purpose of the mark was to enable the master mason to keep an eye on the productivity of individual masons and to trace the culprit if a stone was found to be defective. In some churches masons' marks appear on only a few of the plain stones, perhaps indicating those stones dressed by casual workers with whom the master mason was unfamiliar and on whom he would want to keep a special check. Marks are more plentiful on churches built in a hurry by a large workforce in which many masons may have been employed on 'piece-work' rates. On smaller building projects, the master mason could be more familiar with who was doing what, so marks were less necessary. Elaborate sections of masonry were usually unmarked since everyone would have known who had worked them, though occasionally the mason added his mark to a particularly splendid piece out of conscious pride. At Berden Church in Essex the mason signed his name in Lombardic letters beside the chancel arch: *Gefrai Limathum*, Geoffrey the Mason. Though some marks may have been issued on the site to lower grades of mason, generally they belonged to individual men, and by matching marks in different churches the journeyman's travels can be traced. Often they were hereditary, handed down with slight modifications at each generation to record the mason's 'pedigree'. Such marks were important status symbols whose use depended ultimately on the authority of the lodges. The regulations of one group of masons on the Continent reveal that the granting of the mark to an apprentice was a cause for celebration, it being the custom for his master to provide dinner for the apprentice and ten of his fellows. The Continental masons seem to have been less self-effacing than their English counterparts. On the tomb of Matthew Böblinger in the Frauenkirche at Esslingen in

St Giles', Skelton, near York, one of the most complete churches of the Early English period of Gothic architecture.

Germany, his mason's mark is displayed as proudly as any knight's coat of arms; and in Prague Cathedral there are contemporary portrait busts of the master masons from 1344 onwards. In England the nearest equivalents are the stained-glass figures of master mason William Wynford, and master carpenter Hugh Herland in the chapel of Winchester College.

Masons' marks are not to be confused with the *position marks* also to be found on dressed stones. Position marks, usually roman numerals, indicated to the *walling mason* or *setter* the sequence in which he was to set, say, the voussoirs of an arch. As stone was set on stone, the new church began to emerge. Building usually started with the chancel and proceeded westwards ending with the tower, often the most costly part of the structure.

The plan of the early Gothic parish church remained straightforward, either the two-celled, rectangular plan or the simple cruciform. St Giles' at Skelton, near York, built around the year 1240, gives us perhaps the most perfect glimpse of the small Early English parish church. With no later structural additions and only the most sympathetic of restorations, carried out at the beginning of the last century by one Henry Graham at the rather remarkable age of nineteen, St Giles' stands today very much as its master mason intended it to be. Its ground plan is devised with an economy that sets the tone for the elegant simplicity of the whole church. A basic rectangle is divided by arcades running the length of the building which mark off aisles to north and south. In small Early English churches the aisles are rather narrow because they were set under a continuation of the steep slope of the nave roof. Towards the east

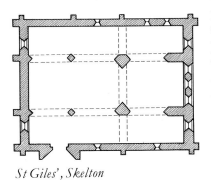

St Giles', Skelton

end, a single arch bridges the two arcades and separates the chancel from the nave. This chancel arch supports a *bell-cote* which expresses the internal division of the ground plan on the outside of the church. The rigid H-shaped formation of arches and piers provides the structural 'skeleton' of the building. At the ends of the arcades, half piers, called *responds*, correspond to external buttresses which carry the outward thrust of the arcades to ground. Many churches of this period are still quite small – the nave of St Giles' has only two bays. For larger churches the cruciform plan was more usual, perhaps as a result of monastic influence. St Mary's at Potterne in Wiltshire and the Church of the Assumption of St Mary the Virgin at Uffington in Oxfordshire are excellent examples of cruciform churches built in the Early English style.

A pier from the nave arcade of St Mary's, West Walton, Norfolk, showing detached shafts 'tied' back to the main shaft by annulet rings. The shafts were originally of dark Purbeck marble.

Let us suppose that the setters have just finished laying the last stones of the repeating bays that make up the nave arcades of our thirteenth-century church, and the master mason and patron stand back to survey the work. The first feature that catches the eye in each bay is the pointed arch, dramatically outlined by the rounds and hollows of its deeply cut mouldings. In the Early English style, arches are often more acutely pointed than in any other period, as if the masons revelled in their new-found liberation from the classical semi-circular arch. Among the round *roll mouldings* of the arch, the masons might have inserted the more elaborate *dogtooth* moulding, evolved from the earlier chevron of the Normans. The free use of dogtooth moulding throughout the church is a special feature of thirteenth century work. Another common ornament is *nailhead* moulding, made up of strings of small stone pyramids.

The shafts of the piers that support the arch are usually round, although octagonal piers are gaining in popularity. In some churches the round piers have four half-shafts grafted on, rather like the compound piers of Romanesque architecture. Occasionally complete detached shafts are grouped around the main shaft and held in place at intervals along their length by *annulet rings*, circular stones bonded back into the central column. The detached shafts are often made of the dark Purbeck marble, and their use both around piers and in wall arcading is a particular characteristic of the Early English style.

The bases of piers usually have two thick roll mouldings with a deep hollow between, known as a *water holding moulding*. Capitals are moulded too. A single roll moulding where the capital meets the shaft and, usually, a double roll moulding where it meets the roll mouldings of the circular abacus, give the capital the appearance of an inverted bell, hence the descriptive name *bell capital*. In some churches the space between the lower and upper roll mouldings is filled with one of the fancier mouldings. Nailhead moulding is used at St Giles', Skelton, for instance. In others the space is filled with beautifully stylised *stiff-leaf foliage* rising from long elegant stalks. The sparing use of carving in Early English churches contrasts strongly with the vigorous, sprawling sculpture of the Romanesque style. Where carving is used, however, it is always exquisitely executed. The overall effect is one of delicate restraint, a mellow reflection of the more austere simplicity of the Cistercian Abbeys in which the Gothic style had been nurtured.

With the turn of the fourteenth century, Gothic architecture evolves into the Decorated style. As Rickman's term implies, the simple, linear quality of Early English gives way to greater elaboration. The plan of the church begins to expand both by elongation of nave and chancel and by the addition of aisles and sometimes transepts. The lateral expansion of the ground plan is one of the major differences between the development of the parish church and that of abbeys and cathedrals. The general plan of a church in the Decorated style is still an unaisled chancel and an aisled nave, but now with north and south porches and a western tower added. There are, however, many variations. Although it was no longer so much in favour, some churches retained the cruciform plan even when they were completely rebuilt in the Decorated style. The result can sometimes be stunning:

Above
St Mary's, Eaton Bray, Bedford-shire, houses some of the most elegant examples of the stiff-leaf foliage capitals that are typical of the Early English period. This group, from the north arcade, was carved around 1240.

Right
The interior of St Giles', Skelton, near York, where the narrow side aisles are set under the continued slope of the nave roof. The church's bell capitals are enriched with a bold nail-head moulding.

St Patrick's, Patrington, Humberside – a handsome Decorated Gothic
church built on the cruciform plan.
The interior (above) shows that this
is one of the few parish churches where
the transepts, as well as the nave, have
aisles. The result is a forest of graceful piers and arches. The exterior
(left): the tower and spire, ringed by
an octagonal corona, form the soaring
central focus of this church.

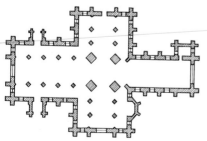

St Patrick's, Patrington

St Patrick's Church at Patrington in Humberside, for example, has a
cruciform plan in which both nave and transepts are aisled. In all
directions a forest of graceful shafted piers fills the view. In each
transept there is provision for three side chapels, and over the
crossing a tower and magnificent spire are raised.

How does a bay of our Decorated church compare with that of
the church built a century earlier? In smaller churches round shafted
piers have fallen out of favour, and octagonal piers are most often
used instead. In larger churches, piers are formed by diamond-shaped
clusters of shafts, or, as they sometimes were earlier, a central column
with four shafts attached. A flat strip of stone, called a *fillet*, often
runs up the outside of each shaft.

The bases of piers consist of two or three roll mouldings, more
widely spaced than before, and sometimes set on an octagonal plinth.
Capitals are still predominantly moulded, but of greater variety.
When set on an octagonal shaft, the capital usually assumes a matching octagonal plan. Some capitals are still foliated, but the stylised
leaves of early Gothic work are gone, replaced by life-like leaves and
flowers, ivy and oak being particular favourites. The foliage is beautifully carved in a dense mass that gives the capital a slightly bulbous
outline. On occasion there are no capitals at all, and the clustered
shafts of the piers blend into the mouldings of the arch above without
interruption.

Arches are generally less acutely pointed than before, and, although there are more mouldings round their edges, the carving is shallower, producing a softer, rippling effect rather than the more dramatic contrast of light and shade. The most common decorative moulding is the *ball-flower*. A small ball enclosed by three petals to form a globular flower and set in a concave moulding, this ornament is as typical of fourteenth-century work as the dogtooth is of thirteenth. The squarish *four-leaf flower* or *tablet flower* is also popular.

Perhaps the most important distinguishing feature of the Decorated style is the introduction of the *ogee* arch. It is formed by two shallow S-shaped, ogee curves meeting in a sharp point, and is most frequently used above sedilia, piscinae and the *niches* which held devotional statues. Sometimes an ordinary pointed arch is framed in an ogee arch. Although its sinuous curve suggests some exotic Eastern origin, the ogee probably derives from the more homely double-curved cross-braces of timber construction. If the arrival of the pointed arch marks the birth of Gothic, then the ogee brings the style of age. Its distinctive outline is a pervasive influence in Decorated churches, weaving webs of stone tracery across windows, and liberating the profiles of mouldings and shafts from their restrained, compass arcs by giving them more luxurious, free-flowing lines. The ogee arch is not a constructional form and so is mainly confined to decorative features, where it is seldom found without an encrustation of *crockets*, small volutes shaped like buds or curled leaves. Its apex usually grows upwards into a leaf-shaped termination, called a *finial*. This budding

Above
Early clerestories often had circular windows, like these at St Margaret's, Cley-next-the-Sea, Norfolk.

Opposite

Above
Capitals at St Patrick's, Patrington, have the densely packed and naturalistically carved foliage of the Decorated style that contrasts with the stylised stiff-leaf foliage of earlier Gothic work.

Below
A doorway at St Lawrence's, Keyston, Cambridgeshire, showing the ogee arch which was introduced during the Decorated Gothic period.

foliage underlines the feeling of potential and movement that is inherent in the flexed curves of the ogee arch. Wherever they could the masons used foliated finials and crockets in profusion, and together with the flowing ogee line, they conspire to give the Decorated style a restless, organic energy which contrasts strongly with the stillness of Early English work.

By now, the first half of the fourteenth century, we are more likely to find a *clerestory* above the nave arcade of our church. Many small churches were still built without clerestories, however, and early ones are tentatively low, often with circular window openings. The introduction of the clerestory in parish churches was made possible by a reduction in the pitch of the roof. As we have seen, in early Gothic parish churches one steep roof sheltered both nave and aisles, so there was room for only the narrowest of aisles if their outside walls were to be of any height at all. The roof was generally thatched or covered with wooden shingles. In the great churches, the church builders had begun to use lead as a roofing material at the end of the preceding century, and its use soon spread to the parish church since the metal was readily available – England being the Continent's main supplier of lead. Lead was far more weather-proof and durable than the earlier roofing materials, but on a steeply sloping roof it presented a problem: its weight, combined with a high coefficient of expansion, made it slip or 'creep' down the slope. The solution was to build roofs with a lower pitch. Where the nave roof of a church meets the wall of its tower, tell-tale weathering marks can sometimes be seen

The development of window tracery during the Early English and Decorated periods:

Left to right

Triple lancets
St Peter's, Maidstone, Kent

Plate tracery
St Mary Magdalene's, Baunton, Gloucestershire

Geometrical tracery
Priory Church of St Peter and St Paul, Leominster, Hereford and Worcester

Reticulated tracery
St Lawrence's, Ludlow, Salop

Kentish tracery
St Mary's, Chartham, Kent

Curvilinear tracery
St James', Great Horwood, Buckinghamshire

indicating the steeper slope of an earlier roof. Lowering the pitch of the roof enabled nave and aisles to be roofed separately, making room for tall clerestories with larger windows. The new clerestories not only let more light into the nave, they also provided the mason and glazier with further opportunities to demonstrate their skills with stone tracery and stained glass. The development of the traceried window was one of the chief glories of the Gothic era, but early on only the east window behind the high altar was large enough to offer the craftsmen any scope for grandeur. Now, as all the walls of the church rose higher to meet the flatter roof, the world was their oyster.

Window tracery, the hall mark of the Gothic style, was not invented – it evolved. And although the beauty of Gothic tracery lies in its infinite variety, it is possible to follow the stages of its development in our parish churches. Early in medieval times even plain glass had been too costly for most parishes, and the small round-headed windows of their churches were probably 'glazed' with oiled linen stretched on wooden frames, translucent enough to let some light in while keeping the weather out. As in domestic buildings, the windows usually had wooden shutters, not hinged but wedged into the window opening. At the Battle of Hastings, King Harold's struggling army is said to have used such shutters as makeshift shields.

In the thirteenth century, the sharply pointed *lancet window* made its appearance in Early English style parish churches. The lancet window was tall and thin, keeping the amount of expensive glass to a minimum. The glass was set into the window in small diamond-shaped panes called *quarries*. Sometimes lancet windows were set in pairs or larger groups of three or five, especially at the east end of the church. Outside, it was now usual to protect the window from rain-water running down the wall by providing it with a *dripstone*, or *hood*

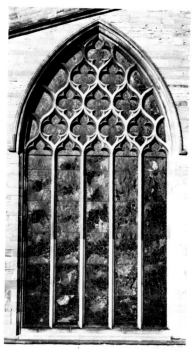

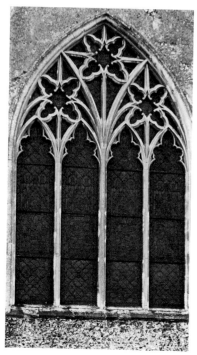

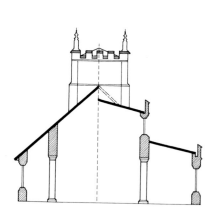

Lowering the pitch of the church roof enabled aisles to be built wider and made it easier to provide a clerestory.

mould, a projecting arch-shaped moulding above a window or a doorway. The dripstone ended on each side of the window in a *stop*, which was usually carved as a head or an animal, or simply foliated. When a pair of lancet windows each had their own dripstone, the point at which the two dripstones met between the windows formed a dip that collected water instead of throwing it off. So the masons began to group the two, and sometimes three windows under a single dripstone. This inevitably brought the windows closer together, reducing the masonry between them to a thin strip. At the same time a rather ugly flat area of walling was left between the heads of the windows and the point of the dripstone above. It was not long before the masons pierced this blank area with some simple geometric opening: a circle, a lozenge, or the four-lobed shape called a *quatrefoil*. The result is known as *plate tracery*. Where the pierced shapes came close to the windows below, the mouldings round them were allowed to run down the thin strips of masonry that separated the windows. A turning point had been reached. Where there had been two or three windows with a pierced opening above them, there was now a single window divided into two or three *lights* by vertical stone bars called *mullions*, and with *bar-tracery* at its head. This was the real beginning of Gothic tracery.

Towards the end of the thirteenth century, the number of lights in windows increased, especially in the east window which now became one of the most important visual focal points of the whole building. This meant that the tracery above the light became more complicated, but since it was still based on relatively simple geometric shapes it is known as *geometric tracery*. Early geometric tracery consists of single or grouped circles, the result perhaps of the master mason experimentally 'doodling' with his compasses, as in the window 'sketch' in Leighton Buzzard Church. At first the circles were plain, but soon they were given *cusps*, projecting points that divided the inside of the circle into a number of arcs or lobes. By the turn of the fourteenth century and the beginning of the Decorated style, geometric tracery was still in vogue but its stone bars were more elaborately moulded and cusped, and traced out a greater variety of geometric forms. The three-lobed *trefoil* became popular, and sometimes one lobe of the quatrefoil was extended to form a dagger-like shape. *Intersecting tracery* was also common at this time, each mullion forking into two curves, of the same radius as the arch of the window head, which then intersect with their neighbours to create pointed arches within pointed arches. More often than not, each point is cusped. Some geometric tracery has an especially intricate centre-piece; some has no particular focus at all. In Kent a local, rather spiky form of tracery developed, which is known as *Kentish tracery*. The design possibilities were virtually unlimited, and the traceried window became the master mason's chief vehicle for inventive expression.

As the influence of the Decorated style grew stronger, softer flowing forms began to supplant the more rigid shapes of geometric tracery. The new ogee curve was woven into a network of stone called *reticulated tracery*. In its precise repetition reticulated tracery still retains something of the earlier geometric style, and it is in the succeeding *curvilinear tracery* that we find the true epitome of the Decorated style. As its name implies, curvilinear tracery emphasises freely curving lines, but at the expense of the openings they define. In geometric tracery the attention had been drawn to the shapes of the window spaces, but now the eye is seduced by the meandering lines of the stonework itself.

In France the curvilinear style of tracery developed into the even more fanciful *flamboyant tracery*, named not so much for its extravagance as for the flame – *flambe* – shape formed by parallel but staggered ogee curves. English and French architecture had run side by side since the Conquest, but now, in the middle of the fourteenth century, they parted company. Perhaps it is not just coincidence that the two countries were at war, ostensibly over Edward III's claim to the French throne, but in fact to protect English economic interests in the wool trade with Flanders. In France, the masons continued to exploit the graceful, flowing lines of the Decorated style and evolved the Flamboyant style of Gothic which held sway there until well into the sixteenth century. By contrast, in England a more orderly and rectilinear style, Perpendicular, was coming.

But that was still a generation away. For the time being the masons worked uninhibited by the more sober spirits that prevailed after the Black Death, and the tracery of their windows continues to follow the exuberant lines of the Decorated style. As the arches and piers of the nave arcade mark out the bays inside a church, so, on the outside, each bay is defined by two buttresses with a window or doorway set between. As windows grew larger, the area of walling between them became smaller and the buttresses of necessity played an increasingly important structural role. So parallel with the evolution of Gothic windows was a corresponding development in buttress design.

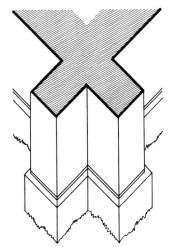

Thirteenth-century corner buttresses at right angles

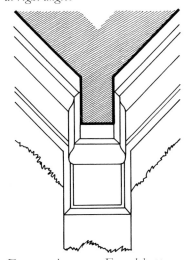

Fourteenth-century French buttress

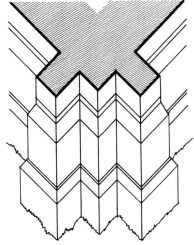

Fifteenth-century buttresses at right angles set back to reveal corner

In the old Romanesque style, buttresses had been little more than wide, flat strips of stone, pale reflections of the classical pilaster, serving no real structural purpose at all. Throughout the Gothic era, buttresses decreased in width and increased in projection as they were required to accommodate more of the outward thrust of the walls. Projection was greatest at the base and was reduced in three of four steps as the buttress rose. Each step was capped with a sloping *set-off* to shed rain-water. In the thirteenth century, buttresses in the Early English style did not always reach the full height of the church. They usually ended in a gabled coping or were just angled away into the wall. By the fourteenth century, the masons working in the Decorated style had learned the principle of top loading and weighted their buttresses at the top with *pinnacles*. The weight of the pinnacle acting downwards helped the buttress to sustain the outward thrust of the wall, and its elegantly tapering profile, enriched with crockets and a foliated finial, provided the perfect visual finish. Beneath the pinnacle, the last stage of the buttresses of a particularly prestigious church might be hollowed out to form a niche. The niche, decorated with blind tracery or cusping and holding a statue, combined with the pinnacle above to impart a special grandeur to such buttresses. The *flying buttress*, a half-arch carrying the thrust of a clerestory wall over the roof of an aisle to a main buttress, also came into use in England in the fourteenth century, but was rarely employed in parochial architecture for other than decorative reasons. The construction of buttresses at the corners of the building provides a useful guide to dating. In the thirteenth century there were two buttresses at each corner set at right angles to each other. At the turn of the fourteenth century this form was abandoned and replaced by a single buttress set diagonally at the corner, the *French buttress*. The French buttress remained in use until the very end of the Gothic era when there was a return to paired corner buttresses. Unlike the thirteenth century however, the corner of the building was allowed to project between the two buttresses producing a more visually interesting composition.

The vertical stages of the buttress are not arbitrary. They were designed so that their set-offs line up with the *string courses* which run around the church like string around a parcel. String courses are horizontal projecting bands of stone moulding, usually carved with one of the ornaments of the period. As buttresses beat out the rhythm of the bays along the length of the wall, so string courses mark out more subtle divisions of its height. Setting windows and other features on this grid of buttresses and string courses gave unity and order to the exterior elevations of the church. The first string course is usually immediately above the plinth on which the building 'sits'; the second runs level with the sills of the windows; another often runs along at the height of the springing point of the window arches and was sometimes looped up over them to double as their dripstones; and the final string course is found along the top of the wall beneath the *parapet*.

The parapet was another new feature associated with the introduction of lead roofing and the consequent lowering of the pitch of the roof. At the beginning of the Gothic era, the steeply pitched church roof was still supported at the eaves by a corbel table as it had

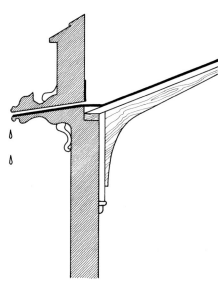

With the introduction of lead for roofing, the steeply pitched roof supported at the eaves by a corbel table (top) *became replaced by a low pitched roof ending in a gutter behind a parapet* (above). *Rain-water escaped from the gutter through gargoyles.*

been in Romanesque buildings. The roof overlapped the corbel table so that rain-water was thrown clear of the walls. With the coming of flatter roofs this arrangement was changed. Instead the roof now ended in a gutter behind a parapet, a vertical extension of the wall stretching between the tops of the buttresses. Sometimes the parapet was quite plain, simply finished with an angled or gabled coping. More usually it was *battlemented*, the solid sections being known as *merlons* and the square spaces between them as *embrasures*. The merlons were often enriched with blind tracery, or flushwork in the eastern counties, and sometimes they were pierced with some geometric shape, a quatrefoil or cross-shaped *oylet* for instance. The parapet may rise flush with the wall, the division between the two being indicated only by a string course, or the corbel table may be retained to support a slightly projecting parapet which made space for a wider gutter behind. Rain-water escaped from the gutter through spouts called *gargoyles* which projected through the wall immediately beneath the parapet. More often than not the gargoyles are elaborately carved, often humorously or grotesquely. Up and down the country, many a fantastic monster spouts rain-water into the churchyard through its gaping mouth, and on occasion, in less delicate fashion.

These innovations had transformed the sky-line of the parish church. Visually, the early Gothic churches had still been dominated by the blank areas of their steep roofs. The straight skyline of the roof ridge, relieved only perhaps by *gable crosses* at its ends, had kept the church earth-bound. Now, as the style reached maturity, the walls of the church rose up, crowned with battlements and spiky pinnacles, to meet the sky like a plant stretching up to the light.

Though the roof was all but hidden from view by the parapet and pinnacles, it remained, of course, a practical necessity, and its construction was the main task of the carpenters. The master carpenter ranked second only to the master mason in the hierarchy of the medieval building trade, and his skilfully constructed roof with its time-worn timbers is the most charming interior feature of many a parish church. The equivalents of the masons' quarries were the saw-pits in the great forests, where huge logs of oak and, by the fourteenth century, elm were sawn up by sawyers working in pairs, or perhaps by a water-powered saw-mill. Choice of good timber was as important as choice of building stone, and the master carpenter might spend much time and trouble finding the best. Even so, wood decays and few twelfth and thirteenth century roofs have survived unaltered. Although there is a great variety of design in roof structures, we may pick out several basic types which the master carpenter selected, combined and adapted to suit the situation in hand.

The most common forms of roof construction in the thirteenth century were probably the *trussed-rafter roof* and the *tie-beam roof*. The tie-beam roof was the simplest roof structure used in medieval times. Hefty timbers, the *tie beams*, were laid across from wall to wall. On their ends rested the bottoms of the main rafters, the *principals*, which met at the roof ridge. The principals were given extra support by a central *king post*. The king post rested on the tie beam and sometimes branched into two or more *struts* at the top. Instead of a king post a

Above	Below
Parts of a king-post roof	*Parts of an arch-braced roof (with collar beams on the common rafters)*
Principal	Principal
Purlin	Purlin
–	Collar beam
Arch brace (under tie beam)	Arch brace
Wall post	Wall post
Wall plate	Wall plate
Strut (longitudinal)	Strut
Common rafter	Common rafter
Tie beam	–
King post	–
Strut (transverse)	–
Ridge piece	–

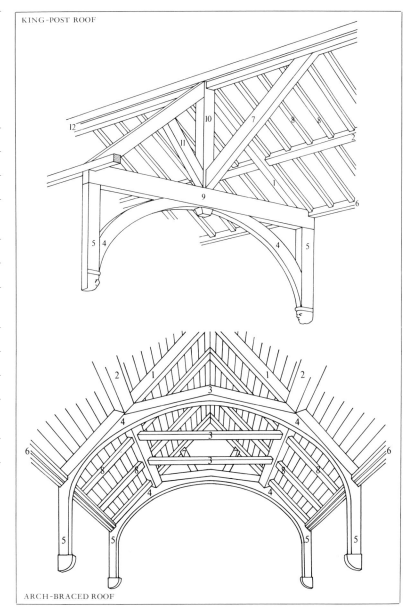

KING-POST ROOF

ARCH-BRACED ROOF

pair of shorter *queen posts* might be used on either side of the centre. This braced triangular shape formed the basic *truss* of the roof. Between these trusses ran the longitudinal members: the *ridge* at the top, the *wall plates* directly on top of the walls, and, half-way between, the *purlins* which carried the sloping *common rafters*. The heavy tie beams were very prone to sagging in the middle and were often cambered to counteract this tendency and given support underneath by a pair of *arch braces* curving down to *wall posts*, which were in turn supported by stone corbels bonded into the nave walls. The tie beams, wall plates and king or queen posts might be treated to some decorative mouldings, but the rest of the roof was quite plain. It was not until the fourteenth century that the roof was intended to be a major decorative feature of the church.

In some areas, the western counties in particular, timbers of sufficient bulk and length for tie beams were not always readily available, so the carpenters sometimes used the *trussed-rafter roof*, a structure that dispensed with both tie beams and principals. Instead, each pair of common rafters carried an equal share of the load and was supported by struts at their feet and tied together just below the ridge with a short, horizontal *collar beam* to prevent them from spreading apart. Intersecting beams placed diagonally between opposite rafters, called *scissor beams*, were another means of bracing the rafters and were sometimes used instead of, or as well as, collar beams.

During the first half of the fourteenth century the tie beam roof fell out of favour and was largely replaced by the *arch-braced* roof. In the arch-braced roof, the principals were supported by continuously curved arch braces which sprang from wall posts to prevent the roof from spreading outwards. The arch braces were tied together towards the top of the roof by a collar beam, so they acted, in effect, as a wooden arch supporting the principals. Purlins and common rafters were set between the principals as they had been in the earlier roofs. Occasionally the spaces between the principals were boarded with panels which were sometimes carved and painted, but this was rare, and it was more common to board only the extreme eastern end of the roof to make a *ceilure*, a richly painted wooden canopy over the Rood.

Instead of arch-bracing principals, the carpenters sometimes added curved braces to all the rafters to give the roof a continuous tunnel-like form. This was the *wagon* or *barrel roof*, and is particularly characteristic of the West Country. This type of roof was usually plastered between the rafters, which gives it a rather domestic feel.

In any form of roof construction, the joints where the various members intersected were now often covered with carved *bosses*. Some bosses were foliated, while others represented saints or mythical characters. Many bosses are carved as faces, portraits perhaps of real people of the parish and the church builders themselves. More complex bosses sometimes condense whole scenes from the Bible into their rounded shapes. They were always painted in bright colours and gilded. Not only was the master carpenter of the Decorative style more inventive in his combination of roof structures, he was also

Above
The wagon or barrel roof at St John the Baptist's, Littlehampton, Devon.

Above right
A second, diminutive tower at the east end of St Nicholas', at Blakeney on the Norfolk coast, housed a lantern which guided sailors safely into harbour.

anxious to show the world that he and his men could do more than just build a roof that stayed up – they could make it a thing of beauty in its own right. This was only the start, however, and nothing had yet been achieved to compare with the magnificent carpentry of the Perpendicular style. But these were glories to come.

Our Gothic church is nearly complete, but it still lacks its most striking feature – the tower, crowned perhaps by a graceful spire. Where would an English village be without its church tower? Though some coastal towers may have served defensive purposes in earlier days, the main function of the church tower was to house the bells that summoned the people to worship. In medieval times the sound of bells was much more common than it is today. Bells were rung at baptisms, weddings, funerals and Church festivals; they tolled for joy, sorrow and emergencies. It was believed that the clanging of bells could drive away the evil spirits of storm and tempest. The records of Spalding Church in Lincolnshire show that the ringers were paid three pence for 'ringing when the tempest was'. Before the Reformation the passing bell was tolled not after death but when a person was thought to be on the point of dying, so that the clamour of the bell might clear the air of the demons who sought to clutch at the departing soul in its most vulnerable moment, and that the parishioners might pray for the soul's safe passage. Most parish churches had two or three bells. To begin with they had been hung on simple spindles but around the turn of the fourteenth century the ringers achieved more control over the sound of the bells by hanging them on wooden quarter-wheels, and later half-wheels. The bells were often dedicated to a particular saint and inscribed with holy symbols and sometimes a prayer or motto. 'I to the Church the living call, and to the grave do summon all' reads one such motto. Over 3,000 medieval bells still survive up and down the country, East Anglia, Devon and Somerset being particularly fortunate in this respect.

Church towers also served as landmarks. As night fell, many a weary traveller must have been comforted to see the profile of a familiar church tower against the dusky sky. Several towers are known to have held lanterns. At Blakeney on the Norfolk coast, the parish church, as well as having a west tower, is provided with a

St Andrew's, Whissendine, Leicester-shire. The Gothic church tower, usually rising from the west end of the church, is the most conspicuous landmark in villages and towns throughout the country.

second slender tower at the north-east corner of the chancel from which a light still shines. Perhaps the medieval sailor was guided safely into harbour by lining up the church's two towers, or by triangulation with neighbouring church towers. In the fifteenth century, the tower of Dundry Church in Somerset was actually paid for by the Merchant Adventurers of Bristol who intended that it should be used as a navigation mark from the Bristol Channel.

Visually, the rising tower imparts dignity and a monumental quality to the parish church. Although a central tower could give a sense of unity to the church by providing a central core, a western tower of the same height, being seen to rise from the ground, was more impressive. Throughout the Gothic era the masons opted for a west tower wherever possible. Sometimes out of practical necessity the tower was built slightly to one side, and sometimes it was absorbed into the main body of the church by the later extension of the nave aisles on either side.

At the beginning of the thirteenth century some towers still retained the basic appearance of their Norman Romanesque predecessors, but where blind arcading was used it had pointed instead of semi-circular arches, and the belfry windows became more prominent. Many of the smaller churches had no towers, and their bells were hung in bell-cotes instead.

The most important development of the Early English style was the spire, which replaced the blunt pyramid-shaped roof of earlier towers. The first spires were built of timber and covered with wooden shingles or lead, and the influence of their design can still be seen in the stone spires of the thirteenth century. The basic problem facing the builders was how to fit an octagonal spire neatly and securely on to a square tower. The first solution to this problem was the *broach spire*. The broach spire effected the transition from square section to octagonal with four *broaches* – half-pyramid shaped sections of masonry at the corners of the tower which died away into the angled sides of the spire at the top, and completed the square of the tower at the bottom. Inside the spire, the weight of the diagonal sides was carried on arches bridging the corners of the tower, called *squinch arches*. The broach spire overlapped the tower walls like a timber roof and was supported by a substantial corbel table. Often the cardinal faces of the spire were set with dormer-like openings called *lucarnes* or *spirelights*. They were unglazed, usually gabled and traceried, and often repeated in diminishing scale as the spire ascended. A major disadvantage of the broach spire was its inaccessibility; if repairs were needed, ladders or costly scaffolding had to be set up from the ground. The corbel table construction was becoming old-fashioned too and although an occasional broach spire was built here and there after the turn of the fourteenth century, its use was confined mainly to the thirteenth century.

With the advent of the Decorated style and the traceried window, the church tower, in its Gothic form, was perfected. Tower and spire were treated as a single architectural composition. It is interesting that medieval records use the word 'steeple' to denote a church tower whether or not it has a spire. Once again a basic pattern evolved upon which the masons played endless variations. There were usually four

Above
The first spires were extensions of the pyramid-like roofs of Norman towers, built of timber and covered with wooden shingles, as at St Mary's, Patrixbourne, Kent.

Above centre
One of the finest lead-covered timber spires of the fourteenth century at St Mary's, Hemel Hempstead, Hertfordshire.

Above right
The thirteenth-century broach spire of St Mary's, Ketton, Leicestershire is typical of the Early English period.

stages to a tower, defined on the outside by string courses: the ground floor, which opened into the nave through a tall archway; the ringers' gallery from which the bells were rung; the belfry; and finally the roof or spire.

The preference for a west tower denied the masons the opportunity of turning the west façade of the parish church into the broad architectural showpiece it provided on the Continent and in the greater English churches. They concentrated instead on achieving an impression of height and making the tower the monumental focus of the church exterior. At the foot of the tower there was usually a door. This west door was used only on special occasions like the Palm Sunday procession, the normal entrance to the church being almost invariably through the south porch. The west door could be quite impressively decorated and was often given a square dripstone called a *label mould*. The triangular spaces between the pointed arch of the doorway and the square label mould are called *spandrels*. They were usually filled with carving, commonly the coat of arms or heraldic device of the patron, or the emblems of the Crucifixion displayed on shields, a reference perhaps to the use of the door on Palm Sunday. Over the doorway was a single large window, second only in size and elaboration of tracery to the great east window. A spiral staircase set into one corner of the tower led up to the ringers' gallery which was lit by one or two smaller windows usually rather underplayed in their

Above
Broach spires went out of fashion by the Decorated period and were replaced in popularity by parapet spires, like this at St John the Baptist's, Chaceley, Gloucestershire.

Opposite
The steeple of All Saints', Moulton, Lincolnshire, shows how the masons used pinnacles and flying buttresses to blend tower and spire into a unified composition.

decoration in deference to the belfry windows above. The belfry stage was now the most prominent feature of the tower elevation. It usually had a pair of windows on each of its faces. Each window was of two lights with a geometric opening, such as a quatrefoil, set at their heads and surrounded by rich mouldings. In later centuries the face of the church clock was often squeezed in between the belfry and the ringers' gallery, but in medieval days the rudimentary clocks of parish churches had no dials, and the hour was simply struck on a bell.

The tower relied for much of its effect on the buttresses at its corners. In the Decorated style they are almost always of the diagonally placed 'French' type. The carefully proportioned reduction in the projection of the buttresses from their bases upwards served to emphasise the vertical perspective of the tower, sweeping the eye up to their crowning pinnacles and the spire beyond.

By the fourteenth century the broach spire had been all but abandoned in favour of the *parapet spire*. Instead of overlapping the tower walls, the spire was set back behind a parapet. This had the practical advantage of enabling scaffolding or ladders for repair work to be set up in the space between parapet and spire. Springing from a smaller base, this type of spire tended to be more slender and graceful than the broach spire. Lucarnes or spirelights were still sometimes let into the cardinal faces of the spire, and its edges were often em-

bellished with the ubiquitous crocket. At the corners of the parapet the pinnacles, repeating in miniature the form of the spire, helped unify spire and tower. A rather elegant refinement was to link the pinnacles to the spire with slender flying buttresses. They served no structural purpose, but were intended to help smooth the visual transition between the two parts of the steeple. Sometimes the tower was given an octagonal top stage to the same end, and at Patrington Church, Humberside, the masons girdled the base of the spire with an octagonal *corona*, a crown of traceried arches and pinnacles.

With the building of the tower, several years of work for the masons and carpenters was reaching its culmination. In the parish, excitement mounted for months as the day set aside for the consecration of the church approached. The formal consecration of the church by a bishop marked its official opening as a place of worship. A procedure for the consecration of churches had been established in the seventh century, but it was as late as 1076 before it was strictly prohibited to celebrate Mass in an unconsecrated church. Inside the church, the walls were painted or incised with twelve *consecration crosses*. Outside, a grand procession headed by the bishop and his attendants followed by the other clergy and the parishioners, circled the building three times, anointing twelve consecration crosses on the outside walls with holy oil as they passed. Arriving at the main entrance to the church, the bishop struck the threshold three times with his crozier, and the door was thrown open. While the laity remained outside, the floor of the church was strewn with ashes and sand in the shape of a cross, to the chanting of the Litany. Then, in a solemn procession, the interior consecration crosses and finally the High Altar were hallowed with consecrated wine and holy water. The bells rang out, and the parishioners joined the clergy in the celebration of the church's first Mass.

At the consecration ceremony the church was dedicated in the name of its patron saint. Dedications to St Peter, keeper of the keys of heaven, St Michael, the Church's knight in armour, and All Saints were very popular. England's own martyr, St Thomas of Canterbury, had a good following too, though his popularity in medieval times was somewhat obscured when Henry VIII decreed that his name be removed from the Church's Calendar, and many parishes prudently changed the dedication of their churches from 'St Thomas the Martyr' to 'St Thomas the Apostle'. It was, however, the Virgin Mary who, as 'Queen of Heaven' stood indisputably at the head of the ranks of patron saints, and dedications to her greatly outnumber any others. Of the 1001 churches selected for the appendix of this book, well over a quarter are dedicated to the Virgin in one of her guises. Every great church, whatever its dedication, had a Lady Chapel beyond the High Altar, and many parish churches now had side chapels or altars devoted to her worship.

The Virgin Mary supplied Christianity with its mother figure, a vital dimension of most religions, and her cult had been growing steadily throughout the early Gothic period, nurtured partly by the romantic notions of chivalry. According to its code, absolute devotion and service to women was one of the knight's highest ideals, and the Virgin Mary, purest, most beautiful and gracious of women ever,

The cult of the Virgin exemplified by the Wilton Diptych showing Richard II being presented to Mary and the Infant Christ.

represented the ultimate 'fair lady'. The affection and respect she commanded is summed up in this popular medieval carol:

> I sing of a maiden
>   That is matchless;
> King of all Kings
>   To her son she chose.
>
> He came all so still
>   To his mother's bower,
> As dew in April
>   That falleth on the flower.
>
> Mother and maiden
>   Was never none but she;
> Well may such a lady
>   God's mother be.

The Gothic church itself, with its light, flowing lines and delicate tracery, had acquired much of the gracious and feminine qualities of the 'fair lady'. The robust masculinity of the Romanesque styles was now long forgotten. But if our church is a fair lady, she is as yet unadorned, and now that the masons have finished their work we must leave the glaziers, the painters, the wood carvers and the metal workers to dress her in her finery.

5: Church Life

One of the loveliest two-storey south
porches is at St Peter and St Paul's,
Northleach, Gloucestershire.

The medieval Church was 'the Mother of us all'. In the bosom of the parish church the baby was baptised, the adult married, and the dead laid to rest. The parish churches with their towers and spires rising above the villages dominated the countryside, not only architecturally but socially too. The shadow of the church fell across matters secular as well as religious, and inextricably bound the everyday working life of the village to its spiritual life. The year was ordered according to the Church's Calendar, the seasons were marked by its festivals, and its holy days were the people's holidays. The majority of the villagers probably held no particularly deep religious convictions; they simply went along with what tradition demanded. No easy alternative existed. There was one religion, and to be excluded from that great body of believers meant social isolation or worse, so open dissent was rarely heard. Among ordinary folk superstition still ruled the day, and the clergy did little or nothing to discourage superstitious beliefs. Many a popular 'miracle' story told by priest or travelling friar centred on some miracle-working holy relic or the 'magical' properties of the consecrated Host, and so actively encouraged superstition. In the medieval mind, the world was a battlefield in which supernatural powers of good and evil fought for and against man's interests. The Church offered the invocation of the benevolent magic of the Saints, without whose blessings the works of devilry and witchcraft would prevail. Crops would fail, lambs would fall prey to wild beasts, and sickness would sweep the village. Life depended on a fruitful harvest, the increase of livestock and the health of the workers, so it was with good reason that the village heeded the tolling of the bells and turned their footsteps to the church door. Now that the masons' fellow craftsmen and artists have played their part in making our parish church the pride of its community, let's follow the villagers' procession and find out what we might have expected to see there.

The churchyard path led the congregation up to the south porch. Since the thirteenth century the south porch had become an indispensable part of all but the smallest of churches, and from the fourteenth century onwards, it often had a small room built over it known as the *parvis* chamber. Above the archway opening into the porch, we would be likely to find a niche holding a statue, perhaps the church's patron saint, but more usually the Virgin with the infant Christ. The statue was often painted in life-like colours, and on the Virgin's head there may have been a delicately wrought and gilded metal crown. A window on each side of the niche, or a single, larger and traceried window, lit the parvis. Strictly speaking the use of this term for the upper room of a porch is incorrect, a true parvis being an enclosed area in front of the main entrance of a church, but the misnomer is so common as to be widely accepted. The parvis may have been used to house important parish records safely, to store weapons in times of trouble, and to provide a place where the priest could teach the children of the village to recite the *Paternoster*, the *Ave* and the *Credo*. The remains of a fireplace in many of these rooms suggest that they may sometimes have provided accommodation for a sexton or other church custodian. At the church of St Peter and St Paul at Northleach in Gloucestershire the porch has the flue of its

Page 115
*A child being baptised, from a
bench end at St John the Baptist's,
Tideswell, Derbyshire.*

The closing ring of the south door at St John the Baptist's, Adel, West Yorkshire, shaped like the head of a bear. On reaching it, a fugitive could claim the sanctuary of the church.

fireplace built rather ingeniously into one of its buttresses. The upper room could obviously provide a custodian with a good vantage point for keeping an eye on the comings and goings in the churchyard, and there was often another window in the north wall that looked directly down into the nave of the church. The façade of the south porch was completed with a steeply pitched gable roof with a plain or battlemented parapet.

Scratched on to one of the jambs of the archway leading into the porch, or on a nearby south-facing buttress, there was usually a *mass dial*, sometimes called a *scratch dial* – a set of radiating lines or dots, or a combination of both, which can be mistaken at first sight for the idle scrawlings of a vandal's penknife. The mass dial was used like a sun-dial to indicate the times of church services. They vary a great deal in size and detail, and there are often more than one, perhaps for use at different times of the year. All have a central hole in which the gnomon was set and from which a number of lines radiate. Often one of the lines is more prominent than the rest to show the hour for the saying of Mass, usually around nine o'clock in the morning.

The porch was the village meeting place for discussing parish affairs and for preparing and signing business documents and contracts. Along the side walls, stone benches provided seating both for these official meetings and for the casual gossiping of a warm evening. The porch held many memories for the villagers. Part of the marriage ceremony was still held here until the middle of the sixteenth century, when it was decreed that the whole of the service should take place in the body of the church. Here too they brought their children for baptism, the child's sponsors taking their vows in the porch before carrying the child into the church for immersion in the font.

The doorway at the back of the porch was usually built in recessed orders with mouldings and capitals decorated according to the fashion of the time. The door itself was very heavy with an enormous lock and often a prominent and decorative door handle. The door handle is sometimes called a *sanctuary knocker*, since an offender managing to reach it before being apprehended was entitled to the sanctuary of the church until a trial could be arranged. The church of St John the Baptist at Adel in West Yorkshire has a particularly interesting early example. The door itself was now shaped to fit the arch of the doorway exactly, so no space was left for a tympanum which had been such a feature of the doorways of Romanesque architecture. Two thicknesses of boarding made up the door, the boards running vertically on the outside and horizontally inside. Each of its hinges was formed by an iron strap fixed to the door and then doubled back on itself to make a loop which was hooked over a vertical iron pin set in the masonry of the door jamb. These iron straps were extended across the door to provide both reinforcement and decoration. The iron work often spread across the face of the door, skilfully wrought into convoluted dragons or, more commonly, foliated scrolls. Sometimes, as at the church of St Saviour, Dartmouth in Devon, the door was completely encased in iron. One of the most elegant examples of iron scroll work is to be seen on the door of St Mary's Church, Eaton Bray in Bedfordshire. It is the work of Thomas de Leighton, one of the master smiths of the thirteenth

*Wrought iron work was used both to
reinforce and to decorate church doors:*

Above
St Saviour's, Dartmouth, Devon.

Above right
St Mary's, Eaton Bray, Bedfordshire.

century. He was also probably responsible for the doors of the nearby
churches of All Saints, Leighton Buzzard, and All Saints, Turvey. It
seems likely that he had his own workshop in this area of Bedfordshire,
perhaps at Leighton Buzzard. The quality of his work must have been
well-known because when the royal smith to Edward I, Henry de
Lewes, died in 1291, the king chose Thomas de Leighton to design
and make the grille of Queen Eleanor's tomb in Westminster Abbey.
Grilles and screens of the thirteenth century, like the wrought iron of
the doors, were made up of foliated scroll work. But at the turn of the
fourteenth century scroll work was abandoned in favour of lattice-
like screens of straight interlacing bars. And in the final century of the
Gothic style the sinuous and tensile qualities of wrought iron were to
be completely repressed in work designed to imitate woodwork. By
the middle of the fourteenth century the meandering iron work of the
door disappeared too, and it became the fashion to cover it with
panels of wooden moulding carved like window tracery.

On the right hand side of the door was a *stoup* for holy water,
usually set in a small niche, sometimes supported by a carved bracket
or a slender shaft. As they passed through the church door, the
villagers dipped the fingers of their right hands into the holy water
and crossed themselves, a token of the renewal of their baptism. At
the west end of the church was the font in which they, and probably
generations of their forefathers, had been baptised. Comparatively
few new fonts were carved in the thirteenth and fourteenth centuries

Above left to right

The round-bowled font supported by columns at St Mary's, Cricklade, Wiltshire, is typical of the Early English period.

By the Decorated period, fonts usually had octagonal bowls with carved panels, like this from St Mary's, Wendover, Buckinghamshire.

The carved panels of the font at St Lawrence's, North Hinksey, Oxfordshire, clearly reflect the window tracery of the Decorated period.

Opposite left to right

The spectacular, eighteen-foot high font cover at St Mary's, Ufford, Suffolk, is constructed so that the lower sections telescope together.

The font at St Botolph's, Trunch, Norfolk, is covered by an extraordinary freestanding wooden canopy.

At St Mary's, Luton, Bedfordshire, a similar structure built in stone forms a unique enclosure, rather like a baptistry, around the font.

since the fonts of Norman days, sturdy and often very decorative, were still serviceable. In the Early English period octagonal bowls became increasingly common, and figure carving, so popular in Norman work, almost disappeared. By the advent of the Decorated style at the beginning of the fourteenth century the octagonal bowl had become standard, and the font was often raised on a stepped platform. Arcading round the bowl was more deeply moulded, often with crocketed, ogee-shaped arches or with tracery like that of Decorated style windows. Figure sculpture on fonts occasionally reappears, but with a new restraint and naturalism that contrasts with the vigorous, grotesque images of Norman sculpture.

The font was always fitted with a wooden cover that could be locked to prevent the holy water from being stolen for superstitious purposes. The marks where the original fastenings would have been can still be found on the rims of many fonts even though the covers themselves may have long since disappeared. The earliest covers were simply flat lids, but as the Gothic style evolved, they became elaborate spire-like structures. Many of these covers were so large and heavy that they had to be suspended from a beam in the roof or a specially built bracket. Sometimes the font was also provided with a freestanding canopy, like that at the church of St Botolph, Trunch in Norfolk, which is a quite extraordinary piece of medieval woodwork. At St Mary's Church in Luton, Bedfordshire, the thirteenth-century Purbeck marble font is enclosed by a unique, octagonal stone structure of the fourteenth century which forms a kind of baptistry. The bases of its sides are panelled, and an open traceried stage above rises to a vaulted and gabled roof which is enriched with crockets and topped by finials.

As the villagers filed past the font, men and women parted and took up their places on either side of the nave, a custom that is still practised at the church of the Holy Trinity at Staunton Harold in Leicestershire. Mass was celebrated daily and, in theory, it was everyone's duty to attend. The lords of the manor, however, were

loath to give their workers the time off to spend unproductively in church, so in practice, most attended mass only on Sundays and the more important of the forty or so holy days: Christmas, Easter, the feasts of the Virgin and the name-day of the saint to whom their church was dedicated. On most days people were content to pause briefly from their labours as the sound of the tolling mass bell drifted across the village fields:

> And if thou may not come to church,
> Wherever that thou do work,
> When thou hearest the mass knell,
> Pray to God with a heart that's still.

On Sunday, however, the whole village was to be found in the church. There was no respectful silence as the congregation waited for the arrival of the clergy. Instead a hubbub of chatter filled the church. Children played and squabbled, and dogs scratched among the straw or rushes that covered the floor for warmth and to soak up the mud. The patterned encaustic tiles found in the greater churches were too expensive to be used other than around the high altar in parish churches. The rest of the church may have been paved with plain reddish tiles or flagstones, but more usually the floor was of beaten earth perhaps sealed with ox blood.

Dogs were a common sight in churches for several centuries. If they were uncontrolled they could be a great nuisance – the story is told of one hungry dog who made off with the consecrated Host. So the church sometimes employed a useful, if not exalted, official – the dog-whipper. The churchwarden's accounts at Ludlow in Salop record that one Thomas Payver was paid eight pence in 1543 for whipping dogs out of church. By the seventeenth century, it seems that dogs had become a real problem, and the Archbishop of Canterbury, William Laud, decreed that altars should be surrounded by railings to keep dogs away and to emphasise the sanctity of the altar.

A woodcut showing the celebration of mass from a medieval prayer book. The church's dog-whipper can be seen on the left, and to the right the clergy occupy their places in the sedilia.

Altar rails are seen in most churches and a few still retain their original *Laudian rails*. If all else failed, and a noisy dog still interrupted the proceedings, the fiercest of animals could be ejected safely with a pair of *dog tongs*, usually made of wood, sometimes of metal, with long handles and a set of fearsome-looking teeth to grip the dog round its neck.

Conversation among the congregation was brought to a temporary halt by the arrival of the priest, and in the seclusion of the chancel the celebration of mass began. The chancel was now larger and better furnished than it had been in earlier times. During the thirteenth and fourteenth centuries many chancels were lengthened to make space for more elaborate liturgical movement, and seating for priests and choristers. These *choir stalls*, as they were called, were set against opposite walls towards the west end of the chancel. To begin with they were just plain benches but they soon became beautifully carved permanent fixtures. Monasteries and abbeys needed more choir stalls than the parish churches, and they were grander and more elaborately carved, often with crocketed wooden canopies. When the monasteries were disbanded in Henry VIII's reign, many of their choir stalls were rescued from the bonfire by astute churchwardens and given new homes in the parish churches. When a rather ordinary parish church boasts an unexpectedly fine set of choir stalls, some clue in their carving, like a coat of arms or a rebus, will usually betray their original setting. The stalls of the church of St Mary the Virgin at Richmond in North Yorkshire, for instance, are known to have come from nearby Easby Abbey since the rebus of one of its abbots, Abbot Brampton, is carved on them. The choir stalls were usually fitted with hinged seats. Medieval services were very long and the clergy was called upon to stand for most of the proceedings. On the underside of each hinged seat was a projecting ledge supported by a carved bracket, so that when the seat was tipped up the occupant could prop himself up on this ledge while still giving the appearance of standing. These projecting ledges are known as *misericords*, an Old French word derived from the Latin 'misericors', meaning 'compassionate'. For the clergy actively involved in the celebration of the mass, the officiating priest, deacon and sub-deacon, there were still the stone sedilia built into the south wall of the chancel near the altar. During the Decorated period, the sedilia were likely to have ogee-shaped canopies richly ornamented with crockets as at the church of St Patrick, Patrington in Humberside, and All Saints, Hawton in Nottinghamshire. The piscina was sometimes grouped together with the sedilia, or had a matching canopy of its own. By the end of the thirteenth century double piscinae were becoming popular. The sacred vessels used in the mass were kept in a small cupboard, called the *aumbry*, in the north wall of the chancel. Unlike the other fixtures of the chancel, the aumbry was usually very simple, with a plain rectangular oak door and devoid of decoration.

The aumbry might also have provided a safe keeping-place for any relics the church possessed. During medieval times there was a brisk trade in relics and any church wanting to make its mark acquired some miracle-working part of a saint's body or clothes. According to Bede, when St Augustine was sent to convert the pagan

Angles, his mission was later supplied from Rome with all things necessary to furnish his new churches, including 'relics of the Holy Saints and Martyrs'. Relics gave a church status; they also attracted pilgrims, and their cash. Six shillings and four pence was collected when a chest of relics from the church of St Augustine at Hedon in Humberside was paraded through the town on the feast of St Mary Magdalene. Relics were kept in richly decorated *reliquaries*. At the church of St Edmund in Salisbury, Wiltshire, the hand of its patron saint was kept in a hand-shaped reliquary. At St Lawrence, Reading in Berkshire, a relic of the saint was contained in a silver casket shaped like the gridiron on which the martyr had been roasted to death. In the Lady Chapel of Patrington Church, Humberside, there is a strange, square roof boss which has been extended downwards and hollowed out to form a kind of box. It is carved on three sides, with the Annunciation, St John the Baptist and St Katherine, but the fourth side, facing the altar, is left open. Various ideas have been put forward to explain this unusual feature, among them the suggestion that the box-like boss, high above the altar, provided a suitably secure place for a small relic.

At the back of the altar, beneath the east window which dominated the chancel, was the *reredos*, also known as the *retable*. The reredos took many forms. At its simplest it was a devotional image painted directly on the wall behind the altar. Sometimes a rich hanging served as a reredos, and later in the Gothic period, sets of carved and painted alabaster panels showing scenes from the Passion, or the Life of the Virgin, were popular. Most commonly the reredos was made up of a row of niches holding statues or a group of painted

Right
A panel from the delicately carved fifteenth-century alabaster reredos at St Peter's, Drayton, Oxfordshire.

Opposite
The bolder and perhaps more expressive imagery of the painted wooden reredos at St Mary's, Thornham Parva, Suffolk – one of the few surviving examples of English fourteenth-century painting.

wooden panels like those at the church of St Mary, Thornham Parva in Suffolk. Two or three panels might be hinged together to make a freestanding altar-piece called, respectively, a *diptych* or *triptych*, which could be closed up to protect the painting from dirt and damage. To the north of the altar a separate niche or bracket held a statue of the church's patron saint.

The *lectern*, the wooden or brass desk from which the Gospel was read, also stood in the chancel in these days and was not moved out into its familiar place in the nave until after the Reformation. There were two types of lectern. The reading desk type had a central column supporting one or more sloping sides on which the books rested. Where the lectern was double- or four-sided, it also served as a music stand for the large music books used in complex antiphonal singing. A lectern of this kind at St Helen's, Ranworth in Norfolk,

Above left and centre
From St Helen's, Ranworth, Norfolk, a lectern of the reading desk type, and an illuminated letter showing a similar lectern in use for antiphonal singing, from the 'Sarum Antiphonal' – an exquisite book that first rested on that very lectern in the fifteenth century.

Above right
An early example of the popular eagle lectern. This one was made in the fourteenth century for St Mary's, Ottery St Mary, Devon.

has music painted on its desk. Miraculously, one of the music books that must have rested there still survives, the priceless 'Sarum Antiphonal', written and beautifully illuminated by monks of Langley Abbey around the year 1400. Most medieval lecterns, however, took the form of an eagle perched on a globe with its outstretched wings serving as the book rest. The church of St Mary, at Ottery St Mary in Devon, has a particularly charming example, given to the church by Bishop Grandisson in the fourteenth century. The popularity of eagle lecterns was, perhaps, due to the eagle being the symbol of St John the Evangelist, the most honoured of the Gospel-makers.

The wider chancel arch of the Gothic church did not separate chancel and nave as completely as in earlier times, so the seclusion of the chancel was maintained by a *rood screen* which ran the full width of the archway. A doorway in the screen linked the two parts of the church but was kept locked or bolted except when worship was in progress. It was called a rood screen because it supported the Rood, the figure of Christ on the Cross, usually with the Virgin Mary and St John the Evangelist on either side. In parish churches, the rood screen was usually built of wood, though a few stone examples do exist. The church of St Mary the Virgin at Stebbing in Essex has a remarkable stone screen which was conceived as a huge traceried window of three lights, completely filling the chancel arch. The present screen is a nineteenth-century copy of the fourteenth-century original, as is a similar stone screen at nearby Great Bardfield. From their design and method of construction, it would seem that the carpenters first used wood as a convenient substitute for stone, the difference being negligible once the screen had been painted and gilded. In its earliest form it was three open arches carried on columns, the central opening being the doorway into the chancel. Very few rood screens of earlier than the fourteenth century remain. The survival of the mid-thirteenth-century screen at St Michael's Church, Stanton Harcourt in Oxfordshire, complete with hinges,

Right
*The impressive stone rood screen
at St Mary the Virgin, Stebbing,
Essex, which completely fills the
chancel arch.*

Above
A detail of the screen's carving.

locks and bolts, is quite exceptional. The solid lower part of the
screen is randomly pierced with quatrefoil openings of various sizes.
These peep-holes, or squints, were made so that children who were
not tall enough to look over the rail of the rood screen could see
through into the chancel. But for the finest rood screens we must
wait until the Perpendicular style of Gothic, when the carpenter's art
was at its zenith and woodwork throughout the church reached a
particular excellence.

Standing in the nave of the church, the congregation peered
through the rood screen at what was happening in the chancel. They

The wooden rood screen at St Michael's, Stanton Harcourt, Oxfordshire, dates from the thirteenth century and is the oldest surviving in the country.

Opposite
The fourteenth-century stained glass window at St Mary's, Shrewsbury, Salop, showing the Tree of Jesse – the lineage of Christ depicted as a tree springing from the recumbent figure of Jesse at the bottom of the window.

could play no active part in the ritual; rather, they were there as witnesses to it. They knew that the words and gestures had symbolic importance, but few would be able to expound their meaning. Those with sharp ears might have been able to pick out the occasional *oremus* and *amen* that punctuated the mumbled Latin of the service, but the larger part of the proceedings remained a mystery, awesome or otherwise. English was used only on the rare days when the priest delivered a sermon in which he was expected to explain the meaning of the sacraments.

Conversation among the villagers began again in fits and starts, and the attention of even the most pious wandered to the paintings on the church walls and the stained glass in its windows. It was from these vivid images, rather than the incomprehensible services that their knowledge of the Faith had been gleaned. As one thirteenth-century bishop wrote: 'Pictures and ornaments in churches are the lessons and scriptures of the laity . . . for what writing supplies to him who can read, that does a picture supply to him who is unlearned and can only look.' In theory, the scenes depicted on the church walls were chosen according to guidelines laid down by the Church as early as the eighth century. But in practice, the choice was more influenced by the popular legends of the saints and the religious cults of the day. As might be expected, events from the Life of the Virgin figured prominently in many churches from the thirteenth century onwards. Easily the most common of surviving wall paintings, however, is the *Doom*, a graphic representation of the Last Judgement. Well over a hundred examples are still to be seen and it seems certain that every church had its Doom. It was usually painted on the wall above the chancel arch. When a church had no clerestory, there was very little wall space left between the top of the arch and the roof above, so the Doom was sometimes painted on a tympanum of wooden boards

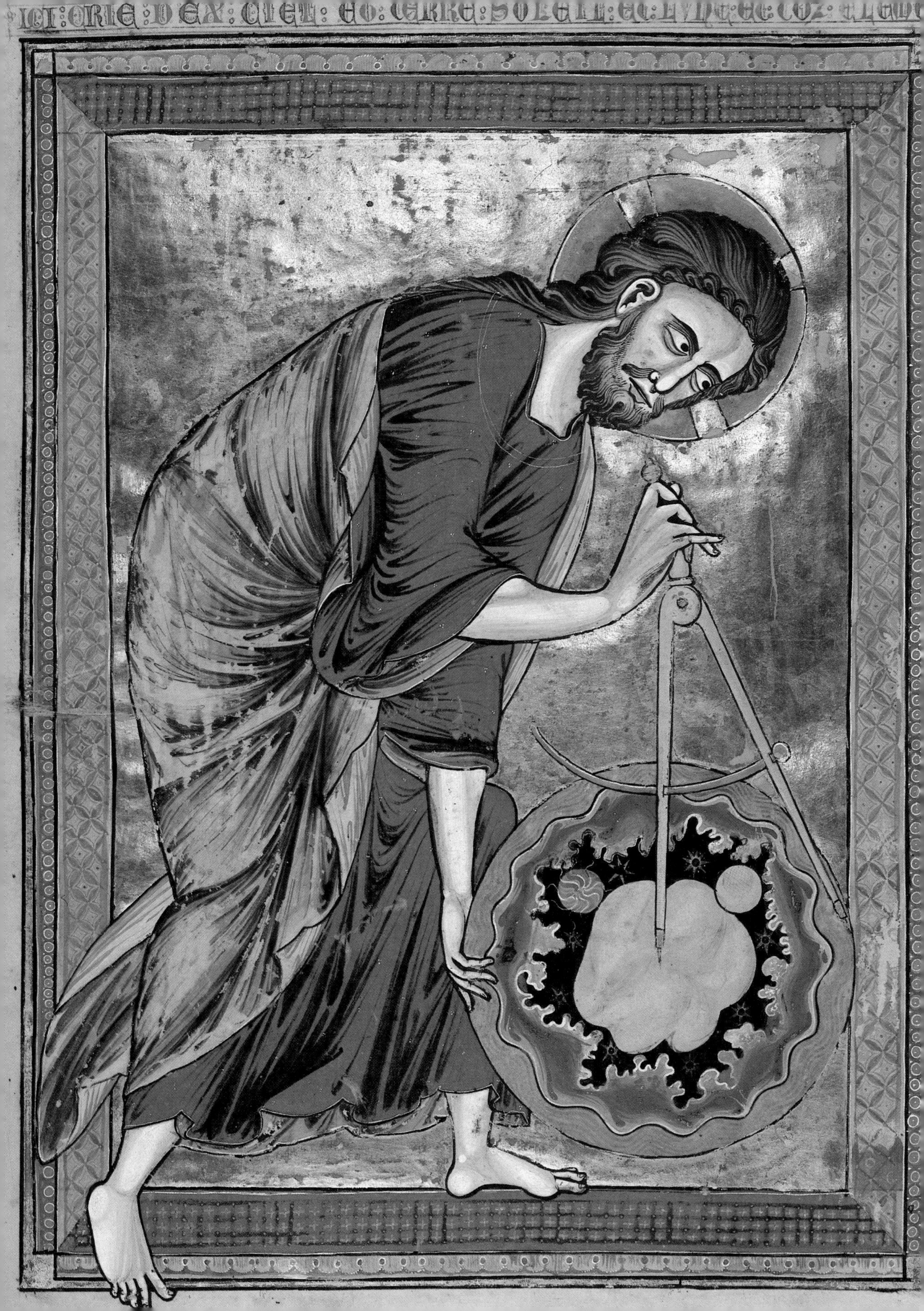
ICI: CRIE DEX: CIEL: ET: TERRE: SOLEIL: ET: LUNE: ET: TOZ:

Above
The Doom from St Peter's, Wenhaston, Suffolk, painted on a tympanum of wooden boards which originally filled the top of the chancel arch and provided a dramatic background to the carved figures of the Rood group.

Left
The craft of the master mason was held in such esteem in medieval times that God Himself could be portrayed as the architect of the universe holding the world in His compass, from a medieval Old Testament.

which fitted under the arch. The layout of this scene of the Last Judgement is more or less standard. At the top, Christ appears in majesty to judge the living and the dead. He is usually enthroned on a rainbow and often accompanied by saints, martyrs and the host of Heaven. At the bottom, the graves open and send forth the souls of the dead. In the centre, St Michael the Archangel, dressed in armour, holds the scales in which the souls are weighed. Often a small demon tries to tip the scales against the righteous, and sometimes the Virgin Mary is on hand to tip them the other way. To the left of the picture are the stairs to Heaven. There St Peter greets the souls of the blessed who are guided by angels up to the New Jerusalem, singing the praises of the Lord. Meanwhile to the right, fearsome demons herd the tortured souls of the damned into the gaping jaws of the monster that represents Hell. This terrifying vision of what was to come must surely have grasped the imagination of the congregation more than any sermon.

Closely related to the Doom is the painting of the Ladder of Salvation which can be seen on the west wall of the church of St Peter and St Paul at Chaldon in Surrey. It was painted around the year 1200 and is the only example of this subject found in England. In fact the subject is rare throughout the Western Church, and is of Byzantine origin. A Greek treatise on church painting, known as the 'Manual of Pauselinos', describes how the Ladder of Salvation should be painted,

and the inscription which the author suggests should be written underneath shows clearly its instructional and devotional purpose:

> Approach the ladder and climb with courage.
> You have the choir of angels for defenders;
> You will escape the snares of evil demons.
> Once at the gate of Heaven,
> You will gain the Crown of Life from the Lord's hands.

After the Doom, the Crucifixion and scenes from Christ's Passion and the Life of the Virgin are the most common of the big narrative subjects. Among individual subjects, St Christopher was unequalled in popularity until the fifteenth century. The patron saint of travellers was usually shown larger than life, wading across a river with the Infant Christ on his shoulder. It was the practice to paint the saint on the north wall opposite the entrance to the church, so that a villager had only to look in through the door to see the image of St Christopher and receive his protection, for superstition had it that whoever beheld his image was safe that day from sudden death.

After the remarkable success of the Battle of Agincourt in 1415, a wave of patriotism swept the country, and St George, England's new patron saint, and his dragon became almost as popular as St Christopher. Among the ladies, a preference was shown for St Katherine, usually identified by her wheel, and St Margaret. A less frequent, but rather charming subject, that must have had much appeal for the village workers, was Christ blessing the Trades. It showed the figure of Christ surrounded by agricultural and other tools.

Wall paintings in English churches are not usually frescoes. They were painted on the walls once the plaster had dried, not while it was still wet. St Mary's Church at Kempley in Gloucestershire has one of the few collections of true frescoes. They show Christ in Majesty, the Apostles and other figures, and date from before the middle of the twelfth century. Being frescoes, the pigments were 'fixed' by the setting of the plaster and the images have survived a little better than

The artist at work – Irene, daughter of Cratinus, shown painting a church wall in an illustration from a medieval manuscript.

other contemporary wall paintings. The most readily available pigments were red and yellow ochre made from oxides of iron, black from soot or charcoal, white from lime, and less common, green from a naturally occurring carbonate of copper. Other pigments were rare and precious, mostly imported from distant countries. The limited palette at the painter's disposal produced a rather monochromatic, reddish-brown effect. The impermanent nature of much wall painting seems to have been taken for granted, and it was quite usual to repaint subjects now and then, or to paint more fashionable new ones on top of the old. Sometimes the walls were painted according to a coherent plan, as at the church of St Mary the Virgin, Chalgrove in Oxfordshire. But more often, with the exception of the Doom over the chancel arch and St Christopher opposite the door, the layout of the various scenes was arbitrary and bore little or no relationship to the architecture of the church. At Pickering in West Yorkshire, the church of St Peter and St Paul gives a good impression of what the overall effect must have been like, though a closer look reveals the 'touching-up' of the modern paintbrush. All our church wall paintings were whitewashed over in the days of the iconoclasts, and those which have subsequently been uncovered have inevitably needed much restoration.

Judging from what has survived, there was a great variation in the quality of wall painting. Some are undoubted masterpieces, like the Virgin and Child painted at St Mary's Church, Great Canfield in Essex, in the middle of the thirteenth century. But much work was not so skilfully executed. The Coronation of the Virgin at Sutton Bingham Church in Somerset, for instance, compares poorly with the Great Canfield Virgin, even though it was painted some fifty years later. In contemporary accounts the painter is generally paid less than other craftsmen, which is rather surprising considering the expensive pigments and gold leaf with which he or she often worked. The cost of painting a wooden statue could easily exceed that of carving it in the first place. Could it be that there were two classes of painter? The first, the professional artists who designed and painted their own pictures within the constraints of conventional iconography; and the second and more common, craftsmen of some other kind who could also turn their hands to 'decorating' and who worked from existing patterns. Fifteenth-century paintings of St Christopher, for example, were often copied from an illustration in the 'Golden Legend', a popular book printed in 1483 by William Caxton and based on a collection of lives of the saints written by a thirteenth-century friar, Jacobus de Voragine.

The glaziers who produced the glowing, richly-coloured glass windows that complemented the wall paintings, also probably worked from designs supplied to them. Like the tapestry weavers and the embroiderers, their job was to translate the artist's conception into a reality using their knowledge of the virtues and limitations of their own particular medium. Small pieces of coloured glass set in mosaic-like geometric patterns had been used in the windows of important churches from early Christian times, but stained glass as we know it did not appear until the twelfth century and is generally considered to have reached its peak in the thirteenth and fourteenth centuries.

The artistic standard of the wall-painters was very variable:

Above
The hand of a master shows in this beautiful Virgin and Child painted on the east wall of St Mary's, Canfield, Essex.

Below
By contrast, the Coronation of the Virgin at All Saints', Sutton Bingham, Somerset, is a rather workaday effort.

Fourteenth-century stained glass from St Mary's, Deerhurst, Gloucestershire, depicting St Katherine with her wheel.

The full-sized design for each panel of the window was drawn up on the whitewashed top of a wooden table, rather like the master mason's tracing board. The outline of each piece of glass and details, like faces and folds in drapery, were painted boldly in black or red so that the lines could be seen clearly through the coloured glass. Later the glaziers drew their patterns on parchment so that the same design could be re-used with slight alterations. One window in the Priory Church at Great Malvern, Hereford and Worcester, has six figures of ecclesiastics all worked from the same basic drawing.

Although plain greenish-white glass was made in England from the early thirteenth century onwards, coloured glass was not manufactured here until the late sixteenth century. So all coloured glass had to be imported from the Continent and was sold in this country by middle-men. The glass came mainly from the glassmaking centres of Normandy and Burgundy, Hesse and Lorraine, and to a lesser extent, Venice and the Low countries.

The molten glass was made into flat sheets, sometimes called *tables*, by one of two means: the *muff* method or the *crown* method. Crown glass was made by blowing the molten glass into a small bubble which was then burst and spun out into a disc some sixty centimetres (twenty-four inches) in diameter, thicker in the middle and thinner at its edge. Using the muff method a larger bubble was blown and then stretched into a sausage-shaped balloon by swinging and twisting. The two ends of the 'sausage' were cut off to make a short fat tube which was split along its length, allowed to cool, and then flattened out by re-heating to form a rather uneven rectangular sheet usually about sixty by thirty-eight centimetres (twenty-four by fifteen inches). These two methods of production can be distinguished in the end product by examining the tiny air bubbles trapped in the glass. Where the muff method was used the bubbles tend to run in straight parallel lines; in crown glass they run in concentric circles or arcs.

There were two different types of coloured glass: *pot-metal* and *flashed*. Pot-metal glass was coloured all the way through by adding various metallic oxides to the ingredients of the glass. The colour that resulted depended on the temperature to which the glass was fired and on the metal used. The rich red 'ruby' glass was made by adding copper oxide, manganese was used for purple, cobalt oxide for blue, and iron oxide for a variety of yellows and greens. Flashed glass was white glass covered with a thin layer of coloured glass. Before being spun or blown out into a sheet, the white glass was dipped into the molten coloured glass. The technique was originally developed because ruby glass became too opaque in thick sheets, and the glassmakers found that its deep red colour was shown to better advantage by a thin film on a white glass support. Other colours were later treated in the same way.

The sheets of glass were laid on the glazier's table and cut to fit the shapes of his design. They were not scored with a diamond and snapped, as today, but cracked by touching gently with a red hot *dividing iron* and then nibbled into shape with a *grosing iron*. The cut pieces were then placed over the working-drawing and the details traced on the glass. Of necessity the painted lines were simple and spontaneous; in glass-painting there was little opportunity for second

Glassmakers at work, from a medieval manuscript.

thoughts. This gave a strength of line and an almost primitive economy of design that matched perfectly the brilliant hues of the glass. The glass-painter used a paint made of copper or iron oxide and a flux of ground soft glass mixed together with wine or urine. The painted glass was fired in a simple clay oven on an iron plate covered with quicklime or ashes. The glass flux melted at a lower temperature than the window glass and so fused the pigment into the surface of the glass.

At the beginning of the fourteenth century, glaziers began to use a solution of silver sulphide or chloride, painted on the glass and fired at a low temperature, to give plain glass a beautiful yellow stain which varied from pale lemon to orange according to the temperature of firing. This discovery added a new richness to the glazier's 'palette' allowing features like haloes, beards, hair, and patterns in drapery, to be picked out with this lovely golden stain. The range of picture-making techniques was further extended in the following century when glaziers began to abrade or scratch the coloured coating off flashed glass to expose white patches or lines.

The finished pieces of glass were built up like a jigsaw on the glazier's table and temporarily held in place by nails round their edges. For the first time the craftsmen could see how successful this particular panel of the window was going to be. Meanwhile, long thin strips of lead had been cast with an H-shaped section. These were the *cames* which were used to hold all the pieces of glass together. The cames were soldered at each joint, and finally, some kind of putty or cement was grouted in between glass and lead to make the whole panel watertight and ready to be mounted on the grid of iron bars that supported it in the window.

Obviously windows made in this way were very fragile, and much of the glass that managed to survive the winds and storms of centuries was eventually lost at the hands of the iconoclasts. So it is not surprising that so little early glass survives. The best collection of twelfth- and thirteenth-century glass is at Canterbury Cathedral. Among parish churches the oldest glass is at St Mary's Church, Brabourne in Kent. St Peter and St Paul at Dorchester in Oxfordshire has four small windows of twelfth-century glass, and there are fragments of thirteenth-century work at a number of churches up and down the country. Pieces of fourteenth- and fifteenth-century windows are more common, but the church of St Mary at Fairford in Gloucestershire is unique in having twenty-eight almost complete windows dating from the close of the fifteenth century. The windows were a gift from the patron of the church, John Tame, a wealthy wool merchant who had bought the manor of Fairford from the Crown. The glass was made by a team of English and Flemish craftsmen working probably at Westminster and perhaps under the direction of Barnard Flower who was glass-painter to King Henry VII. The remarkable survival of the windows gives rise to the assumption that they were taken down and hidden when glass elsewhere was being deliberately destroyed.

The windows at Fairford were intended as a sermon in glass, linking together themes and stories from the Bible into a coherent expression of religious belief. The sequence starts with the Fall from

Grace and ends with the Day of Judgement. The narrative planning of the windows is very sophisticated. At a simple level they follow the story of the Life of the Virgin and Christ's Passion, but at the same time they illustrate more philosophical aspects of medieval belief, for instance, the nature of Redemption, and the idea of the New Testament being the fulfilment of the Old. The twelve Apostles of the New Testament are therefore set in the south aisle windows opposite the twelve Old Testament Prophets in the north aisle windows. The Apostles are identified by their various emblems, and each has a scroll which carries a line of the Creed; the Apostles' Creed was traditionally believed to have been written in committee, the Apostles each contributing one phrase, before they went out into the world to spread the Word. Their counterparts, the Prophets, have scrolls with texts from the Old Testament which parallel those of the Apostles. This kind of subject pairing of part and counterpart, type and antitype, was a key device in both medieval philosophy and design. A manuscript called *Speculum Humanae Salvationis*, the 'Mirror of Man's Salvation', has a pair of pictures on each page, one from the Old Testament and one from the New, with a column of text beneath each. Copies of this manuscript were widely circulated and, like the later 'Golden Legend', provided the designers of the day with much of their religious material.

Windows were expensive to produce, and the donor often made sure that his coat of arms appeared somewhere in the design. Sometimes a portrait of the donor was included, usually as a kneeling figure at the bottom of the picture. The designers knew little about the Middle East and nothing of life there in Biblical times. They drew their inspiration from the world about them, painting their figures in the costume of the day and setting them in houses and gardens like their own. The New Jerusalem of the Fairford windows, with crows flying round its crocketed pinnacles, is far removed from the Middle East. And St John's house, where the crucified Christ appears to the Virgin Mary, is a rather comfortable Tudor apartment. With its Gothic architecture, its everyday costume and its lush green landscape, the Holy Land had a solid Englishness about it that must have made the Bible stories seem very close to home.

The Church used every means to bridge the communication gap between clergy and laity, except the one obvious and certain way: conducting services in English. This was as yet unthinkable, and the mere possession of an English translation of the Bible was considered to be heresy until the end of the medieval period. As well as painting, music and the symbolism of the rituals themselves were intended to help the congregation understand the Faith. On important days in the Church's Calendar, the relevant events of the Bible might be enacted simply by the clergy. On Palm Sunday, for instance, the priest led a procession around the churchyard and into the church through the west door, if it had one. This represented Christ's triumphant entry into Jerusalem. A few churches have a west porch or vestibule usually called a *galilee*, probably referring to its use in this Palm Sunday ceremony. Sometimes a wooden gallery at the west end of the church, or over the south door, housed a group of singers who waved palm branches and showered flowers over the procession as it entered.

The carved stone Easter sepulchre at St Patrick's, Patrington, Humberside, a reminder of the liturgical drama that accompanied the medieval celebration of Easter.

The carved stone Easter sepulchre at St Patrick's, Patrington, Humberside, a reminder of the liturgical drama that accompanied the medieval celebration of Easter.

The Easter ceremonies sometimes amounted to full-scale liturgical drama. On Maundy Thursday the consecrated Host, representing the body of Christ, was 'entombed' in an *Easter sepulchre*. Generally, the Easter sepulchre was a richly draped wooden cupboard set up to the north of the altar, but some churches had permanent, elaborately carved sepulchres set in the north wall of their chancels. Splendid stone sepulchres can be seen in the churches of St Andrew at Heckington in Lincolnshire, All Saints at Hawton in Nottinghamshire, and St Patrick at Patrington in Humberside. At Patrington the Easter sepulchre has three rectangular panels set one above the other under a crocketed ogee arch. The bottom panel shows the soldiers asleep at their posts. Like the wall and glass painters, the sculptor modelled his figures on the people he saw around him, and the Roman soldiers are portrayed, rather paradoxically, as Christian knights dressed in contemporary armour. In the central panel Christ rises from the dead, stepping out of a coffin, another anachronism. He gives the sign of the Benediction, and on each side angels waving censers fill the air with incense. Between these two panels is the niche which held the Host. The carving in the top panel has been destroyed, but it almost certainly would have shown the scene of the Ascension, like that at Hawton. Once the Host had been entombed, watch was kept day and night. One penny was paid 'for bread and drink for them that watched the sepulchre' at All Hallows-on-the-Wall in London, according to the churchwardens' accounts. Then on Easter morning three priests processed to the sepulchre, taking the parts of the women who found the tomb empty, and reciting, in Latin of course, their conversation with the angel they met there. The Host was 'resurrected' from the sepulchre, and High Mass was celebrated.

It was a small step from this liturgical symbolism to the dramatisation of stories from the Bible in English and their performance in costume with simple properties and rudimentary scenery in the nave of the church or on wooden stages set up in the churchyard. The churchwardens' accounts for the church of St Nicholas at Great Yarmouth detailed the buying of materials for making a movable star, which no doubt led the Magi across the boards to the stable of the Nativity. These *miracle-plays* evolved into epic cycles like those of York, Coventry and Chester, and called for casts too large to be recruited entirely from the clergy. Laymen became more and more involved, and the responsibility for the production of miracle-plays shifted from the Church to the town's Guilds. The Biblical dialogue ascribed to the main protagonists was supplemented with verse written for the less important characters who supplied boisterous 'comic relief'.

How much the average villager learned of the Faith from all this is questionable. The miracle-plays were concerned with telling a good story, and the audience was not to know what was religious dogma and what was theatrical interpolation. Their vivid spectacle, costumes and scenery, must have made an impression on the artists, perhaps influencing the pictures they painted and perpetuating on the church walls the extra 'business' of the players. As the unlettered man's Bible, the parish church had its shortcomings. The painted images told relatively little of Old Testament history or the teaching of the New Testament; a saint wrestling with some fearsome monster or a martyr dying in torment was more to the liking of both painter and congregation. And those scenes that were validated by the Bible were, more often than not, distorted by legend and folk-lore. The symbolism of the rituals was vague and open to misinterpretation. The layman's only guide through this bewildering maze of imagery was the parish priest.

It was the duty of the parish priest to 'expound to the people in the common tongue, without any fantastic texture of subtlety, the fourteen articles of Faith, the Ten Commandments, the two precepts of the Gospel . . . the seven Works of Mercy, the seven Deadly Sins with their progeny, the seven chief Virtues, and the seven Sacraments of Grace', four times a year according to the decree of 1281 by John Peckham, Archbishop of Canterbury. These sermons were formal and seldom eloquent; the skill of preaching was beyond the average parish priest. Despite pressure from the bishops throughout the thirteenth century to increase the frequency of sermons, the sermon remained a rare event. So it is not surprising that few pulpits dating from before the end of the fourteenth century are found in our churches. Preaching was left to the wandering Friars whose fiery rhetoric pulled crowds in market-places and village greens. Though popular with the people, the Friars were distrusted by the resident clergy whose authority they threatened and, eventually, undermined. The records show that many parish priests had difficulty not just with sermons, but with Latin services too. The clergy, it seems, was often far from efficient. Reports of the regular episcopal visitations to the parishes reveal priests who could not recite the words of the mass correctly, and others who, like the priest of Clyst Honiton, near Exeter, 'hath been there twenty-two years, honestly fulfilling his priestly office in all that pertaineth to a parish priest: but he is now broken with age and insufficient for the cure of the parish.' It was clear, even to the bishops of the day, that the parish priest was the weakest link. To quote Archbishop Peckham again, 'The ignorance of the priests casts the people into the ditch of error: and the folly or unlearning of the clergy . . . tends rather to error than to sound doctrine.'

The root of the problem lay in a system of appointing parish clergy which somehow managed to ensure that those with the education lacked motivation, and those with motivation had little education. Broadly speaking, there were two classes of parish priest, the well-off rectors and the poor vicars. In many parishes the right to choose the rector of the church was held by the lord of the manor. The future of his eldest son being assured by inheritance, it had become a well-established tradition to provide the second son with a guaranteed income by appointing him to the living of the church. This had good consequences and bad. On the credit side, the rector was well placed to act as a mediator between the parishioners and their lord, and was a man likely to command the respect of the people. On the debit side, this link between church and manor brought the two controlling forces in village life into the hands of one family. It also gave the church a rector who probably had little or no sense of vocation and whose interests ranged wider than the parish borders. He needed to gain only the lowest of minor holy orders in order to qualify for his post, and once appointed he could claim a year's absence for further study, a pilgrimage, or some other worthy-sounding excuse for travel. This sabbatical year could be extended to two or three years, or more. In many ways joining the Church in medieval times was, rather like joining the Party in a communist country today, a prerequisite for getting on in the world. The rector, in effect, used the income of the church to finance his own education, leaving the spiritual needs of the parish to be met by a paid substitute priest, the vicar. When, after the Black Death, the relative value of the churches' livings fell, the number of aristocratic rectors fell too.

The vicars, appointed where there were absentee rectors or where churches had been appropriated to religious institutions, and the rectors of churches with poor livings, formed a second class of parish clergy. They were drawn not from the aristocracy, but, like Chaucer's poor parson who was the ploughman's brother, from the ranks of the workers. Their expectations were lower and they were willing to take the livings that were not lucrative enough to interest the sons of the gentry. We may suspect that the peasant-priest also had the stronger sense of vocation. As a boy, he had probably shown an interest in the Church and been allowed to act as server to the priest. The priest would have taken a promising lad under his wing and encouraged him to learn enough Latin to follow the services and perhaps take part in the responses. If his father could afford to pay the fine that the lord of the manor demanded from any of his villeins who joined the clergy, the boy might begin to progress through the first minor holy orders. The office of the holy water clerk, who helped take care of the church and read the Epistle and the responses as well as carrying the holy water, was a common first step since it carried with it a small income which made it possible to buy private tuition or attend a grammar school. By and large the education he received was restricted to a working knowledge of written and spoken Latin and the form and meaning of the Church's services. With such limited training, the chief virtue of the peasant-priest was, no doubt, his affinity with the parishioners whose souls were in his care. He may not have had the intellectual calibre of the aristocratic rector, but at least he was there, and could provide the villagers with advice and support when they needed it. For better or worse, he was their *parson*, the chief 'person' of the village, and by dint of his office he stood for something beyond the mundane world of everyday working-life.

The vicar lived on a stipend paid by the absentee rector or the appropriating institution. Besides himself, he often had junior clergy, like the holy water clerk, to provide for, and, although it was expressly against Church Law, a mistress to keep. In allowing its clergy to marry, the reformed Church of England was to do no more than legalise a situation that had been commonplace throughout medieval times. The stipend was only a fraction of the church's revenue, and the priest usually supplemented his income by farming the *glebe*, the land in the village assigned to the church, either by letting to tenants or by the sweat of his own brow. But if the priest was the rector of the church, he had its entire revenue at his disposal.

The main part of the church's revenues derived from the *tithes*. The rector was entitled to take one tenth of the annual income of each man in the parish. From a labourer the church would expect a tenth of his wages and the produce of his garden; if he had land to farm, the church could take every tenth sheaf of corn at harvest time, and a tenth of the increase in his livestock during the year. The tithes were divided into the *great tithes*, the valuable tithes of cattle and crops, and the *lesser tithes*, the church's share of everything else the villager produced. The tithes were often enforced with pitiless attention to detail, the wool tithe, for instance, being considered to include even the down shed by geese. Where the church had been appropriated or there was an absentee rector, the vicar was usually left with only the lesser tithe which, unfortunately, was not only less valuable but also harder to collect, so the income from the glebe became all the more important to him. The third source of revenue was the *altarage*, the contributions that the parishioners were obliged to make when they received communion on one of the major holy days or when they buried their dead in the churchyard. On the latter occasion the rector might also be entitled to claim the dead man's second-best beast as a *mortuary*, the best beast going as a *heriot* to the lord of the manor. Not surprisingly, the villagers paid their tithes grudgingly. It seemed

quite unreasonable that they should have to give part of what little they had either to a vicar who was at least as well-off as they were, or to a rector who, by comparison, was positively wealthy.

From his income the rector not only had to provide for himself but, as has been noted earlier, he was also responsible for maintaining the fabric of the chancel in good repair and sometimes for supporting several junior clergymen as well. On top of this it was his duty to give alms and hospitality to the needy. In theory, between one quarter and one third of his income was to be spent on such charity. The laity played its part in the relief of poverty too. Every church had its *poor-box* for the collecting of alms. But even in those days, it seems security was a problem, and the poor-box in the church of St Agnes, at Cawston in Norfolk, illustrates the precautions that were taken to prevent pilfering. The poor-box is carved from a single piece of oak, bound by iron straps and capped with a sturdy iron lid with a slit for the money. Inside, an iron cup suspended upside-down prevented money dropped into the box from being retrieved through the slit with a knife or stick. The lid was secured by three locks. The main lock has a cover which cannot be lifted until two dials on the outside are set into a certain position – a primitive combination lock. The rector held the key to this lock, and the keys to the others were kept by the two churchwardens.

The churchwardens were the elected representatives of the parishioners, their office having been set up in 1129 by the Council of London. Acting on behalf of the parishioners, they were responsible for the building and maintenance of the parts of the church used by the laity. They also had to provide certain of the church's furnishings, according to the decree of Archbishop Winchelsea: 'a pyx for the Body of Christ, a proper Lenten veil, a banner for Rogation Days, bells with ropes, a bier for the dead, a vessel for holy water, a pax, a candelabrum for the Easter candle, a font with a lock, images in the church, a principal image in the chancel.' In addition, the parish might sometimes have to provide wages for the parish clerk and sexton. So the churchwardens' job involved raising and spending a considerable amount of money, and much of what is known of medieval church life is drawn from the detailed accounts they kept.

One of the most popular ways of raising money was to hold a parish feast called a *church-ale*, the forerunner of today's church fêtes and bazaars, in the nave of the church. The churchwardens bought or were given large amounts of malt, which was brewed into ale at the nearby parish brew house. The revellers paid for the ale that they drank, and the profits went to the church. A sexton-ale might be held to raise the salary for a sexton, a tower-ale to finance the building of a new tower, or a bride-ale to provide a poor bride with a dowry. The ale was strong and the dancing usually merry. A good time was had by all, judging by the fact that a certain William the bellringer was paid as much as eight pence for clearing up after one such ale at St Edmund's Church in Salisbury. The ales sometimes degenerated into riotous secular events, and the more sober-minded churchmen and magistrates made many attempts to stop them, with a conspicuous lack of success. But eventually the ballad singer sang too profane a song, and the piper led too free a dance to be tolerated by an increasingly puritanical climate, and the practice of holding ales in the nave of the church was slowly to die out.

The church-ales had their origins in the pagan feasts which the church had wisely absorbed into the Christian Calendar, and which were attuned to the rhythm of the agricultural year. The tilling of the soil played such an important part in parish life that many country churches had a *plough rood* set up at the west end of the church. The plough rood was maintained by the local guild of ploughmen. For them it acted as a shrine to the guild's patron saint whose statue would have stood in front of a carved wooden *plough screen*. At Cawston Church in Norfolk a fragment of the ancient plough screen still survives. It is carved with a lively and suitably down to earth inscription: 'God spede the plow and send us ale corn enow our purpose for to make: At crow of cok of the plowlete of Sygate; Be mery and glade wat good ale yis work mad.' *Wat good ale* is believed to be a pun on the name of a man who is said to have been one of the churchwardens of the time, *Watt Goodall*. Ale corn was the barley that provided the malt from which ale was brewed, a very important commodity in the days when bread and ale formed a large part of the ordinary man's diet. The plough guild usually had its meeting place, or guild hall, over an inn, which is why so many public houses today are called 'The Plough'. At Cawston the plough guild met at an inn in the nearby village of Sygate, mentioned in the inscription, which was renamed Southgate in Victorian times. It is said that the inn was originally called the 'Plough Lights', after the candles which were always kept burning on the plough rood. Money was often bequeathed to pay for these candles. When William Herward of Cawston died in 1490, he left sixpence for the maintenance of the plough lights.

Candles burned before all the devotional statues in the church and cast their flickering light across the painted walls. The comparative splendour of their parish church gave the villagers the nearest glimpse their earthly life could permit of Heaven itself. There they saw mirrored the idealised relationships of their own childhood: a stern

The elevation of the consecrated Host, the central moment of the mass, as it is shown in one of seven sacramental scenes on the font of All Saints', Gresham, Norfolk.

but just Father, an obedient Son and a caring Mother. The faces of the saints and martyrs, staring out protectively, evoked a sense of security; the pictures, from the Garden of Eden to the terrible Day of Judgement, spelt out man's place in the cosmology of the medieval world, and the penalties for stepping outside it. As the villager's gaze wandered across the familiar images, memories were evoked of life's turning points, of good times and bad.

The sudden ringing of the Sanctus bell punctuated the day-dreaming and idle conversation of the congregation and returned their attention to the chancel. The most solemn and awesome moment of the mass had been reached. The priest elevated the Host. Every one of the congregation was aware that the miracle of the mass had been accomplished. Somehow the Body and Blood of Christ, their only hope of Redemption, was there among them, and they did what they could to join in by reciting the *Paternoster* and *Ave* over and over again.

In some churches there was another witness to the mass, the solitary *anchorite*. An anchorite was a pious recluse of either sex who lived in a cell built against the wall of a monastic or parish church. Once ceremonially installed in his cell by the bishop, the anchorite was cut off from all worldly distractions, and the rest of his life was spent in religious contemplation. A small opening in the church wall allowed the anchorite to see and hear the mass, and in the outer wall another opening enabled him to receive food and water, for which he was totally dependent on charity. There was no normal position for the anchorite's cell, though they generally seem to have been set against the dark north side of the church and often by the chancel. In later centuries, such a cell was conveniently placed for conversion into a vestry for the priest.

The men and women who withdrew from the world into their anchorites' cells were for the most part from the educated laity. Many spent their solitary years writing devotional treatises. They wrote primarily for other anchorites and for members of religious communities, but their vividly imaginative and spiritually incisive writings found a wider audience among the clergy employed in secular administration and the educated class of lay society. One such writer was Juliana, an anchoress at a church in Norwich who was made famous by her 'Revelations of Divine Love'. In this treatise she empathises with Christ's Passion and tries to recreate His suffering within herself by describing, with cold and precise attention to anatomical detail, the wounding of Christ and its physical effects. It was a literary counterpart to the agonies of Christ pictured on the church walls. Both anchorite in his cell and unlettered villager in the nave contemplated the images of Christ and His saints, but they did so through very different eyes. Receiving such little spiritual instruction, the villagers took the images at face value, and if they saw beyond them at all it was to ascribe to them the superstitious qualities of talismans. But for the devotional writers, these images were only the starting places that pointed the way along a road hedged on one side by divine contemplation, and on the other by self-analysis, which led ultimately to an apprehension of spiritual truths. The very images that overtly symbolised the unity of the Church were, in fact, feeding a growing divergence. The popularity of devotional writings revealed a rising

Right

Although everyone attended mass at least once a week, communion was only taken on special occasions, the most important being during the Last Rites when it was believed that the forces of good and evil fought for possession of the departing soul. In this medieval deathbed scene an angel rescues the soul from the clutches of a demon.

Opposite page

Details of late fifteenth-century stained glass from the Last Judgment window at St Mary the Virgin, Fairford, Gloucestershire. A blue demon pushes a soul in a wheelbarrow (top left) to Hell which, paradoxically, is depicted as a glassmakers' factory where souls are ground in a pigment grinder (top right) and roasted in a furnace (bottom left) under the gloating eye of the Devil himself (bottom right) who is shown as a two-headed, fish-like monster.

level of spiritual awareness among the well-educated laity which began to leave most parish clergy way behind, and which contributed, in the centuries that followed, to the breaking of the religious monopoly of the medieval Church.

In the chancel the clergy ate the Body and drank the Blood of Christ. Although everyone in the village attended Mass at least once a week, it was rare for laymen to receive communion more than three times a year, and some were content to do so only on their death beds with the Last Rites. For the sake of his immortal soul a man had to die in a 'state of Grace'. 'In the place where the tree falleth, there shall it lie', taught the Church, and all round the congregation were reminders that the spectre of Death was never far away.

The tombs of those important enough to be buried within the church itself jostled for position near the altars. Even in death the social distinction was maintained between the noble, or at least wealthy, who were buried inside, and the common-folk who were

Left

A roof boss from Sherborne Abbey, Dorset, showing a mermaid holding a comb and looking-glass, a subject derived from the 'Physiologus', a book of real and mythical animals.

Right

A table tomb from All Saints', Ashwellthorpe, Norfolk, bearing the life-size effigy of Sir Edmund de Thorpe dressed in full armour.

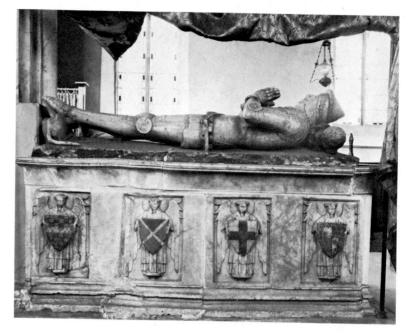

laid to rest outside in the churchyard. A distinction which was to be even more evident by the eighteenth century and which is neatly summed up by an epitaph of 1793 on a grave by the door of St Edmund's Church at Kingsbridge in Devon:

> 'Here I lie at the chancel door,
> Here I lie because I'm poor:
> The further in the more you pay:
> Here I lie as warm as they.'

During the twelfth century, tombs had been simple coffin-shaped slabs of stone laid flush with the floor of the church. They were incised with foliated crosses and often a symbol which gives a clue to the occupation of the deceased: a sword for a knight, a chalice for a priest, a pair of shears for a wool merchant.

The first carved life-size effigies recumbent upon their box-like *table tombs* date from the thirteenth century. Their poses are rigid with hands set together in pious supplication. No attempt was made at a realistic representation of the deceased; the effigies were personalised by heraldry and details of costume. A knight was always shown in full armour, his head resting on his tilting helm and his feet on his heraldic beast or some other animal. The earliest effigies are of Purbeck marble, but alabaster was most commonly used. There are also a few wooden effigies surviving, like the two knights and their ladies at Clifton Reynes Church in Buckinghamshire. Whatever material they were carved from, the finished monuments were painted in life-like colours.

Occasionally a diminutive stone effigy of a knight is found. In medieval times it was not unusual for an important man's heart and body to be buried in different places. Where the heart lay, a small figure was placed usually shown holding a heart in his hands. A small Purbeck marble effigy at the church of St Mary, Bottesford in

Leicestershire, is accompanied by a tablet set in the wall which reads in Latin: 'Here lies the heart of William de Roos whose body is buried at Kirkham'. William de Roos died in 1285 and his monument is the earliest among a quite remarkable collection housed in the chancel of Bottesford Church. They are the monuments of the Lords of Belvoir Castle who later became the Dukes of Rutland, and housed under one roof are the tombs of eight successive earls, representing a slice of history of nearly four hundred years.

Round the sides of the table tombs there were usually small carved figures, called *weepers*, praying for the soul of the deceased. On early tombs they are often angels, each shown in an identical, rather stiff, pose. Later the weepers become more individual, and sometimes, especially if they are kneeling, they may represent the dead person's children. Sometimes a kneeling child is shown holding a skull, a convention which indicated that the child had died before its parent.

During the fourteenth century a greater variety is found in the design of monuments. They are often set under vaulted stone canopies. The poses of the effigies become more relaxed, and they begin to take on individual characteristics which approach portraiture. In the centuries that followed, poses were to change from relaxed to positively casual in some instances. At the church of St Mary, Swinbrook, in Oxfordshire, the members of the Fettiplace family lounge idly on their elbows to await the Day of Judgement.

From the last part of the thirteenth century until the end of the fifteenth, *monumental brasses* were a popular alternative to stone monuments, less expensive and more durable. They were made not from brass, but from a very similar alloy of copper and zinc with traces of lead and tin. The resulting metal, called *latten*, was extremely hard and

HERE LIETH THE
BODY OF S[r] EDMVND
FETIPLACE KNIGHT
SONNE AND HEYRE
TO WILLIAM FETI
PLACE ESQVIER
HE ESPOVSED ANNE
DAVGHTER OF ROGER
ALFORDE ESQVIER

NVLLO VE
VNE

HERE RELIETH THE BODY OF WILLIAM FETIPLACE ESQVIER SONNE AND HEY
OF ALEXANDER FETIPLACE ESQVIER POWSED ELIZABETH ASHFIELD DAVGHTER AND
HEYROF SEDMVND ASHFIELD KNIGHT HE HA SVE3 SONNS HE DECEASO FEI 10 DAY OF MAY 1562

HEARE LVETH THE BODY OF ALEXAND FETIPLACE SONNE AND HEYREOF ANTH
NVE FETIPLACE ESQVIER HE WAS FIRST ESPO WSED TO A MEDA VGHTER AND HEYR OF WILLIAM
ESQVIER FENTODORITY ASHEILO HE HAD IS VE3 NNS AND 7 DAVGHTERS HE DISCESEO FEI 20F SEPTEMBE

monumental brasses have better withstood the tests of time and the vandal's penknife than have stone monuments of a similar age which are often worn or mutilated beyond recognition. Although most of the metal was imported from the Continent, England has more medieval brasses than the rest of Europe put together. The craftsmen who made them were called *latteners*, and their designs, like those of the monumental sculptors, provide a wealth of information about the history of costume. The design was painted on a sheet of latten which was then engraved and cut to shape. The engraved brass was set in its *indent* in a stone slab and the engraved lines filled with pitch or some other dark material. Certain other sections would be inlaid with coloured enamels. The oldest surviving brass in the country, that of Sir John d'Aubernoun at Stoke D'Abernon Church in Surrey, has a shield with a blue enamel design. The figure was often framed with a patterned or inscribed border, and sheltered under an elaborate canopy which sometimes included a miniature representation of the Holy Trinity or the Virgin and Child. Because monumental brasses were less costly than carved stone effigies, we meet a wider cross section of medieval society through them. As well as archbishops we find humble parish priests; alongside knights and their ladies, traders and their wives. Knights are shown in full armour with a precise attention to detail that reflects the latest contemporary developments and so provides a unique record of the history of armour. Their ladies' costumes mirror as faithfully the more fanciful dictates of fashion, their head-dresses ranging from a simple veil worn about the head and shoulders to the flamboyant *butterfly* head-dresses of the second half of the fifteenth century. Costumes worn by the clergy, however, remained virtually unchanged. Archbishops portrayed in full pontificals provide some of the most impressive brasses. The richly detailed borders, or *orphreys*, of their vestments are often engraved with charming pictures of the saints.

Costume, particularly armour, gives the best guide to dating a monument, but the language of an inscription and the type of lettering in which it is written may be helpful too. Latin was universal on memorials to the clergy, but on other monuments it is mainly confined to the fifteenth century, being preceeded by Norman French in the fourteenth, and followed by English in the sixteenth. Writing is generally in Lombardic letters until the middle of the fourteenth century, 'black-letter' until the seventeenth, and Roman thereafter.

The constant cry of inscriptions on memorials was *ora pro anima*, 'pray for the soul (of). . . .' It was a plea that struck to the heart of the congregation as they looked up at the Doom painting and saw the torments that beset the souls of the damned. Other wall paintings, like *Les Trois Rois vifs et morts*, a popular subject showing three kings in the prime of life confronted by three skeleton kings, reminded them yet again that earthly life was short for all. Death was a certainty; Redemption was not and the mass now over, many of the congregation must have carried this thought with them out into the morning sunshine. Beneath their feet the green sward of the church-yard covered generations of their forefathers, and they knew that sooner or later they too would pass for a last time under the *lychgate* which stood at its entrance. The lychgate was a roofed gateway which

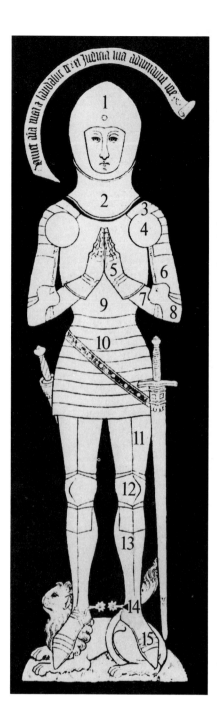

1 bascinet
2 gorget
3 spaulder
4 besagew
5 gauntlet
6 rerebrace
7 vambrace
8 couter
9 breast plate
10 skirt of taces
11 cuisse
12 poleyn
13 greave
14 rowel spurs
15 pointed sabaton

The brass of Sir Lawrence Fyton at St Andrew's, Sonning, Berkshire, shows the knight wearing armour that is typical of the first half of the fifteenth century. The chain mail seen in the thirteenth-century brass of Sir John d'Aubernoun (see page 153) has been completely replaced by solid plate armour.

The elegant brass of Margaret Dayrell at St Nicholas', Lillingstone Dayrell, Buckinghamshire, dating from the end of the fifteenth century, presents a charming portrait of the lady and shows her wearing the flamboyant butterfly head-dress that was all the rage with fashionable women in the closing years of Edward IV's reign.

1 amice
2 chasuble
3 maniple
4 ends
   of stole
5 alb
6 orphrey
   of alb

Clerical dress was less subject to the whims of fashion. This brass, dated 1395, from St Mary the Virgin, Edlesborough, Buckinghamshire, shows John de Swynsted dressed in the vestments he would have worn to celebrate mass. Priests are often shown holding a chalice and wafer. John's kindly face is particularly well drawn and full of character.

The brass of Geoffrey Kidwelly at St Peter's, Little Wittenham, Oxfordshire, dates from the end of the fifteenth century and is a good example of the comparatively sober costume of civilians. He is wearing a plain mantle with a hood slung over his left shoulder and a purse and prayer beads, often worn as a symbol of piety, hanging from his belt.

The Black Death brought death on an unprecedented scale. In this medieval illustration survivors struggle to keep pace with the burying of victims of the plague.

took its name from the Old English word *lych*, meaning 'corpse'. Only the well-to-do could afford coffins, and most people were buried in simple woollen or linen shrouds. The lychgate provided a shelter for the body until the priest arrived to lead the funeral procession into the churchyard.

Medieval men were familiar with death, but none could have imagined the sudden and hideous fate that was travelling westwards across Europe. The Black Death reached England in 1348, and in the years that followed over a third of the population was wiped out. The catastrophe sent shock waves through the social and economic structure of the country that were still being felt a generation later. In some places whole villages disappeared. The despair of the people is expressed in these pitiful words, scratched in rough Latin by an unknown hand on the tower wall of Ashwell Church in Kent:

'1350. Wretched, savage and violent.
Only the dregs of the people are left to tell the tale.'

6: Civic Pride

Gloucester Cathedral, the birth-
place of the Perpendicular style of
Gothic architecture.

Previous page
*Profits from the flourishing wool
trade provided for the building of
many rich churches like St Mary the
Virgin, Fairford, Gloucestershire
– from the 'Discovering English
Churches' television series.*

The effect of the Black Death was catastrophic. With the drastic
reduction of the population, the economic life of the villages floun-
dered, and for a time church building was robbed of both its financial
and its practical resources. New churches were left half-finished,
sometimes for a generation or more. When work began again, a new
style spread across the country – the final phase of Gothic architecture, Perpendicular. By this time the Hundred Years' War had
distanced England from the influence of France, the cultural pace-
setter of Europe, and the development of the Perpendicular style in
this country was a contribution to the history of architecture that was
uniquely English.

The seeds of the new style had already germinated in the years
immediately before the Black Death, at Gloucester in the Abbey
Church of St Peter, now the Cathedral. There the tomb of Edward II,
who had been brutally murdered at nearby Berkeley Castle in 1327,
attracted a large number of pilgrims whose offerings had greatly
swelled the church's coffers. So much so that during the 1330s a
reconstruction was begun of the transepts and choir of the Old
Norman church. Since the massive Norman piers and arches were

The four-centred arch, so-called because the lower parts of the arch curve on a smaller radius than the upper parts.

still structurally sound, instead of demolishing them, the masons concealed them behind a stone screen of open tracery with mullions rising directly from the ground to an elegant vault which canopied the choir. The emphatic upward lines of these mullions laid bare the verticality which had always been at the heart of Gothic and set the tone for almost two centuries of architecture.

In the Perpendicular style, the grid-like laying out of architectural features reached its logical conclusion with spaces and surfaces ruled into tall rectangles by a lattice of vertical and horizontal lines. Because of this emphasis on the straight line, Perpendicular is sometimes also referred to as the *Rectilinear* style of Gothic. The sinuous curves and convolutions of the Decorated style were replaced by predominant right angles and straight lines. It was as though the set square and the rule had become the mason's favourite tools, while his compasses hung idly on the wall.

Although the style originated at Gloucester, the best of Perpendicular work is not to be found in the great churches of the monasteries, as in earlier styles, but in the parishes. The fortunes of the monasteries were now in decline. Endowments to religious houses had already been discouraged by the constraints of the Statute of Mortmain, and during the Hundred Years' War it became unpatriotic to endow any establishment whose wealth eventually filtered back to a mother house in enemy France. So the monasteries, with the exception of those growing rich on the wool trade, had no money to spare for lavish rebuilding. Not that any new building was much needed. The Black Death had severely depleted the numbers of monks and nuns so existing accommodation was usually more than adequate. At St Albans Abbey, for instance, only thirteen of the sixty brethren survived. Falling numbers had to be made up in a hurry and the monasteries were in no position to be choosy. Standards of recruitment dropped and with them public estimation of the religious Establishment. Lay benefactors turned their attention from the monastery to the parish church which was closer to home in spirit as well as geographically. In the period between the mid-fourteenth and sixteenth centuries, parish churches grew wealthier than ever before or since, and many of them were partially or completely rebuilt. Consequently, parochial architecture is dominated by the style of that time, and more than a third of England's ancient churches are Perpendicular in part or whole.

In a typical bay of an arcade the pointed arch is flatter than in earlier Gothic styles and is often softened into the more subtle shape of the four-centred arch, in which the lower parts of the arch curve on a smaller radius than the upper parts. When built in brickwork, the four-centred arch is sometimes also known as a *Tudor arch*. The piers supporting the arch are more slender than before, usually with plain octagonal shafts, but sometimes diamond-shaped with four or more half-shafts. The half-shafts often carry on the mouldings of the arch, and, in East Anglia especially, the spaces between them may be scooped out into wide shallow hollows. Where arch mouldings flow into the shafts of the piers in this way, the capitals are usually rather insignificant or omitted altogether. In the west country capitals decorated with carved foliage or figures, usually angels holding

shields, are still found, but elsewhere the simple moulded capital is most common. The bases of piers are also still moulded, but they are now taller and often set on a high plinth.

The flattening of the arches alters the proportions of the arcade: a larger part of its height is now taken up by the piers. The piers being both taller and thinner make the arcade appear loftier and produce the impression of height and lightness of structure that is so characteristic of the Perpendicular style. This effect is enhanced by the addition of the clerestory, now almost a routine feature of the parish church. Clerestory windows are larger than before, and sometimes there are even two to each bay. In the Cotswolds area a window was sometimes inserted above the chancel arch, a local peculiarity which effectively continues the clerestory right round the nave, as at the Church of St James, Chipping Campden in Gloucestershire.

The preference for straight lines during the Perpendicular period shows particularly clearly in window tracery. There the vertical mullions that divide a window into its lights rise almost without interruption to the head of the window, ruling its tracery into tiers of rectangular compartments. The art of stained glass was reaching its peak, and the glaziers no doubt breathed a sigh of relief as the awkward shapes marked out by the flowing tracery of the Decorated style were replaced by the neat rectangles of the Perpendicular. Each of the cusped panels could now conveniently accommodate one painted saint or angel. The glass painter was given every opportunity to demonstrate his expertise as windows were made larger and larger. The east window often occupies almost all of the east wall of the chancel. As the number of lights in a window increased, its framework needed to be strengthened, so the masons tied the mullions together with horizontal bands of stone called *transoms*. Transoms

The graceful geometry of Perpendicular window tracery illustrated by St Mary's, Saffron Walden, Essex.

were sometimes added to windows of an earlier date and where a transom is found together with flowing or geometrical tracery, a change in the colour or texture of the stone work will often confirm the suspicion that it was inserted later. Like the arches of the arcades, window heads are generally flatter and the four-centred arch is often used. Smaller windows, especially those of the clerestory and at the ends of aisles may even be square-headed.

The four-leafed flower set in a hollow moulding remains a popular ornament, though more square in shape than before. Wall surfaces, especially parapets and spandrels, are sometimes decorated

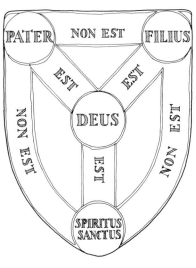

An example of religious 'heraldry' from Holy Trinity, Blythburgh, Suffolk, in the shape of an angel from a bench end bearing a shield with the 'arms' of the Holy Trinity – an abstract graphic device which expresses the mystic paradox of the unity and individuality of the Trinity.

with broad bands of blind quatrefoil panelling. Each quatrefoil may enclose a four-leafed flower or perhaps a shield with armorial bearings or some other heraldic device. Heraldry and the repeated decorative use of secular emblems, like the Tudor rose and portcullis, are typical of the Perpendicular period and underline the more worldly air of the parish church after the decline of the monasteries. Even orthodox symbolism was tinged with the secular and recast into a kind of religious heraldry. Shields are emblazoned with the emblems of the Passion for instance, and the saints are assigned badges bearing their personal symbols.

One of the most characteristic decorative elements of the Perpendicular style is the use of cusped rectangular panelling to enrich the surfaces of walls, doors and buttresses. The panels echo the shapes of window tracery of the period and, at their best, provide a rich setting that unifies the major architectural features of the church. Sometimes, however, excessive repetition of identical panels over large areas of walling has a monotonous effect and contributes to the impression that imagination and invention were flagging in some later work of the period.

There is a certain ambiguity about the Perpendicular style. Some architectural historians have seen it as the climax of Gothic architecture, others as a degeneration in which the energy and innovation of the earlier styles were dissipated in the tired repetition of formula solutions. Was Perpendicular the consummate refinement of Gothic, or was it no more than a simplification? The creation of a more rectilinear style that was simpler to execute is sometimes ascribed to the lack of experienced masons after the Black Death. But, since the style had already appeared at Gloucester before the coming of the plague, it must be acknowledged that it had at least been born of aesthetic choice rather than practical necessity.

The portrayal of Perpendicular as the degeneration of the Gothic style has been strengthened in the past by the notion that everything in life is cyclic: a time of birth and growth, followed by blossoming and fruition, ending in a period of decay after which new growth can start again. In this way the Early English style was seen as growth, the Decorated as maturity, and Perpendicular as the inevitable decline. This analogy between Nature and Art is, however, a questionable philosophy. It led the historians of the nineteenth century generally to prefer the Early English and Decorated styles. But what reason is there to suppose that the search for solutions should necessarily produce 'better' or more 'noble' architecture than the sure-footed application of known solutions? In practice it is more useful to talk of good and bad standards of design and workmanship rather than the doubtful analogies of climax and decay. All the Gothic styles produced some architecture that was good and some not so good. The Perpendicular phase of Gothic was to last nearly two hundred years, longer than Early English and Decorated put together, so it is not surprising that something of its freshness was lost in later years. But the best work is at least the equal of earlier Gothic and sometimes the confidence and self-assertiveness of the style place it a cut above. In the well-off parishes in particular, churches were raised in noble scale, set with elegant architectural detail and very richly furnished.

The cash for building these sumptuous new parish churches was made available by the wider distribution of wealth that resulted from the wages' explosion following the Black Death, and the continuing expansion of domestic and foreign trade. The pestilence left labour in short supply, and on the manors the first flexing was felt of what we today would call 'industrial muscle'. Labourers who were freemen refused to work for low wages, and villeins bound to the lord of the manor struggled for freedom. The tottering feudal system, which had concentrated wealth in the hands of the great landowners, collapsed. As a little more money found its way into a few more pockets, business prospered for the small trader and craftsman. In groups or sometimes even as individuals, they too could now afford to bestow patronage and expensive gifts upon their church. At St Agnes, Cawston in Norfolk, for instance, the roof of the south transept was paid for by the local Weavers' Guild. Its bosses are carved as portraits

to commemorate the particular generosity of individual members of
the Guild, some of whom are shown wearing their distinctive weavers'
caps. Thus commoners often replaced the great landowning nobles as
the new patrons of the churches. This was especially true in the
expanding towns. In the hundred years following the Black Death
the population rose again to its former level, but it grew much more
rapidly in the towns than in the countryside. Many a newly-freed
villein must have left his manor in search of adventure and fortune in
the towns where the streets were paved, if not with gold, then at least
with opportunity. The towns developed a strong sense of corporate
identity which paralleled the growing national spirit of patriotism,
and a magnificent town church was both the outward show of
commercial success and a symbol of civic pride.

The richest traders raised the richest churches, and those built by
the wool merchants, often called 'wool' churches, are among the
finest in the land. The wool trade, not being labour intensive, had
survived the turmoils of the mid-fourteenth century unscathed. In
fact in some ways the shortage of labour proved a benefit, since
landowners who were unable or unwilling to pay the higher price for
labour turned the land they could no longer afford to keep under
cultivation over to sheep farming. English wool, judged to be the
best in Europe, was much sought after, and the flourishing wool
trade provided the economic backbone of medieval England. In
international affairs, the country's strength rested, as did the Lord
Chancellor himself, on the wool sack. Some wool merchants became
very wealthy. Investing their money in land, diversifying into other
businesses, becoming financiers and speculators, they laid the foundations for Tudor capitalism. William de la Pole, for instance, a
merchant of Hull, lent money to the King to finance the wars with
France. Edward III was desperate, and William was astute, acquiring
for himself such favourable terms that he achieved both privilege and
position. As the first merchant to found a noble family, he led the way
for many who were to climb from humble traders to the ranks of the
nobility on the woolly backs of their sheep. It is no wonder that the
Agnus Dei, the lamb of God, became such a popular merchant's mark.

The churches the wool merchants endowed reflected their wealth
and status. East Anglia, conveniently facing Europe, was the first
major centre of the English wool trade. But after the discovery of the

One of the carved armed merchant ships from St Peter's, Tiverton, Devon, a church which benefitted from the business acumen of the merchant John Greenway.

Americas, trade routes became more orientated towards the New World. As ports facing the Atlantic, like Bristol, became more important, wool production moved to the west country. In East Anglia the wool towns and ports went into decline. Today, wandering through the becalmed little village of Blythburgh in Suffolk, it would be difficult to imagine that this was once a busy port, one of the dozen or so largest in England, were it not for the spacious church of the Holy Trinity. There it stands, like many of East Anglia's churches, incongruously large, stripped by time and iconoclasm of most of its fifteenth-century richness, yet with the resilient dignity of one accustomed to better times. Even before the end of the fifteenth century, trade had begun to decline here. Received '16d. and no more', the church's accounts for 1478 state despondently, 'because the Bretons did not come this year . . .'

Meanwhile, in the west country business was booming, and so was church building. Many of the churches record their debt to the wool trade in the carved details of their stonework. At Cullompton in Devon, St Andrew's church was richly endowed by John Lane, the leading merchant of the town, and the sixteenth-century Lane aisle named after him has carvings of sheep-shears and merchant ships. John Lane's great rival was John Greenway of nearby Tiverton. Greenway was an extremely successful merchant who traded English cloth for oil and wine from France and Spain. At St Peter's, Tiverton, the chapel which bears his name, built in 1517, is carved with various emblems of the merchant's trade: barrels of wine, bales of wool and, as at Cullompton, various sailing ships. It was during these years that the Tudor monarchs began building the supremacy of English sea-power, and the collection of armed merchant ships at Tiverton is of special interest to the student of naval history.

The influence of the affluent merchant class showed itself not just in the scale and lavishness of the new parish churches, but in their planning and fittings as well. Two factors, both results of the wider distribution of wealth, may be singled out: first, the generosity of individuals in the face of death, and second, the accelerated growth of the educated section of the laity.

To begin with the first factor, it must be remembered that the generosity of the benefactors of the parish churches was not without an element of self-interest. Death was an ever-present reality that had been intensified by war and plague. The Last Judgement, as it was shown on the walls and in the windows of the churches, presented a frightening prospect, and the only way up the heavenly staircase was through the earthly Church. The funeral service in early times took the form of a Requiem Mass, and later it became the custom to say mass for the soul of the deceased at regular intervals, every year or even every month. These masses were called the *year's mind* and the *month's mind*. It was popularly believed that such memorial masses could ease the passage of the departed soul through Purgatory, and people from all walks of life willed large sums of money to be used to pay for their memorial masses or other prayers for the dead. Those who could afford it made more permanent arrangements for the repose of their souls. With an eye to success in the next world as well as this one, a man of means might found a chapel within the church

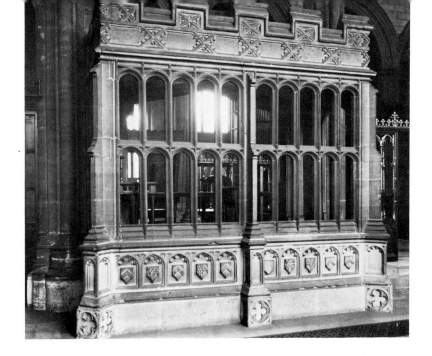

and provide an endowment, usually of land, to pay the salary of a full-time priest who prayed daily for the souls of the dead benefactor and his family. These were called *chantry chapels*. The foundation of chantries was welcomed by the Church since the chantry-priest provided an extra pair of ecclesiastical hands and usually assisted with other duties besides those of his own chapel.

Endowing a chantry was, of course, beyond the means of all but the richest individuals. So in many places chapels were founded by groups of people instead, most often a craft guild but sometimes a fraternity set up specially for the purpose. At the church of St John the Baptist at Cirencester in Gloucestershire, for instance, the chapel of the Holy Trinity was endowed in 1430 by two knights connected with the wool trade, Sir Richard Dixton and Sir William Prelatte, in association with the town's Guild of Weavers. They provided the chapel with land enough to maintain two chantry-priests. The brass of one of them, Ralph Parsons who died in 1478, is still to be seen in the chapel. He is shown, as priests generally were, holding a chalice and wearing the vestments he would have worn for the celebration of mass. In another corner of the church a part of the cope Ralph Parsons actually wore is preserved in a glass case, and its rich embroidery gives us a glimpse of the splendour the wealth of the merchants brought to the parish church.

This proliferation of chantry and guild chapels had a major effect on the ground plan of the parish church. They were usually set up in part of an aisle, or occasionally a transept, and fenced off from the rest of the church by open screens of wood or stone, called *parclose* screens. Many churches, however, were not big enough to accommodate the growing number of chapels in this way and the building had to be extended. Often whole aisles were added. The result was that the church expanded sideways, until in some cases, like St John the Baptist, Cirencester, the church grew almost as wide as it was long. The church of St Michael in Coventry (which became the city's

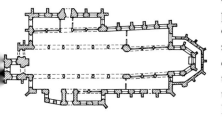

St Michael's, Coventry

167

Cathedral in 1918 and was almost completely destroyed during the Second World War) provided a good example of this expansion of the ground plan of a parish church. Altogether the church had seven guild chapels. Much partial rebuilding and extension of the parish churches during the Gothic period meant that the ground plan evolved, almost haphazardly in some places, into a great diversity of forms, and by the time of the Perpendicular style it is hard to discern any one 'typical' plan. However, the favourite position for chantry chapels was close to the altar, and if a chancel had no convenient aisles, they were often added specially. In this way the cruciform plan of many earlier churches became submerged and tended towards a simple rectangle. The preference for a more rectangular plan is quite marked in churches completely rebuilt in the Perpendicular style. The aisled rectangle of the church of St Nicholas at King's Lynn in Norfolk, for example, engulfs the thirteenth century tower and is almost severe in its simplicity.

The aisled rectangle plan also received indirect support from the second of the two factors mentioned earlier: the growth of the educated section of the laity. The thirst for knowledge of a larger part of the congregation made the sermon, the only part of the service spoken in English, more and more popular and emphasised the function of the church nave as an auditorium.

The early medieval church and the rituals that took place there had been designed for a congregation that was passive and illiterate. They could witness the 'theatre' of the Church but were excluded from participation both by the layout of the church and by their own lack of education. However poorly educated the clergy may have been, they had always remained one step ahead – until now. That advantage was now being eroded. The rising level of literacy and the dissemination of devotional treatises were expanding the spiritual awareness of the lay population. Esoteric religious topics became talking points at the dinner tables of merchants and craftsmen. Devotional treatises stressed the individual's role in achieving his own salvation, and by doing so inevitably detracted from that of the established Church and lowered the status of the clergy still further. Furthermore, for a large part of the fourteenth century the Papal Court was held at Avignon – too close for comfort to the borders of France, the national enemy, in the eyes of many Englishmen. And the Great Schism of 1378, which lasted well into the fifteenth century, did nothing to restore confidence by splitting Christendom between two rival Popes. The medieval Church began to lose its grip on the common mind. With better education, resentment became articulated criticism and the sermon became important to the clergy too, as an instrument with which to silence the whisper of heresy.

The main voice of dissent in the fourteenth century was that of John Wycliffe, an Oxford don who was at his most active during the 1370s. His early work propounded rather welcome theoretical justifications for curbing Papal intrusion into national affairs and won him support within the ranks of the nobility and the intellectual establishment. But this support fell away as the more far-reaching implications of his ideas became apparent. He held that God and man were in direct contact and that the Church's role was not that of a mediator

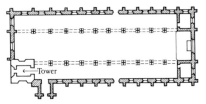

St Nicholas', King's Lynn, Norfolk

*John Wycliffe whose teachings
inspired the Lollard movement.*

but of a teacher. The clergy should, therefore, set a living example to the laity. He called for a service in English and produced the first complete translation of the Bible in the common tongue. Vernacular versions had already been made available under special licence to nuns and certain wealthy patrons, but the Church had always actively resisted making an English version of the Bible available to the laity in general. It feared that its authority would be diminished, even challenged, if the ordinary man were allowed to read the Bible and interpret it for himself, and for more than another hundred years, possession of an English Bible continued to be evidence of heresy. Wycliffe's criticism of the Church bit deep. He questioned the divine authority of popes, scorned the worship of relics and images, condemned the sale of pardons and masses for souls, and denied the theory of transubstantiation, according to which the elements of the Sacrament are miraculously transformed.

Such subversive notions lost Wycliffe many influential friends and must have seemed especially dangerous at a time that was already threatened by social unrest on the labour front. The repressive Statutes of Labourers had bottled up discontent, and now discontent was fermented by heavier taxes levied to pay for the wars with France. In May 1381 the situation exploded. The Peasants' Revolt broke out in Kent and spread quickly to London. Although John Wycliffe was not involved in any way with the rising, it was to affect his influence by making the climate even less hospitable to change and, more directly, by bringing an old adversary to a position of power. In London the mob sacked the Lambeth residence of Simon Sudbury, Chancellor and Archbishop of Canterbury, and publicly beheaded him at Tower Hill. Two hundred years earlier the murder of an Archbishop of Canterbury had caused public outrage and earned Thomas à Becket his canonisation. That Sudbury should have been so lightly disposed of gives a chilling measure of the disregard in which the high-ranking clergy were now held. Sudbury's successor, William Courtenay, had no love for Wycliffe or his beliefs. At Oxford he instigated a witch-hunt that purged the University of Wycliffites.

Wycliffe was no fiery evangelist. At heart he was a scholar writing for other scholars, and it had been his hope to achieve reform from within the Church by academic persuasion rather than open dissent. Having lost his intellectual footing at Oxford, this was no longer possible. Paradoxically, it was with the middle and working classes that his new ideas were to find favour. While Wycliffe maintained a low public profile until his death in 1384, those of his followers with more evangelical zeal spread the word to eager ears. These followers, known as Lollards, often preached with more enthusiasm than knowledge however, and many who espoused the Lollard cause knew little or nothing of Wycliffe's writings. The popular appeal of the movement doubtless lay as much in its anti-authoritarian tone as in its actual principles. Whatever the reasons, Lollardy took firm root throughout the country and the establishment was to resort to desperate means to combat it. In 1401, the statute *De Heretico Comburendo* was passed, making it legal to burn heretics. That the State shared the anxiety and insecurity of the Church is shown by the obligation put upon local secular authorities to initiate the tracking down and

Three pulpits from the fifteenth century:

Left to right
The wooden pulpit from All Saints', Trull, Somerset, carved with the figures of the Doctors of the Church.

The hexagonal painted pulpit from St Margaret's, Burnham Norton, Norfolk.

The stone 'wine glass' pulpit from St John the Baptist's, Cirencester, Gloucestershire.

prosecution of heretics as well as merely to assist the clergy in their persecution. Understandably, Lollardy lost its last vestiges of political support. The politicians, in any case, had less need of anti-Rome propaganda since the Great Schism had already temporarily weakened the Papacy to such an extent that it posed no real threat to England's internal affairs. In fact, with the nations of Europe each deciding for themselves which of the two Popes to support, the boot was rather on the other foot. In 1414, the firm suppression of the Lollard Revolt by the ultra-orthodox Henry V served to drive Lollardy still further underground. In the long term this was perhaps no bad thing. The religious values of the movement were both purified and strengthened by persecution, and the foundations were laid for the non-conformity of later centuries.

The increasing importance of the sermon in church services led to the greater prominence of the *pulpit* after the middle of the fourteenth century. There is some evidence to suggest that portable wooden pulpits had been used earlier, but the pulpit now became an indispensable fixture, set in the nave near the rood screen and often attached to a pier of the arcade. Some 160 medieval pulpits still survive, most of them in East Anglia and the west country. The majority are made of wood and usually date from the fifteenth century. Whether of wood or stone, pulpits are generally octagonal in form and decorated with the ubiquitous cusped panelling of the Perpendicular period. The panels of wooden pulpits were often carved or painted with saints or other devotional figures. The church of All Saints at Trull in Somerset, a treasury of fifteenth-century woodwork, has a splendid pulpit carved in high relief with the figures of St John the Baptist and the four *Doctors of the Church* – St Gregory the Great, St Ambrose, St Jerome and St Augustine of Hippo. In East Anglia the panels are more often painted. The pulpit of St

During the fifteenth century figure sculpture reappeared in the design of fonts:

Left to right
The Seven Sacraments font from All Saints', Walsoken, Norfolk, a type found almost exclusively in East Anglia.

A detail from the Seven Sacrament font at St John the Baptist's, Badingham, Suffolk, showing the sacrament of Holy Matrimony.

From St Mary's, Happisburgh, Norfolk, a font with the symbols of the Evangelists around the bowl and lions and wild men around the stem.

Margaret's Church at Burnham Norton in Norfolk, complete with its original painting of around 1475, is a particularly fine example. It is also one of the few hexagonal pulpits. To modern eyes, more accustomed to the tub-like pulpits of Victorian times, medieval pulpits often seem rather tall and thin. They are usually supported on slender, tapering stems which can sometimes appear uncomfortably fragile! At the church of St John the Baptist, Cirencester in Gloucestershire, the stem of the stone pulpit spreads upwards into elegant panels of lace-like open tracery which form the actual pulpit. This very graceful type of pulpit is known as a *wine glass pulpit* for obvious reasons. Whether they were carved with figures or not, stone pulpits, like wooden ones, were lavishly enriched with gilding and painting and in design and craftsmanship they came to rival the other main fitting of the nave – the font.

Fonts too were now cast in the Perpendicular mould, and more survive from this period than any other since that of the Normans. With very few exceptions, the font bowl is octagonal and supported on a central stem. The stem is usually panelled, and sometimes carved figures are set in the panels or in niches. Occasionally the stem is formed by four angels with outspread wings. The sides of the octagonal bowl are often quite restrained in their decoration, perhaps a simple cusped panel or blind tracery in keeping with the general architectural style. The typical font of the period has a square quatrefoil on each face, or a circular quatrefoil set in a square panel. In the centre of the quatrefoil there is very often an heraldic device, a shield bearing the arms of a benefactor or some religious emblem, for example. Not all fonts were so conservative however. The fifteenth century also saw a revival of figure sculpture in font decoration. The figures are usually angels or saints, and their carving is calmer and more life-like than the restless, almost abstract work of the Normans

some four hundred years earlier. The most attractive of these fonts are to be found in East Anglia where comparative affluence enabled the parishes to afford the finest craftsmen. The accounts of the church of St Nicholas at East Dereham in Norfolk show that the parish raised over twelve pounds for a new font, a very considerable sum in 1468. The font that their money paid for is one of the *Seven Sacrament fonts* found almost exclusively in East Anglia. They are so called because each side of the bowl is carved with a scene depicting one of the Seven Sacraments of the Church – Baptism, Confirmation, Mass, Marriage, Ordination, Penance and Extreme Unction. The number of subjects was usually made up to eight by including a scene of the Crucifixion or the Baptism of Christ. East Anglian fonts are sometimes also carved with the symbols of the four *Evangelists* – a winged man for St Matthew, a winged lion for St Mark, a winged ox for St Luke and an eagle for St John. The symbols are alternated with angels bearing shields or musical instruments, and there are often four grotesque 'wild men' or seated lions around the base.

Another change which, like the pulpit, may be associated with the growing importance of the church nave as an auditorium, was the permanent provision of seating in the nave. In early days the congregation had been expected to stand or kneel throughout the services, but during the thirteenth century a few wooden benches began to appear, perhaps for the use of the infirm, and by the fifteenth century they had become normal and often highly decorative fixtures of church furnishing.

The earliest benches had plain, solid ends, but later these *bench ends* were often elaborately carved. Once again the richest examples are be found in East Anglia and the west country. In the south west, bench ends are usually flat-topped. They are carved in relief with a large variety of subjects ranging from emblems of the Passion to windmills and even a bag-pipe player. Elsewhere bench ends were

Above
A dog washing itself, carved on a bench end at St Agnes', Cawston, Norfolk.

Above right
The exceptionally richly carved bench ends at St Mary the Virgin, The Wiggenhalls, Norfolk.

usually topped with an elegant finial called a *poppyhead*, a name derived from the Latin *puppis*, meaning the figurehead of a ship. The poppyhead is commonly foliated, but often takes the form of a carved figure or animal. Holy Trinity Church at Blythburgh in Suffolk has a remarkable collection of poppyhead bench ends among which are spirited representations of the Seven Deadly Sins. Mermaids and other mythological creatures are also to be found on bench ends. The carving sometimes extends along the backs of the benches and more figures and animals often nestle on the armrests. As noted earlier, dogs were a familiar sight in medieval churches and it is said that many kept a bench reserved for shepherds and others who brought their dogs to church with them. At St Agnes, Cawston in Norfolk, one of the benches has a charming carving of a dog washing itself. Since it is also the back bench of the church, it is tempting to suppose that this was the bench reserved for local dog owners. The letting of the new seating became a profitable source of income for the church. In one year the churchwardens of St Edmund's Church in Salisbury collected 10s 6d from renting just thirteen seats. It is not clear whether parishioners were yet allocated their own particular seats, but the records do suggest that seats were sometimes 'priced' according to their position and that preference was given to women.

As far as church furnishings are concerned, the fifteenth century was without doubt a Golden Age, due in no small part to the expert skills of the carpenters and woodcarvers. The variety of their designs and the quality of their workmanship gave church interiors an almost sensual luxury. In every corner a wealth of inventive detail greeted the eye. Of all woodwork, it is perhaps the chancel or rood screen that demonstrates their craft at its best, and for the very best we must turn yet again to the churches of the west country and East Anglia. In these areas the main part of the screen is usually a series of traceried openings which are, in effect, unglazed Gothic windows built of

The rood screen at St John the Baptist's, Plymtree, Devon, with its wooden vaulting and rich bressummer is one of the most elegant examples of a west country screen.

wood. In early examples the tracery is quite simple, but by the fifteenth century it had become more elaborate. Elsewhere in the country the screen is most commonly made up of a series of open panels with tracery at the top. Both types of screen usually have a solid base of wainscoting whose panels correspond to the traceried openings above.

Standing between the nave and the chancel, the rood screen symbolised the division between Earth and Heaven, and was, therefore, the perfect place for images of the apostles and saints who, everyone believed, could intercede between Man and God. So each panel of the wainscoting was painted with the figure of a saint or sometimes an angel. Occasionally the figures were grouped together to represent a story from the Bible or an incident from the Life of the Virgin. The saints are identifiable by their emblems which were far more familiar to the medieval congregation than they are to us today. Behind each figure, the background was usually painted or gilded with a delicate *diaper* pattern, a design made up of a small motif repeated in squares or diamond-shapes. The rood screen in St Helen's Church at Ranworth in Norfolk has perhaps the best painting in the country. It was built during the last quarter of the fifteenth century and is extended on both sides of the chancel to form reredoses for side altars in the nave. Sometimes the painters used *gesso* to give subtle relief to the decoration, as at St Edmund's Church, Southwold, in Suffolk, where the background to St James, for example, has a relief diaper pattern of tiny shells, the saint's emblem. At St Michael's Church, Barton Turf in Norfolk, the screen has paintings of all *Nine Orders of Angels*. The Nine Orders of Angels were first postulated by the sixth-century mystical theologian, Dionysius, whose writings blended classical philosophy with Christianity. In his 'Celestial Hierarchies' he explains how nine kinds of celestial beings mediate God's will, and arranges them in three hierarchies, each containing three *choirs*: the *Seraphim*, *Cherubim* and *Thrones*; the *Dominations*, *Virtues* and *Powers*; and the *Principalities*, *Archangels* and *Angels*.

Lavish painting and gilding was not confined to the panels of the wainscoting; it often covered the entire rood screen. The vertical *muntins* between the open panels or 'windows' of the screens were decorated with spiralling bands of colour and pattern. At their tops, the muntins usually spread out into vaulting which concealed the struts that supported the floor joists of the rood loft above. The webbing between the ribs was most often painted a dark blue and sprinkled with tiny gilded stars or sometimes flowers. At St Andrew's Church in Bramfield, Suffolk, dainty angels hover between the ribs of the screen's vaulting. The vaulting and tracery of rood screens illustrate the way in which the carpenter and woodcarver drew inspiration for much of their work from stone construction. The sculptor too, borrowed from the mason for his designs; font panels, niches, reredoses and tombs are often canopied with scaled-down vaulting and adorned with diminutive buttresses and pinnacles. This repetition in miniature of structural forms for purely decorative purposes, is very typical of the Perpendicular style.

The vaulting of the rood screen stretched up to the *bressummer*, the main beam which ran across the top of the screen and supported

The accomplished design and painstaking detail of two trails carved as grape vines with birds from the bressummer of the rood screen at St Peter and St Paul's, Bovey Tracey, Devon.

the rood loft – a suitably poetic name for what is the most attractive part of many a west country screen. The bressummer acted as a cornice and was richly carved with three or more *trails*, gilded and picked out in bright colours. A trail is a convex moulding made from a long strip of relatively thin wood which was carved and cut out, rather like fretwork, to form an undulating, leafy stem. Vine-leaves with grapes and oak-leaves with acorns were most popular, and often small animals and birds peek through the dense foliage. The beam behind the trail was hollowed out so that the cut-out shapes of the leaves were set off boldly by a shadowy background.

Above was the rood loft, sometimes called the *solar* or *soller* in medieval records. Access was usually by way of a spiral staircase set in the walling to the north of the chancel arch. It was generally something under two metres (about six feet) deep, large enough to accommodate the statues of the Rood group which were sometimes life-size or larger, an organ and perhaps a few singers, a priest to read the Gospel, and sometimes even an altar. Parapets at front and back of the loft prevented unhappy accidents. The front parapet was sometimes panelled and painted, or pierced with traceried openings. The most impressive were enriched with *tabernacle work*, a series of canopied niches, containing carved figures of the saints or angels.

Today, few rood lofts survive. Most were taken down and burned, along with their images, by the iconoclasts of the sixteenth and seventeenth centuries who sought to rid religion of superstition, and

in the attempt succeeded in destroying much of the rich artistic heritage of the medieval Church. Others were simply abandoned to neglect and later swept away at the hands of well-intentioned nineteenth-century incumbents who wanted something smarter for their church. The west country, however, was comparatively lucky, and for an interesting reason. In Devon and Cornwall particularly, it had become quite common to build churches on the aisled-rectangle plan, discussed earlier, in which the nave aisles are extended to embrace the chancel. This type of church has no chancel arch since without the eastern walls of the nave aisles on either side it was not possible to provide the lateral support, or *abutment*, needed to stabilise a large arch. In the absence of a chancel arch, the rood screen with its loft was the only division between the nave and the chancel, and so, though its images were destroyed, the structure itself was often retained. The west country was, in any case, a rather conservative part of the country where unnecessary destruction was unlikely to be tolerated. Unfortunately, East Anglia did not escape so lightly. There the iconoclasts were particularly diligent, and not only the rood lofts, but usually the bressummers, and often the vaulting were torn down too. As a consequence, many East Anglian screens inevitably seem a little lightweight, and rely for much of their charm on their delicate tracery and exquisite painting. By comparison west country screens are generally shorter, and the prominence of richly-carved bressummer and loft parapet often overshadows the tracery beneath, and gives the design a strongly horizontal emphasis.

The medieval rood screen, beautifully carved, ablaze with gilding and glowing with colour, was the perfect expression of the collaboration between carpenter, woodcarver and painter. It was the crowning feature of every church nave in the country. Yet these days, perhaps fewer than one in ten churches can boast even a mutilated part of their

original rood screen. And all that is left of the rood loft in the vast majority of churches is a sorry reminder high up in the wall to the north of the chancel arch – the doorway which once led on to the rood loft, now, sadly, a doorway to nowhere.

Since the church roof was a practical necessity, and its decoration too inaccessible to be easily damaged by the iconoclasts, it usually escaped relatively unscathed and can often be the most attractive part of a church. Time has mellowed the oak beams of many roofs to a marvellous silver-grey colour which, in some ways, is more appealing to modern eyes than the more strident colours of the original painting. During the Perpendicular period clerestories were added to many churches, which meant that their nave roofs had to be removed and new ones built. Consequently, church roofs often date from this time. Unlike other woodwork, the design of the roof owes nothing at all to the techniques of stone construction; it demonstrates the carpenter's skill at its purest.

The lowering of the pitch of some roofs, associated with the introduction of lead as a covering material, encouraged a return to the tie-beam type of construction that had been widespread during the thirteenth century. But the tie beam was no longer the plain, stout timber of earlier building; instead it was carved with mouldings and decorated with brightly painted patterns and gilding. Additional support was given by arch braces springing from wall posts and curving up to meet the underside of the tie beam. The sides of a tie-beam roof were now frequently boarded in with panelling. In a low-pitched roof the triangular space between the tie beam and the sloping sides of the roof was quite small, and the carpenters might fill it in with delicate open tracery, as they did at St Mary's Church in Westonzoyland, and many others in Somerset and Devon. If the pitch of the roof was flattened still further, it was possible to give the

Above
An angel with a bell from the fifteenth-century roof of St John's, Stamford, Lincolnshire.

Right
St Bartoline's, Barthomley, Cheshire. As roofs became even flatter the tie beam was replaced by the camber beam and roofs came to look like flat coffered ceilings.

tie beam an upward curve, or *camber*, so that it met the sloping sides of the roof and acted, in effect, as a particularly strong principal rafter. The tie beam is then known as a *camber beam*. In some Perpendicular churches the pitch of the roofs became so low that they began to resemble high, coffered ceilings.

In the west country, the curved trussed-rafter roof, boarded in to form a wagon roof, still remained popular. Its many panels were lavishly painted or were decorated with blind tracery, as at the church of St Peter and St Paul, Shepton Mallet, Somerset. The intersections of the mouldings between the panels were covered with beautifully carved bosses. But the carpenters of the Perpendicular period were not content with merely refining and enriching established forms of roof construction; they also produced a striking innovation, the *hammer-beam roof*.

The hammer-beam roof first appeared in the fourteenth century and reached the peak of its popularity in the eastern counties. The practical virtue of the new form of construction was that it enabled the roof to cover a wider span by eliminating the heavy tie beams, which were always prone to sag, and, when they did so, loosened the joints between the rest of the timbers. The tie beam was replaced by a pair of *hammer beams* – hammer-like brackets which rest on top of the wall and project several feet into the nave with the help of supporting wall posts and arch braces. On the hammer beams stand the struts or

The most spectacular development in roof construction during the fifteenth century was the hammer-beam roof – the pride of the East Anglian carpenters. Here at St Wendreda's, March, Cambridgeshire, a host of angels flutters among the timbers of its double hammer-beam roof.

arch braces which in turn support the principal rafters of the roof.

The carpenters continued to design hybrid roofs which combined different types of structure, as thay had in earlier times. At the church of All Saints in Leighton Buzzard, Bedfordshire, tie beams and hammer beams are used alternately. But, in East Anglia especially, the carpenters delighted in their new hammer beams, and, as if to show how pleased they were with themselves, went one step further and developed the *double hammer-beam roof*, with two tiers of hammer beams. Since the upper set of hammer beams cannot rest on the walls, they serve no structural purpose and are there for purely aesthetic reasons – and perhaps, bravado.

Structural considerations aside, the beauty of the moderately-pitched, hammer-beam roof lies in the sense of space it created and the opportunity it afforded for ornamentation, an opportunity the woodcarvers seldom missed. The hammer beams themselves frequently end in carved angels, with oaken wings spread wide; the spandrels between hammer beams, struts and rafters are often filled with intricate tracery; timbers everywhere are moulded and crested; carved bosses look down from the heights; and yet more angels are to be found hovering on wall-posts and cornices, or fluttering along the ridge and collar beams. When the medieval worshippers looked up they must have felt reassured to see a host of angels standing guard over them.

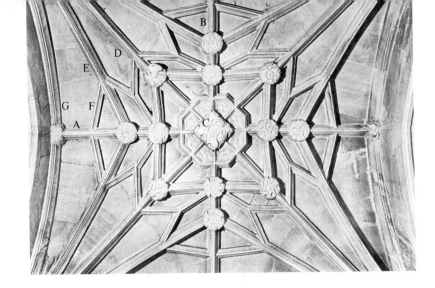

Lierne vaulting from the south aisle of St Mary the Virgin, Steeple Ashton, Wiltshire.

A *Transverse ridge rib*
B *Longitudinal ridge rib*
C *Central boss*
D *Diagonal rib*
E *Tierceron rib*
F *Lierne rib*
G *Longitudinal rib*

Very few indeed were the parishes that could afford that extravagant expression of prosperity, a church roofed with a stone vault. Though common enough in the greater churches, stone vaulting of any extent is rare in parish churches. There are exceptions of course, and the most remarkable is the church of St Mary Redcliffe in Bristol which is vaulted in every part, something quite extraordinary. But St Mary Redcliffe is a church superlative in every way. Its abbey-like proportions and its grand plan, with aisled transepts, hexagonal north porch and an *ambulatory* around the high altar leading to a Lady Chapel beyond, would seem to suggest that this was once the church of some thriving ecclesiastical establishment. In fact, the church has always been parochial and owes its magnificence not to some defunct monastery but to the incredible wealth of the Bristol merchants.

The simplest form of ribbed vault, the *quadripartite vault*, had been used by the masons since Norman times. It was so called because two intersecting diagonal ribs divided the compartment to be vaulted into four equal spaces which were then filled with a skin of masonry called *webbing*. When the masons began using the pointed arch in vaulting, the point of the arch produced a horizontal ridge in the webbing which suggested the introduction of a third rib, the *longitudinal ridge rib*, which ran along the length of the vault and divided it into six unequal parts, creating a *sexpartite vault*. An equivalent rib running across the vault was soon added, the *transverse ridge rib*. The panels to be filled with webbing were then further subdivided by another kind of rib, the *tierceron rib*. Tierceron ribs spring from the same points as the diagonal ribs, the main springers, but instead of meeting in the centre of the vault, they end on one or other of the ridge ribs. Then, in the fourteenth century, the masons began to introduce ribs which had no real structural purpose at all; instead of springing from one of the four main springers or the central boss, these *liernes*, as they are called, were used as decorative links between the main ribs and the tiercerons. Liernes enabled the masons to build vaults in which the ribs formed stunning geometric patterns studded with jewel-like coloured bosses. When the ribs make a star-like pattern the vault is sometimes called a *stellar vault*. The variations were endless. At St Mary Redcliffe alone there are nine different designs of lierne vault.

Vaulting reached its zenith with fan vaulting, like this from St Andrew's, Cullompton, Devon, invented by the masons towards the end of the Perpendicular period.

Even in the affluent fifteenth century a fully vaulted church like St Mary Redcliffe was quite beyond the means of the vast majority of parishes. At Steeple Ashton in Wiltshire, work began on the present church of St Mary the Virgin in 1480. Both nave aisles, chapels and south porch were given charming stone vaults and it was obviously intended to vault the nave as well. Unfortunately, it appears that the parishioners' funds did not match their aspirations and the nave was completed with a timber roof instead. Later, in the seventeenth century, it was replaced by an effective mock vault of wood and plaster that can still be seen today. To vault just an aisle was a more realistic objective for even a rich parish. The Lane aisle, mentioned earlier, at St Andrew's Church, Cullompton, and the Dorset aisle at St Mary's, Ottery St Mary, both in Devon, provide splendid examples of vaulted aisles. Both have *fan vaulting* – for richness of effect, the tour de force of vaulting. Fan vaulting is intimately associated with the late Perpendicular period, and, like the style itself, is an exclusively English development. From the main springing points of the vault, ribs of identical curvature and uniformly spaced spread out like fans over trumpet-shaped semi-cones of masonry. Between the ribs, the masonry is carved with the familiar Perpendicular cusped panels which also radiate like fans. Structural and decorative ribs often become indistinguishable. Sometimes the central boss in each compartment is extended downwards to form a *pendant*. The lacy intricacies of fan vaulting give a wonderful impression of lightness and conceal all overt expression of construction, a sleight of hand which almost persuades the eye that it sees a structural impossibility. For most churches, however, even a vaulted aisle was a dream, and where vaulting is found in a parish church it is most likely to be in the limited, and generally square, spaces of the porch and tower.

The church-browser has little difficulty in finding a Perpendicular tower. Between the Black Death and the middle of the sixteenth century, well over two thousand churches had new towers built or existing ones heightened, and a thousand or so new churches were raised complete with towers. In some areas, spires were still occasionally built, but their heyday was over and the fifteenth century was undoubtedly the age of the tower. For quality and variety, towers of the Perpendicular period are unmatched. The tower became easily the most imposing part of the church exterior. In some places, like Leigh-on-Mendip in Somerset, a tower added in the fifteenth century was of such extravagant scale that it dwarfed the rest of the church building. The contemporary passion for traceried windows found its expression in towers as it did elsewhere. The west elevation of the tower of St Mary Magdalene's Church at Taunton in Somerset (a nineteenth-century rebuilding of the original) has a large traceried window in its lowest stage and a pair of windows in each of the three stages above. Each stage is divided by a band of blind quatrefoil panelling and the walls of the belfry stage have the cusped panelling which we have come to expect of a Perpendicular building. At St Botolph's Church, Boston in Lincolnshire, panelling overlays the whole tower including its buttresses.

During these last years of the Gothic style, instead of using the diagonal corner buttress, the masons often reverted to the earlier arrangement of two buttresses set at right angles to each other. As a variation, however, they were usually set back slightly from the corner so that the angle of the tower projected between them (see page 105). A completely new form of corner buttress also made its first appearance, the *octagonal buttress* topped by a small turret. At St Sampson's Church, Cricklade in Wiltshire, the unusually massive octagonal corner buttresses seem about to engulf the tower.

A typical Perpendicular tower is topped by a battlemented parapet with pinnacles at the corners. The number of pinnacles was often increased by setting more than one at each corner, or adding intermediate pinnacles along the sides and on the set-offs of the buttresses. It was not unusual to make the top stage of a tower octagonal in plan. This rather pleasing device can be seen in upwards of fifty churches, the most spectacular example being the tower of St Botolph's at

Boston, the famous 'Boston stump' which is the tallest tower in
England. St Mary and All Saints at Fotheringhay in Northamptonshire provides another example, designed in the 1430s by the master
mason William Horwood. There are usually pinnacles on all eight
corners of the octagonal stage as well as those on the corners of the
square base, which are sometimes connected to the diagonal faces of
the octagon by slender flying buttresses.

The towers of Somerset are generally agreed to be the finest built
during this period. The area was doubly fortunate in having both a
plentiful supply of high-quality freestone and a school of particularly
talented masons based at the Abbey of Glastonbury. Abbeys still set
the fashion for parochial building to some extent and, when they
could afford it, helped out with funds as well. The influence of
Glastonbury Abbey, which unlike many others was still thriving in

St John's, Glastonbury, Somerset, has a fine example of a Somerset tower topped by a filigree crown of pinnacles.

the fifteenth century, was felt throughout Somerset. St Mary Magdalene in Taunton, for instance, had sculptured angels on its tower bearing shields with the initials of Richard Bere who became Abbot of Glastonbury in 1493, presumably to commemorate his patronage. A distinguishing feature of Somerset towers, although not exclusive to the area, is the use of canopied niches which once held statues, on both sides of windows. But their crowning glory, quite literally, is usually the pinnacled parapet. Here the normally solid battlemented parapet is pierced with traceried geometrical openings or cusped panelling, giving the impression of a lace fringe. There is usually a profusion of pinnacles, which may also be pierced like the spiky skeleton of some sea creature. The pinnacles sometimes stand away from the parapet as if supported by thin air, but in fact resting on artfully placed corbels. The whole effect is of a filigree crown set about the head of the tower.

But it would be wrong to give the impression that all Perpendicular towers were so resplendent. Such towers were the exception rather than the rule, and many are severe in design and sparing in their use of ornament. In East Anglia particularly, tower pinnacles often have a

Above
The richly carved door of St Mary's, Stoke-by-Nayland, Suffolk. By the Perpendicular period iron strap-work on church doors had been abandoned.

Above right
St John the Baptist's, Cirencester, Gloucestershire, is almost over-shadowed by the imposing three-storey south porch from which the Abbots of Cirencester conducted their secular business affairs.

stunted and mean appearance or are omitted altogether. It seems that statues sometimes replaced pinnacles at the corners of towers in this area. Some towers are without even battlements and end abruptly in a straight line. The tower of the church of St Agnes at Cawston has no parapet at all and presents a bleak, uncompromising silhouette against the equally bleak Norfolk sky. Somewhere between these two extremes lie the majority of Perpendicular towers.

If there was money to spare after building a new tower, the second priority was a new porch. By the fifteenth century the south porch was often a small-scale architectural masterpiece. An upper chamber was now commonplace and the lower storey was frequently roofed with a smart stone vault. The church door was no longer reinforced with iron strap-work, but decorated with cusped panelling or wooden tracery after the fashion of Perpendicular windows. The church of St Mary at Stoke-by-Nayland in Suffolk has a double door richly carved with panels of tracery and canopied niches with their carved figures intact. The most spectacular porch in the country is at Cirencester in Gloucestershire. Here the church of St John the Baptist is virtually hidden by a three-storey porch built by the abbot of Cirencester

The fan vaulting of the south porch at St John the Baptist's, Cirencester, Gloucestershire.

Abbey, which lay immediately to the north of the parish church. The ground level has a beautiful fan-vaulted roof, and the two upper stages each have a range of three oriel windows and much decorative carving. This impressive annex to the church acted as a kind of medieval office block from which the abbot conducted his business affairs with agents of the Crown, foreign merchants, and the tradesmen of the town. The size of the porch gives us a good idea of the power the Abbey wielded. In fact, the abbot seems to have exerted almost despotic control over local trade; he even took a cut from the proceeds of the weekly town market.

The Abbey of Cirencester was not alone in its involvement in secular business affairs. With the decline in endowments of ecclesiastical houses and the falling value of tithes from the countryside, all monasteries had to work that much harder to make ends meet. They became more and more persistent in exacting their rents and dues, and inevitably stirred up ill feeling. As incomes from agriculture dwindled, many monasteries turned their eyes to the towns and channelled their resources into industry. Commercial venture was on a small scale at first and remained so in many places, traditional monastic activities, like manuscript copying and illuminating, being developed into fairly lucrative businesses. Some monasteries, however, were more aggressively enterprising. A large corner of the wool trade had long been controlled by the religious houses, and now they

From Beverley Minster, Humberside, a misericord showing a cowled fox preaching to a congregation of geese.

began to move into other industries. Tavistock Abbey, for example, had a profitable stake in the prospering Devon tin mines and, at Durham, the monks had a financial interest in coal mining. Property was, as ever, the best investment and many abbeys turned to speculation, building and renting cottages on land bought up in the rapidly growing towns. The abbots often became adept, and sometimes over-zealous, businessmen. While monks in some monasteries struggled on the bread-line, others lived like princes. All this did nothing to bolster the deteriorating reputation of the clergy. The anti-clerical feeling which had grown up among the laity was directed not against the humble parish clergy who had little opportunity for corruption, but against these high-living magnates of the Church. Fanned by winds of heresy, discontent flared into outright resentment.

That resentment found expression not only in the events of history that were to follow, but in the churches as well. While stained glass windows and painted walls proclaimed the official iconography of the Church, imagery of another kind was to be found in the nooks and crannies of the church where the craftsman could make his own, less inhibited comment on life – humorous, superstitious, sometimes satirical. The misericords of the choir stalls provided one such place. Their designs depict scenes drawn from everyday life, classical and eastern mythology, medieval romantic legends and the animals of the *Physiologus*, a Book of Beasts. Daily life is shown in a comic light, sometimes with seaside-postcard vulgarity. One misericord at the church of St Mary the Virgin at Fairford in Gloucestershire, shows a wife beating her drunken husband, while another presents an obscene picture of a man supporting himself on two large dogs as he crouches to answer a call of nature – quite a find in a church!

The *Physiologus*, a fifth-century catalogue of real and fabulous beasts, furnished the woodcarver with a rich and imaginative source of inspiration. It had been based on a natural history by the classical Roman author, Pliny. Each of his descriptions was amplified by Biblical texts concerning the animal in question and concluded with an exemplary moral. Mermaids and griffins are treated as seriously as lions and elephants, whose description must have seemed just as fantastic to the average Englishman. The *Physiologus*, sometimes known simply as the 'Bestiary', was translated into many languages and ranked with the Lives of the Saints in popularity. Everyone was familiar with its real and imaginary beasts and their appropriate morals. So the significance of portraying an ecclesiastic as a fox was lost on no-one. 'The fox,' says the *Physiologus*, 'is a very crafty and cunning animal. . . .' And that is how the clergy was sometimes satirised in these last days of the medieval Church. At Beverley Minster, Humberside, a fox wearing a habit is shown preaching to a congregation of geese, and his clerk, a monkey, has one unfortunate member of the congregation slung from a stick over his shoulder, ready for supper. At St Botolph's Church in Boston, an abbot or bishop is portrayed as a fox holding a crozier and reading, from a book held up by an ass, to a congregation of five hens and a cock. Is it the preacher or the popular sermon that is being satirised? Either way these carvings reflect the resentment of ecclesiastical authoity that was building up both within the Church and without.

Henry VIII who was to become the first Supreme Head of the Church of England.

Successive English kings had sought slowly but steadily to curb the political and economic influence of Rome by gradually gaining the upper hand in the partnership of Church and State. If the medieval Church had been prepared to make a few concessions to social change, then the reform which was inevitable could have been achieved without conflict. Unfortunately the Church in England was powerless to effect its own reform. What had once been the great strength of the Church now proved its downfall. It was not master of its own destiny but a dependent part of a cosmopolitan hierarchy centred on Rome which was intent on preserving its unity and traditions, and deaf to the particular needs and circumstances of the Church in England.

England was drawing away, socially and politically, from the rest of Europe and defining an increasingly independent national identity. This patriotism was personified by the Tudor monarchs who embodied the power now centralised in Crown and Parliament. And it was a threat to the perpetuation of the Tudor dynasty that was to bring resentment of papal authority to a head and precipitate the country into Reformation.

Henry VIII had been married to Katherine of Aragon for eighteen years, but they had only one surviving child, a daughter, Mary. Henry was already thirty-six and desperately wanted a male heir; Katherine, now in her forties, was nearing the end of her child-bearing years and every day it seemed less likely that she would provide one. The need for a son was no trivial matter of masculine pride. A legitimate male heir was vital for political stability. Katherine had first been married to Henry's elder brother, Arthur, who had died as a youth. Henry began to see her failure to produce a son as a divine judgement on him for marrying his brother's wife, or at least to look upon her previous marriage as a convenient escape clause. Henry's Chancellor, Cardinal Thomas Wolsey, Archbishop of York, was instructed to obtain the Pope's confirmation of the Church's rule forbidding a man to marry his sister-in-law and a declaration of the invalidity of the marriage. Unfortunately, Katherine's nephew was the King of Spain, and the Pope, Clement VII, was in his power. Despite three years of coercion, Henry's request was refused. Incensed by the Pope's refusal to invalidate the marriage and by the interference in English affairs it implied, Henry opted for a complete break with Rome. There was overt opposition in Yorkshire, where a rebellion known as the 'Pilgrimage of Grace' was hastily suppressed, but otherwise little opposition was voiced and the volume of public opinion appears to have been behind the King. In 1534 Parliament passed the Act of Supremacy, declaring that the Pope had no greater jurisdiction over English affairs than any other foreign bishop and affirming Henry as the 'Supreme Head of the Church of England'.

In the years that followed, the religious houses of England were systematically disbanded. This Dissolution of the monasteries served two purposes: it stifled all remaining ideological resistance to Henry's supremacy and it destroyed the economic basis of the Church. The monasteries owned around a quarter of the country, and the King, as Head of the Church of England, considered himself entitled to lay personal claim to this enormous wealth. The lands of the monasteries

Above
Katherine of Aragon, the first wife of Henry VIII, whose failure to produce a male heir provoked the power struggle which eventually split the Church of England from Rome.

Above right
St Mary's Abbey, Whitby, North Yorkshire, one of the many monasteries left to fall into ruin after the Dissolution, its gaunt shell bearing silent testimony to the conflict of Church and State.

were confiscated and their riches plundered. Land and treasure which did not find their way into Henry's hands were snapped up by the local gentry. Furnishings and fittings were auctioned off. Lead, ripped from roofs and torn from smashed stained glass, was melted down on bonfires fuelled by magnificent wooden stalls and screens. In the ransacked shells of the once-proud abbeys, public resentment and royal determination found their satisfaction.

In the parishes, the priests must have looked anxiously over their shoulders at the despoiled monasteries and wondered who would be next. But, for a while at least, the parish churches were safe. The break with Rome had been to achieve political and economic ends; it was not envisaged as a religious revolution. In fact, Henry himself was quite orthodox, and made it clear that he had no intention of questioning the doctrine of the Faith or altering dramatically the character of public worship. The only innovation in this respect was that services were now to be conducted in English, a change meant to underline the independence of the new national Church, but one which also gave the congregation a long overdue accessibility to the Christian ritual. Every church was to provide two Bibles, one in Latin and one in English, for the use of any man who cared to read them. An English version of the Bible was at last officially sanctioned.

This was the 'Great Bible' of 1539, produced under the patronage of the King's chief adviser, Thomas Cromwell, the successor to Thomas Wolsey whose failure to secure the annulment of Henry's first marriage had cost him his job and very nearly his life too. Some fifteen years earlier, the great pioneer of the English Bible had been William Tyndale. Tyndale had long been aware of the ideological need for a Bible in the common tongue and worked abroad, secretly

financed from London by a group of merchants, to produce a masterly translation of the New Testament which was first printed in Cologne in 1525. Many copies found their way back illicitly to England where they were avidly received by Lollards and other dissenters. Tyndale began work on the Old Testament but before he could complete it he was imprisoned for obstinate heresy and eventually executed. Meanwhile, one of his followers, Miles Coverdale, an Augustinian friar who had been exiled abroad for his reformist preaching, completed the first translation of the whole Bible, drawing heavily on Tyndale's work, and published in Zurich in 1535. In England the climate was beginning to change, and Thomas Cromwell's enthusiasm for a new English Bible paved the way for Coverdale's return. By 1538, Coverdale was hard at work revising his earlier translation and incorporating new material from other trans-

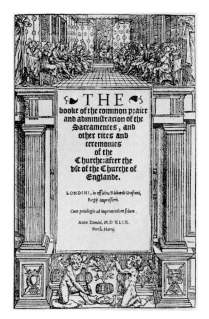

The first Book of Common Prayer, published in 1549, which formed the liturgical basis of the new Church of England.

lators, and the following year the first official English Bible was born. It is impossible to overstate the impact of the English Bible. In many ways it was the most important single event of the Reformation years. Spiritually, it hammered the last nail into the coffin of the medieval Church; culturally, it set the standard of the English language for many years to come, and created a habit of reading and contemplation among ordinary folk which raised the levels of literacy and stimulated the intellectual curiosity of a whole new section of the community.

In 1547 Henry died, and the decade that followed saw the pendulum swing savagely and destructively between the extremes of Protestantism and Catholicism. When Edward VI succeeded to the throne he was nine years old and in ill health. The young king was completely in the hands of advisers led by his Protector, the Duke of Somerset, who was a Protestant. Without the protection afforded by Henry VIII's orthodoxy, the way lay open for more extensive reform and even the parish churches lost their immunity. Measures repressing heresy were repealed, priests were given permission to marry, and the exclusive use of a new 'Book of Common Prayer', more Protestant in tone than the traditional liturgy, was made law by the Act of Uniformity. Though Henry had relieved the monasteries of their wealth, there were still rich pickings to be had in the parish churches where the chantry and guild chapels were often generously endowed and expensively furnished. The government had more than its share of financial troubles. Protector Somerset turned his avaricious eyes towards the parish churches, and the chantry and guild chapels went the way of the monasteries. The dissolution of the chantries had to some extent been pre-empted by the benefactors themselves, many of whom had already prudently reclaimed their endowments. Whether it was the Crown or private hands that gained from the destruction of the chantries, it was the parish churches, stripped of their most splendid chapels, that were the losers. Then in 1548 the despoiling of the churches was taken a step further when the King's Council directed that all things 'corrupt, vain, and superstitious', meaning paintings and statues, including the great Rood, should be taken down and destroyed. Shrines were smashed, wall paintings obliterated with whitewash, and everything of value – gold and silver plate, rings and jewels – whatever its religious significance, was taken. Even the brass of the tombs was ripped out and sold; at St Thomas' Church in Salisbury, the brass fetched thirty-six shillings. Some churches were left with only a chalice and a bell.

By the time Edward died, at the age of fifteen, Protestantism had become identified with greed and corruption, and the accession of Mary, the Catholic daughter of Katherine of Aragon, was greeted with popular enthusiasm. In the parishes, the churches began once more to accumulate the rich trappings of their rituals, but in a few short years they could never replace the splendour that had been built up over generations. The population in general seemed happy to return to the religious position as it had been at the end of Henry's reign, a Catholic Church of England, independent of Rome. Unfortunately this was not good enough for Mary who insisted that England be brought back within the Roman Church, turning the clock back to before the Reformation. To strengthen the English

Counter-Reformation she married Philip II, King of staunchly Catholic Spain. Suddenly England found its hard-won independence lost in subjection both to Rome and to Spain. Popular enthusiasm evaporated. Protestant protest grew, and was suppressed by a vicious revival of the statute *De Heretico Comburendo*, under which some three hundred 'heretics' were consigned to the flames in the space of four years. After a short and violent reign, Mary died childless and despised. The people danced in the streets.

Elizabeth I inherited a kingdom that was demoralised, religiously divided, and near bankrupt. England was perilously beset; France, the country's traditional adversary, was in league with Scotland, and Spain too was soon to become an enemy. Elizabeth was acutely aware that the only hope lay in unity. Fortunately she held no strong sectarian views, and the common-sense religious compromise she imposed was acceptable to all but die-hard Catholics and the most fervent Protestants, now becoming known as Puritans. Ties with Rome were severed again by reassertion of the Act of Supremacy, and the Book of Common Prayer was re-introduced in a somewhat modified form. To keep dissent firmly underground, weekly attendance at church was enforced by law. The wooden *communion table*, which had replaced the stone altar during the purges of Edward VI's time, was brought out of the chancel into the nave or choir of the church so that the congregation could sit or stand around it for morning and evening prayer. Rhyming, metrical versions of the psalms were sung in relatively simple four-part harmony, accompanied perhaps by two or three village musicians on wind and string instruments, now that the organs were gone. When Communion was over, the communion table was re-set against the east wall of the chancel. The laity had finally won an active role both in public worship and the Church itself. Above the rood screen, in the place the medieval Church had reserved for the image of Christ on the Cross, the Royal Coat of Arms was prominently displayed – a firm reminder that the Queen was the earthly Head of the Church. Never again was the Church to have the power in economic and political affairs that it had enjoyed in medieval times.

In these troubled years, church building had been a somewhat foolhardy enterprise. What little was built conformed to the late Perpendicular style, the national style of England. In Italy, the Renaissance was already a century old, but here its influence on architecture was hardly felt. The Perpendicular period of Gothic had lasted as long as the Early English and Decorated put together. The style had ossified, as if to resist the waves of social change that swept around it. But change could not be prevented. As in the Church so in architecture the time had come for something new.

7: The Light of Reason

The churchyard of St Mary the Virgin, Painswick, Gloucestershire. It was in tombs and monuments that the classical influence of the Renaissance was first seen in England.

The religious upheavals of the sixteenth and seventeenth centuries were symptoms of a wider struggle – the struggle of reason to tear itself from the constrictions of medieval superstition. The world was opening up and men's minds had to follow. As the ocean voyages of Elizabethan explorers and merchants expanded the economic and political life of the country, so the study of the Bible and a developing taste for the classical authors expanded its intellectual and cultural life. Elizabeth's successor was James VI of Scotland and I of England. During his reign, the courtier and philosopher, Francis Bacon, was to publish two books of great importance, 'On the Advancement of Learning' (1605) and *Novum Organum* (1620). In his writings Bacon distinguished between philosophical and scientific thought and argued that general laws of nature can be deduced from observation of particular instances. In 1616, the King's physician, William Harvey, proved his theory of the circulation of blood by practical experiment. Meanwhile in Italy, Galileo was making fundamental discoveries which were to pave the way for Newton's laws of motion, and teaching Copernicus' theory that the Earth was not the centre of the universe, but revolved around the sun. His teaching contradicted that of the Church, and the religious authorities eventually imprisoned him for his 'heretical' views.

A world was being revealed which simply would not fit into the medieval picture of the universe. While the Church had been the ultimate authority and guardian of truth, the picture had held together. But now it was being suggested that truth might be derived from observation of the tangible world of here and now rather than contemplation of the world to come, by measurement and experiment rather than by philosophical debate or blind acceptance of what the Church dictated. The comparatively rapid expansion of knowledge provoked a kind of crisis of identity in which man found himself at odds with his world. Medieval cosmology was splitting at the seams, but as yet there was no new order on which to pin belief, no rules with which to build a new model. This sense of dismay found voice in

Previous page
Country life in the eighteenth century was ruled by squire and parson – from the 'Discovering English Churches', television series

The growing taste for the classical was encouraged by men like Thomas Howard, Duke of Arundel, one of the great patrons of the arts, shown here in front of his collection of classical sculpture, one of the first in the country.

the works of the poet John Donne. In his poem 'An Anatomy of the World' he laments that the world is 'all in pieces, all coherence gone', and goes on to say:

> 'For of meridians, and parallels,
> Man hath weav'd out a net, and this net thrown
> Upon the heavens, and now they are his own.
> Loth to go up the hill, or labour thus
> To go to Heaven, we make Heaven come to us.'

The collapse of the medieval world-picture created a climate of intellectual doubt which had two key effects. It finally separated scientific thought from the strait-jacket of religious dogma, and it reinforced the already fashionable interest in ancient Rome. Greece was still in the hands of the Turks and so remained virtually unknown to Englishmen until the eighteenth century. The classical world came to be seen as a Golden Age of order and stability, symbolised by its idealised sculpture and noble architecture. Illustrated books of ancient buildings became obligatory items in the library of any learned gentleman. The most important of these was *De Architectura* by the Roman author, Vitruvius. This treatise, written at the beginning of the first century, is the only classical work on architecture to have survived through the Middle Ages. It was copied and re-copied in manuscript form, and then in the sixteenth century illustrated translations were printed in Italy. In a spirit of rediscovery, architects and designers turned to this Golden Age for the rules and harmonies they sought to re-establish in their own world. Classical ruins were accurately measured and precisely drawn up, details meticulously recorded, and proportions studied religiously as if to reveal some hidden truth. A fashionable taste for the classic grew into a dominating influence that was to hold both religious and secular architecture in its grip until the nineteenth century.

There was, however, little opportunity for classicism to express itself in church architecture until the second half of the seventeenth century. For the time being, the religious and political situation was far from settled, and new churches were to be very few and far between. Although the Elizabethan religious compromise had given a semblance of unity, beneath its surface discontent thrived. Catholics met with severe discrimination and were not allowed to hold office in local or national government. At the other extreme, Puritans were treated with little more tolerance since Elizabeth had no time for what she called 'newfangledness' in religion. The publication of the Authorised Version of the Bible during the reign of James I, represents the last moments of concord between the two religious groups. Puritans, and some Catholics too, began to set sail for the New World, where they hoped to live their lives according to their consciences beyond the shadow of persecution.

During the religious turmoils of the sixteenth century it had been the cleric and the artisan who were sent to prison or the stake; the landed gentry, who had benefited richly from the acquisition of Church lands at the dissolution of the monasteries, had managed discreetly to avoid trouble. This new aristocracy replaced the Church

The south front of Hatfield House, Hertfordshire, where the two Tudor wings are bridged by a loggia with the kind of debased classical forms that were already used in domestic architecture by the turn of the seventeenth century.

as the main patron of builders and craftsmen. So it is in the designs of the tombs and monuments they commissioned and in the grand houses they raised on their country estates that classical influence was first felt. The builders had little accurate knowledge of classical buildings, and debased classical forms, copied second- and third-hand from German and Flemish pattern books, were applied to structures that were basically medieval to give them the fashionable 'Italianate' look. At Hatfield House in Hertfordshire, for instance, built in 1611 for the Earl of Salisbury, a would-be classical *loggia* bridges two wings which are quite Tudor, and therefore essentially medieval, in style. This loggia is often attributed to the architect Inigo Jones who was to build England's first house, first place of worship, and first parish church in completely classical style.

Inigo Jones was the first man in this country of whom the word 'architect' may be used in its modern sense. The architect was a new breed of professional who replaced the medieval master mason. Though the master mason was still a highly skilled craftsman, he now began to work to the architect's designs rather than his own. His role, by the eighteenth century became more that of a contractor, ensuring that the architect's plans were accurately interpreted and soundly constructed. As yet there was no proper system of training for the new architects; they had no alternative but to be self-taught.

Inigo Jones had first visited Italy at the turn of the seventeenth century, chiefly to study Renaissance painting. On his return he

Top
Inigo Jones, the designer and architect who was the father of true classicism in England, drawn by Anthony van Dyck.

Above
A stage design by Inigo Jones for one of the court masques, 'Oberon, or the Fairy Prince'. Such architectural fantasies enabled Jones to experiment freely with classical forms.

found favour at the court of James I and Anne of Denmark as the designer of classical architectural settings and costumes for their royal masques. The masques combined drama, song and dance into extravagant spectaculars with elaborate mechanical stage sets and lavish costumes. They had their origin in Elizabethan times as fêtes staged in honour of the Queen as Gloriana, and during the reign of James I they became the most popular form of court entertainment. Courtiers, the royal family and the King and Queen themselves dressed up and took part in the performance. It was, however, inconceivable that the ladies and gentlemen of the court should be considered as common actors, so speaking parts and set dance pieces were performed by professional players. The masques always carried an allegorical meaning. Generally the players began by portraying a world corrupt and in disarray which was then set to rights by the dramatic entrance of the King or Queen dressed elaborately as some mythical god or virtue. Order having been restored by royal intervention, the masque proper began and the idealised classical world merged with the real world of the court. No expense was spared on these entertainments, and they provided Inigo Jones with almost unlimited opportunities to try out his classical designs.

It was probably as a result of his court connections that Jones was fortunate enough to be chosen to escort Thomas Howard, Duke of Arundel, to Italy in 1613. At the age of twenty-seven, the Duke was already on his way to becoming one of England's greatest collectors and patrons of the arts. On his second trip to Italy, Jones focused his studies more closely on classical and Renaissance architecture. He would already have been familiar with the architectural treatise of Vitruvius and those of sixteenth-century Italian architects like Sebastiano Serlio and Andrea Palladio. As his guide he selected the *Quattro Libri dell' Architettura* by Palladio, who had been Italy's foremost exponent of the classical style. Jones visited the buildings Palladio had illustrated and added his own observations and annotations to the book. In Venice, he met Vincenzo Scamozzi who had been a pupil of Palladio and had now stepped into his master's shoes as Italy's leading architect. The architectural theory and practice of Palladio and Scamozzi were to be the major influences on Inigo Jones' own brand of classicism.

On his return, Jones' advancement at court continued and he was appointed Surveyor to the King's Works, a position which confirmed his status as an architect. During Elizabeth's time there had been little royal building, but her successor was more extravagant and in one three-year period towards the beginning of his reign James had already spent more than £73,000. It was rather a fortuitous moment to become the royal architect. In 1616, Jones began work on the first truly classical building in England, the Queen's House at Greenwich, a villa in the style of Palladio.

James' son, Charles, was to be married to the Spanish Infanta, who was, of course, a Catholic. So in 1623 Inigo Jones was commissioned to build a chapel by St James' Palace for the Infanta's use. Unfortunately, it appears that the romance did not blossom as anticipated, and Charles returned from Spain without his bride. Shortly after his accession as Charles I, however, he married another Catholic, Henrietta

The Queen's Chapel by St James' Palace, the first place of worship to be built in correct classical style, was designed by Inigo Jones for the private use of Henrietta Maria, the Catholic wife of Charles I.

Maria, and in 1627 the chapel by St James' Palace was completed for the new Queen. The Queen's Chapel was the first place of worship in the country to be built in the classical style. And a very impressive building it is too. Its basic shape is a double cube over which stretches an elliptically curved and richly coffered ceiling. The elegant interior is lit at the east end by a triple window of the kind known as a *Venetian window* during the eighteenth century. Despite its name, the Venetian window has no particular connection with Venice. Its design – a central, round-headed light flanked by two shorter, square-headed lights – was derived by Jones from Scamozzi and is, therefore, in the Palladian tradition. Four years after the completion of the Queen's Chapel, Jones was to start work on the first English parish church in the classical style; St Paul's, Covent Garden.

Covent Garden belonged to the fourth Earl of Bedford, and in 1631 he obtained permission to build 'houses and buildings fit for the habitation of Gentlemen and men of ability'. The notion of a systematically planned property development was quite new to the City of London. The focus of the plan was to be the church and square, a combination undoubtedly inspired by the *piazzas* of Italy. The church itself posed a problem. Although a few tumble-down churches had been rebuilt since the Reformation, more or less along traditional lines, no church had been built on an entirely new site. There was, therefore, absolutely no precedent for what a brand new Anglican church should look like. With no guidelines to follow, Inigo Jones

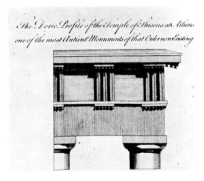

The hypothetical evolution of the Doric order from the primitive wooden hut shown in a treatise of 1759 by Sir William Chambers.

was provided on one hand with tremendous freedom, and on the other with a weighty responsibility to find a form and style that were appropriate and architecturally correct. One limitation was already known. The Earl was what we today would call a 'low church' man. He held views which veered towards the Independent and which kept him at arm's length from the court. The Earl had made it quite clear to Jones that he did not intend to go to any great expense in building the church, and that it was to be not 'much better than a barn'. To which Jones is said to have replied that the Earl should have 'the handsomest barn in England'. For his handsome barn Jones turned to the classical temple as its most fundamental precedent. The key to the design of the whole church lay in deciding which of the classical *orders* of architecture would be the most suitable.

This is perhaps a good moment to consider some aspects of the architecture which had so inspired the architects of the Renaissance. Although the Roman style of architecture was re-discovered and adopted before that of Greece, historically it was Greek architecture that was the precursor of Roman. Greek architecture reached its aesthetic peak during the fifth century BC and continued until 146 BC when Greece came under the rule of Rome. Unlike Gothic architecture, which was to derive much of its brilliance from its myriad variety of form, Greek architecture relied for its beauty on closely observed proportions presented within prescribed limits of variation.

The Greek builders created a system of 'orders' which fixed both the proportions and the basic decorative treatment of the individual parts of the structure. Greek architecture is of *trabeated* construction, that is, based on the structural unit of a horizontal beam – *trabs* in Latin – supported by columns, a form derived directly from the posts and lintels of timber building. Each of the Greek orders describes the set configuration of this unit of construction, consisting of a column with a capital and sometimes a base, supporting an *entablature* (see page 272). The entablature was subdivided into the *architrave*, the *frieze*, and on top, the projecting *cornice*. There were three Greek orders: *Doric*, *Ionic* and *Corinthian* (see page 279). The Doric is the simplest order and its debt to timber construction can still be seen in the carving of its frieze which is divided along its length by a series of *triglyphs*. A triglyph is a raised rectangle of stone, made up of three vertical bands, which is said to represent the sawn-off end of the cross beam as it would have been seen in a timber building. The spaces between the triglyphs are called *metopes*, and are either plain or carved with figures. At each end of a Greek temple the horizontal entablature and the sloping roof form a triangular *pediment* which is often filled with sculpture.

The only ancient literary source for the definition of the various orders is Vitruvius, the first-century Roman writer mentioned earlier. As well as describing the orders in detail he assigns general characters to them. Doric he sees as having the 'proportion, strength and grace of a man's body'; Ionic as 'feminine slenderness'; and Corinthian as the 'slight figure of a girl'. The Romans adapted the three Greek orders is Vitruvius, the first-century Roman writer mentioned earlier. *Tuscan*, rather plain like the Doric, and the *Composite*, which combined elements of both Ionic and Corinthian. Great attention was also paid to precise spacing of the columns. There were five degrees of spacing, each giving the colonnade a distinctive visual rhythm. The closest was the *pycnostyle*, which, at one and a half column diameters, produced a rather tense, defensive effect. At the other extreme, the *araeostyle*, at four diameters, seems to mark out the slow, deliberate strides of some giant. It was such precision that endeared classical architecture to the analytical minds of the Renaissance. Its architects produced their own variations on the five orders, drawing not only on the authority of Vitruvius, but on actual measurement of classical ruins as well. They also suggested appropriate uses for particular orders. Sebastiano Serlio followed Vitruvius' sexual polarisation of the Doric and Corinthian orders, recommending Doric for churches dedicated to the more vigorous male saints; Corinthian for virgin saints, especially the Virgin Mary herself; and Ionic, somewhere between the two, for saintly matrons and men of learning. He makes no recommendation for the Composite order, and the robust Tuscan is seen as fit only for fortified buildings and prisons.

It was the Tuscan order which Inigo Jones decided to use at Covent Garden. In the light of Serlio's recommendations, it was an unlikely choice for a church. But Jones was familiar with the order and, if the church was to be as simple and inexpensive as the Earl of Bedford wanted, then a temple-like building based on the austere Tuscan order seemed practically and philosophically ideal. Although the acknowledged authorities varied in their precise descriptions, all agreed that Tuscan was the plainest, most basic of the orders, the closest to the primitive hut from which they supposed Greek architecture to have developed, and therefore an academically correct classical realisation of the Earl's 'barn'. For his detailed design of the order, Jones turned to the Italian translation of Vitruvius by Daniele Barbaro, illustrated by Palladio, in which translator and architect produced a version of the Tuscan order based solely and literally on the text of Vitruvius. This version presented the most rudimentary form of the order: plain, widely-spaced columns seven diameters and a half high, supporting a bare, unmoulded beam with *mutules* – projecting stone 'battens' immediately beneath the cornice of the entablature – which extended out to one quarter the height of the columns. The design had not been intended as a model for actual construction; it was more of an intellectual exercise in antiquarianism. But the dramatic starkness of this Vitruvian Tuscan struck a chord with Jones, and he used it, with stunning effect, to construct a massive *portico* at the east end of his church. In plan the church is a simple rectangle in the ratio of 2:1, with vestries projecting on either side of the west end. A series of large round-headed windows lights the interior.

The architectural success of St Paul's established Inigo Jones as the innovator of the classical style in England. A hundred years after it had been built, one of the leading architectural critics of the eighteenth century hailed Jones' church as being 'without rival, one of the most perfect pieces of architecture that the art of man can produce'. St Paul's, Covent Garden, was indeed a milestone in English parochial architecture, but the road, for the time being, had come to a halt. The reign of James I had been marred by a continuous struggle for

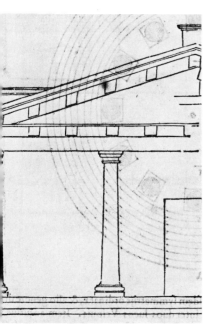

Above right
St Paul's, Covent Garden, London, presents a milestone in the story of parochial architecture. It was the first completely new parish church to be built after the Reformation and the first to be truly classical in form.

Above
Inigo Jones' design for St Paul's, Covent Garden, was derived from this realisation of the Tuscan order drawn by Palladio for an illustrated Italian translation of the first-century treatise 'de Architectura' by Vitruvius.

authority between King and Parliament. Under Charles I, an even less successful statesman than his father, the struggle intensified and in 1642 the country was precipitated into a civil war which was to last, in two phases, for seven years.

By the time of Charles I, the House of Commons had become a body of professional politicians drawn from the ranks of the smaller landed gentry, men who had done rather well for themselves and who had acquired considerable political ability through years of day-to-day management of the business of government. They were not men to take kindly to being lectured like surly children by a man less capable than themselves who seemed determined to impose his will by virtue of some nebulous divine right. This hostility was exacerbated by a clash of religious views. Throughout the country, the Puritan preachers were gathering larger flocks. When civil war broke out, it was between a king claiming by divine right to be Supreme Head of the Anglican Church and a Puritan Parliament whose beliefs had no place for priests let alone a Supreme Head. Parliament officially abolished kingship, declaring it to be 'unnecessary, burdensome, dangerous to the liberty, safety, and public interest of the people'. Generally speaking, the old aristocracy sided with the Crown while merchants and the self-made men of the new squirarchy stood for Parliament. But it was not always social class that drew the battle-lines, and allegiances were more often determined by religious belief. Indeed, families were sometimes divided against themselves. In the twelfth-century church of St Mary at Bromsberrow in Gloucestershire, two flags which once faced each other across the battlefield hang as memorials to two brothers, Rice Yate who commanded a Parliamentary regiment, and John Yate who fought for the Royalist cause.

The Civil War was conducted with an incongruous air of gentlemanly sportsmanship, punctuated by a few instances of wanton

Above
Oliver Cromwell, Lord Protector of England.

Above right
Parliamentarian iconoclasts sit among the shattered remains at 'superstitious' images at St Nicholas', Arundel, West Sussex, in a nineteenth-century painting by John Herring.

violence. The first years were indecisive. Both sides were rather poorly equipped and the fighting was sometimes confused and half-hearted. But in 1645 the balance swung in favour of the Parliamentarians with the formation of the New Model Army, better organised, better disciplined, and spurred by religious fervour. In skirmishes up and down the country, parish churches often provided Royalist troops with a last desperate stronghold. At Alton in Hampshire, eighty Royalists under the command of Colonel Richard Boles were heavily outnumbered by Parliamentarian soldiers. Under cover of smoke from burning houses they withdrew to the churchyard. From dawn to midday they fought a losing battle, eventually barricading themselves in the church itself and preparing for a final stand. The Parliamentary troops broke down the church door and burst in. The bullet-scarred doorway and pillars of the church still record the frantic barrage of fire which left sixty Royalists dead. Colonel Boles, refusing to surrender, was killed as he stood in the pulpit. On hearing the news of his death, the King is reported to have said, 'Bring me a mourning scarf; I have lost one of the best commanders in this kingdom.'

In 1647, Charles himself was captured by the army. He was tried for treason and levying war against Parliament, and found guilty. On 30th January 1649 he went to the block. During the next four years Oliver Cromwell, leader of the victorious army, tried to contain the growing threat of anarchy by ruling the country through the jurisdiction of Parliament. But his political experience was fairly limited, and Parliament would not allow itself to be led by the nose, least of all by the army. In 1653, Cromwell marched into the House of Commons with thirty musketeers at his side and dissolved Parliament on the spot. When his attempts to work through that Parliament's successor also failed, Cromwell took sole charge and proclaimed himself Lord Protector, in his own words, 'a good constable set to keep the peace of the parish'. That peace was kept by a military dictatorship, administered under Cromwell by eleven major generals, each with their

Above
*Sir Robert Shirley who died in 1656 having incurred the anger of Oliver Cromwell three years earlier by building a new church in Gothic style (*above right*) on his estate at Staunton Harold, Leicestershire.*

own districts. The country now had no king, no Parliament, and no Established Church.

In August 1641, the House of Commons had ordered the taking down of 'all scandalous pictures', and Parliamentary Visitors were appointed to ensure that the order was carried out in every parish church. They were empowered to remove all crosses and crucifixes, images of the Trinity and the Virgin Mary, pictures of the saints, and any allegedly superstitious inscriptions like the familiar '*ora pro anima . . .*' Local authorities were required to assist by providing manpower and, if needed, intimidation. The pillage of the monasteries during the Dissolution had been the work of opportunists riding on the back of Henry VIII's political ambitions; a hundred years later, the iconoclasm of Cromwell's rule was fuelled by a compulsion to rid religion of superstition and idolatry. In East Anglia, the local Parliamentary Visitor was William Dowsing, a man notorious for his zealous destruction, who kept a meticulous diary of his activities. At Cambridge he effected a 'godly thorough reformation'; at Wood Ditton 'brake down 50 superstitious pictures and crucifixes'; at Haverhill 'beat down a great stone cross on the top of the church'. In less than fifty days, Dowsing visited more than one hundred and fifty churches, smashing windows, fonts and statues, defacing tombs and monuments, and shooting out with pistols what could not be reached by the ladder. The pious craftsmanship of centuries burned in the fire of Puritan passion.

It was not exactly an auspicious time to build a church for Anglican worship. But in the same year that Cromwell took the title of Lord Protector, in Leicestershire an undaunted Royalist, Sir Robert Shirley, did just that. On his estate at Staunton Harold, he raised a new church that was unashamedly Gothic in design. The traditional style of building still persisted in the country and Sir Robert would have had no trouble finding craftsmen capable of building a church in the late Perpendicular manner. Its ornate style,

however, must have seemed an affront to any decent Puritan and, to Oliver Cromwell, the church's very existence was an act of defiance. He sent to Sir Robert ordering him to provide a regiment of soldiers, reasoning that since he could afford to build a new church, he could afford to pay for a regiment. Sir Robert's refusal earned him a cell in the Tower of London, where he eventually died. Over the west door, whose heavy classical ornament is the only concession made to the Renaissance by this latter-day Gothic church, a tablet records Sir Robert's courage and optimism in a touching epitaph: 'When all things sacred were throughout the nation either demolished or profaned, Sir Robert Shirley, baronet, founded this church; whose singular praise it is to have done the best things in the worst times and hoped them in the most calamitous.'

The Puritans saw no need for grand or inspiring church architecture; the humblest meeting house was good enough, 'for where two or three are gathered together in my name, there am I in the midst of them'. Walpole Chapel in Suffolk was the first non-conformist chapel in East Anglia, and is probably the second oldest now surviving in the country. It was set up in 1647 as a meeting place for Independents, or Congregationalists as they were later to be known. From the outside it looks like any other simple village house. A few gravestones are all there is to show that this is a place of worship. In fact, it was not built as a chapel at all, but converted from an existing building, said to have been a tannery or perhaps a pair of cottages. And inside, there is practically nothing that a medieval church-goer would have recognised – no chancel, the most sacred part of the medieval church, no altar as such, no painted saints, no stained glass windows, not even a cross. Worship in these new chapels centred on the reading of the Bible and the preaching of the sermon, symbolised by the large wooden pulpit which dominates the interior. Above the pulpit a *tester* acted like a sounding board, reflecting the preacher's voice down to the congregation who sat in box pews and wooden galleries arranged around the pulpit. Walpole Chapel has a most evocative atmosphere. The light of day pours in through two large windows, flooding every corner of the building, but revealing not the slightest hint of decoration

A contemporary illustration of Charles II's triumphant return to London after the Restoration of the Monarchy.

on its bleak surfaces. Nothing attracts the eye or distracts the mind from the central purpose of Puritan worship – to hear the word of God. The rugged simplicity of Walpole Chapel reflects the need they felt for a plain and straightforward religion that was unhindered by what they saw as hollow superstition and vanity. The medieval scene of an exclusive priesthood performing the miracle of the Sacrament in the seclusion of the chancel, while the congregation looked on passively, had been replaced by the idea that the Church consisted of an army of believers, each individual responsible for his own faith and salvation. The man who stood in the pulpit was not a priest ordained by a bishop, but a preacher elected by the entire congregation. The only authority they acknowledged was the Bible.

A greater degree of religious tolerance than ever before prevailed throughout the country for all but Catholics and those Anglicans who clung to 'high church' ways. After the Reformation the spiritual life of the land had been splintered and, in the century of turmoil, persecution and uncertainty that had followed, ordinary men and women had had to choose their religion according to their own consciences. Under Cromwell, people were now able to express their views more freely and follow their beliefs without the shadow of State or Church falling across their path although true tolerance was not assured until the nineteenth century. Some of the customs acquired at this time left an indelible mark on everyday life in England – the habit of Bible reading, family prayer, the 'Lord's Day' set aside for rest and quiet contemplation. Although the years of Puritan rule were an austere interlude, the mismanagement of the country's affairs in preceding years was being set to rights and favourable conditions were being established for the growth of national democracy.

Even before the execution of the King, a series of debates had been held by the Parliamentary army in the parish church at Putney, in London, to discuss the nature of democracy and the future government of England. These famous 'Putney Debates' were recorded almost word for word, and both officers and men express a surprisingly sophisticated political awareness: 'the poorest he that is in England hath a life to live as the greatest he,' declared one officer, 'and I do think that the poorest man in England is not at all bound in a strict sense to that government that he hath not had a voice to put himself under.'

On a stormy night in 1658, Cromwell died. His son, Richard, took over as Protector, but he was no fit successor to his father. After a few short months he resigned, leaving the country in the hands of the eleven major generals. The commander of the army in Scotland, General Monck, marched to London and declared for a free Parliament. A new Parliament was elected and one of its first acts was to recall the eldest son of Charles I from exile in France to serve as King. In May 1660, Charles II landed at Dover and was greeted by a huge and enthusiastic crowd led by General Monck. The diarist, John Evelyn recorded an eye-witness account of the King's triumphant entry into the City of London: 'This day, after a sad and long exile, and after calamitous suffering of the king and church for seventeen years, His Majesty King Charles II came to London: this day was also his birthday. He came with a triumph of over twenty thousand horse and foot brandishing their swords and shouting with unexpressable joy.

LONDON

THAMESIS   FLUVIUS

South Warke

LONDON im Brand.

THAMESIS   FLUVIUS.

LA VILLE DE LONDRES   PROSPECTUS LONDINENS

A PROSPECT of the CITY of LONDON.

The changing face of the City
of London:

Above
*Vischer's famous view of the City
as it was in 1616.*

Centre
*The medieval City engulfed by flames
during the Great Fire of 1666.*

Below
*The skyline of the charred City
transformed into a forest of spires by
the rebuilding master-minded by
Christopher Wren.*

The ways were strewn with flowers, the bells were ringing, the streets were hung with tapestry, and the fountains were running with wine.'

The Restoration of the Monarchy also meant the restoration of the Church of England. In the House of Lords, the bishops took their seats once again; in the parishes, the ordained Anglican parsons regained their social status and their livings; and in the churches the prominent display of the Royal Coat of Arms was made compulsory – a reminder that the restored Anglican Church was part and parcel of the revived Establishment with the King at its head.

One of the most important events following the Restoration was the founding, in 1662, of the Royal Society for Improving Natural Knowledge, under the patronage of the King. Its first members read like a catalogue of the fathers of modern science. Among them were Robert Hooke, the great inventor and pioneer of physics; Robert Boyle, originator of modern chemistry; Isaac Newton, whose work on calculus, the nature of light, gravitation and the laws of motion were to win him acclaim as the world's greatest man of science; Christopher Wren, mathematician and Professor of Astronomy at Oxford; and Samuel Pepys, naval administrator and diarist. The Royal Society followed where Francis Bacon had led, and the triumph of knowledge over superstition, of science over magic, did much to set the scene for the increasingly tolerant attitudes and rational religion of the eighteenth century.

But the progress of these early years of Charles II's reign were set against a background of continuing troubles. The relationship between Parliament and the Crown was still uneasy; the country was fighting a sporadic maritime war with the Dutch; the Plague had returned to England; and in 1666, London was all but razed to the ground by the disastrous Great Fire. 'It made me weep to see it' wrote Samuel Pepys in his diary, 'The churches, houses, and all on fire and flaming at once, and a horrid noise the flames made, and the cracking of houses at their ruin.' Pepys' fellow member of the Royal Society, John Evelyn, was there too: 'The stones of St Paul's (Cathedral) flew like grenados, and the lead melted down the streets in a stream. The very pavements glowed with fiery redness, and neither horse nor man was able to tread on them . . . the air all about was so hot and inflamed that, at the last, one was not able to approach it, so that they were forced to stand still and let the flames consume on, which they did for nearly two miles in length and one in breadth. The clouds of smoke also were dismal, and reached, upon computation, nearly fifty miles in length. Thus I left it this afternoon burning, a resemblance of Sodom, or the Last Day. London was, but is no more.'

When the fire finally died away after raging for four days and nights, a large part of the city and eighty-four of its parish churches had been completely destroyed. The enormous undertaking of re-building the city's churches was to be master-minded by one man – Christopher Wren, fellow of the Royal Society. By training Wren was a mathematician and astronomer, and it was not until he was thirty that he began to develop an interest in architecture. By that time he was at the top of the academic tree and acknowledged as one of the finest minds of his time. Christopher Wren was an outstanding example of that special product of the Renaissance, the *uomo universale*

Christopher Wren, astronomer, mathematician and architect.

– the 'universal man' whose talents and knowledge embraced many branches of science and the arts. It seems to have been his skill in drawing and his love of model-making that first led to a desire to design buildings. Before the Great Fire he had already tried his hand, rather successfully, with a large hall at Oxford, the Sheldonian Theatre, built in the grand Roman style. Wren was also on good terms with the King, his family having been staunch Royalists throughout the Civil War, and this no doubt played a part in securing for him the task of supervising the design and building of the city's fifty-one new churches. The cramped and irregular sites left by the Great Fire set Wren a challenge that he was to meet with an astonishing variety of ingenious solutions, and within fifty years he transformed the skyline of the charred city into a forest of graceful spires, and crowned it with his masterpiece, St Paul's Cathedral.

As well as giving Christopher Wren a chance to establish himself as a major architect, the re-building of the city churches provided the opportunity for the classical style to assert itself as the accepted style of church architecture. The new churches were, in the main, classical. But their classicism was not the scholarly, almost archaeological, classicism of Inigo Jones. By the seventeenth century, the static and serene classical style of the early Renaissance had given way to a more flamboyant and theatrical treatment of classical form, called *Baroque*. The Baroque style flourished in Italy and France, where Charles II had spent his exile, and French Baroque in particular had a strong influence on Wren's work. The generation of architects that succeeded him produced a more fully developed Baroque style, but, true to national temperament, English Baroque continued to avoid the excessive extravagance of its Continental counterpart.

With the exception of Inigo Jones' church at Covent Garden, the new city churches were the first to be built expressly for Anglican worship. They were planned not to meet the requirements of medieval ritual, but to suit the liturgy of the Book of Common Prayer. In Wren's view this meant that a parish church should be as large as possible, but not so large that the congregation could not see and hear clearly. 'The Romanists indeed may build larger churches,' he acknowledged, but 'it is enough if they hear the Murmur of the Mass, and see the Elevation of the Host, but ours are fitted for Auditories.' The main function of the church had indeed become that of an auditorium. In London especially, people came to church chiefly to enjoy a good sermon. The sermon had become the central part of a church service, and its importance was matched only by its length! Prayer Book worship minimised the use of the chancel. In existing churches, they became almost redundant and often fell into serious disrepair. In the new churches, the distinction between the chancel and the rest of the church was often implied rather than clearly articulated, and sometimes there was no distinction at all.

These *auditory plan* churches, as they are called, tend to be rectangular in plan like Inigo Jones' 'handsomest barn', although the irregularity of some of the sites left by the Great Fire forced Wren to adopt a wide variety of ground plans. The main concern of the architect was the division of the internal space of the church in ways that were both liturgically acceptable and aesthetically pleasing. In this respect, perhaps the most successful of Wren's churches is that of St Stephen Walbrook, built between 1672 and 1677. It replaced the destroyed fifteenth-century church on the east bank of the Walbrook, a stream which now runs under the street of that name. The rebuilt church is smaller than the medieval one, so the shape of the site presented no restrictions. In plan the church is rectangular, but within that simple space Wren contrived, with characteristic mathematical precision, a series of splendid vistas using sixteen columns with plain shafts and Corinthian capitals. Four columns towards the western end of the rectangle mark off a vestibule area, rather like the *narthex* of a Romanesque church, and leave a perfectly square area to the east. Within this square, twelve columns in four groups of three set out the shape of a symmetrical Greek cross, which defines, in traditional terms, the transepts, aisles, crossing and chancel of the church. The eight inner columns are linked by semi-circular arches which support an impressive coffered dome spanning most of the interior. A lantern at the top lights the dome and throws its plaster panels into dramatic relief. The dome was the first of its kind in parochial architecture and pre-dates that of St Paul's Cathedral. To the north and south of the dome, the areas that correspond to transepts are covered with short barrel vaults and end in large windows. All the windows were originally of clear glass panes. The three eastern windows, however, were filled in 1961 with stained glass which, whatever its artistic merits, cannot but detract from the design of the church as a whole. The existence of a chancel area is inferred by the structure of the church rather than stated by a dividing screen, and the communion table is left with only a neat set of low wooden railings to protect its sanctity. Pride of place, as in all auditory plan churches, is given to the pulpit. Over the chancel area and the four corners of the square, there are groined vaults which enabled Wren to insert two windows at each corner in the manner of a clerestory.

Light floods in from all directions, emphasising the spacious air of the interior. In the subtle division of its ground plan, Wren's church provided the perfect setting for the liturgy of the re-established Anglican Church; in its handling of space, especially the ambitious use of the dome, St Stephen Walbrook placed Wren on a par with the leading European architects of the day; in its use of pure shapes – the square, symmetrical cross, semicircles and hemisphere – it exalted geometry as the basis both of structure and aesthetics; and in its enjoyment of light, it reflected the clarity and curiosity that was to fire the scientific mind of the Age of Reason.

Today, walking into St Stephen Walbrook for the first time is still a stunning experience, even though time has robbed the interior of some important details. The church's sixteen columns, for instance, sit on pedestals which look disproportionately tall until it is remembered that the high box pews formerly set between them would have significantly altered the way in which the proportions appeared to the eye. The congregation of the seventeenth and eighteenth centuries usually sat not on the familiar bench-like pews, but in pews surrounded by wooden panelling often as much as two metres high and fitted with doors. Services were long and the church often cold and

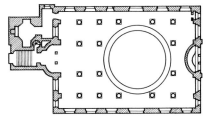

St Stephen Walbrook, London.

draughty, so to be 'boxed in' provided at least a little extra comfort. Contemporary illustrations show that the box pews at St Stephen Walbrook were of the same height as the pedestals of its columns. They were designed as an integral part of a carefully proportioned architectural unit formed at each corner by box pews, columns and entablature. So the lack of box pews inevitably spoils the view of the church at ground level. The inappropriate Victorian mosaic floor which replaced the original elegant white and black marble, does not help in this respect either. For a more complete impression of the furnishing of a city church of this period we must move on a few hundred yards and some fifteen years to another of Wren's churches, St Margaret Lothbury.

Squeezed into a narrow street in the shadow of the Bank of England, St Margaret Lothbury is one of the smaller city churches. The church, built between 1686 and 1693, has always been hemmed in by other buildings, and the cramped site with which Wren was presented after the Great Fire is reflected in the distorted rectangle of the church's one-aisled plan. Inside, the first impression is that of a rather grand house – dark, wood-panelled walls, a flat ceiling with gilded stucco, and gleaming brass chandeliers give the church the comfortable air of some fine drawing-room. The building is essentially human in scale. It does not overawe the visitor; it makes him feel at

home. St Margaret Lothbury is perhaps the best furnished of the city churches, its own original fittings being supplemented by several pieces from now-demolished churches. It is also one of only two Wren churches which retain their contemporary chancel screens. The screen was no longer intended to divide the church into one province for the clergy and another for the laity, but to provide instead two areas for use during different parts of the service. The screen at St Margaret Lothbury is particularly impressive. Constructed around 1689 at the expense of two German merchants living in London, Theodore and Jacob Jacobsen, it stood originally in All Hallows' Church, Thames Street, and was brought to St Margaret's when All Hallows' was demolished in 1894. On either side of the middle entrance there are four open, round-headed sections separated by *balusters*. Each baluster takes the form of a cleverly carved *double helix*, two intertwined spirals – another reminder of the fascination with geometry and mathematics. The entrance itself is bridged by an *open segmental pediment*, a pediment in which the sloping, upper sides of the triangle are replaced by a segment of a circle with a gap in the middle. The use of segmental pediments over doorways and windows is a particular feature of Baroque architecture. Beneath the pediment is a large carved eagle with outspread wings, and above, the compulsory Royal Coat of Arms.

The most prominent feature of the nave is, of course, the pulpit, raised high up so everyone could see it over the tops of their box pews which are now, alas, gone. Both the pulpit and its tester are beautifully carved with flowers and fruit. The tester with its cherubs and swags is particularly fine and came originally, like the chancel screen, from All Hallows', Thames Street. Beyond the screen, the chancel floor is fashionably paved in black and white marble, and leads not to a grand altar, but to a small wooden communion table. The table would have

Above
*Another of Wren's churches,
St Margaret Lothbury.*

Above right
*The richly carved chancel screen, pulpit
and reredos at St Margaret Lothbury.*

Wren's original drawing for the steeple of St Mary-le-Bow, London.

been covered, according to the Canons of the Church, with a 'fair linen cloth' and set with elegant silver vessels for Communion. Sometimes a copy of the Bible was placed upright on a cushion at one end of the table and a Book of Common Prayer at the other. Behind the altar is an impressive reredos of three wooden panels framed by Corinthian columns supporting segmental pediments. On the central panel the Ten Commandments, sometimes called the *Decalogue*, are painted in gold, and on the side panels are the Creed and the Lord's Prayer. This was by far the most popular type of reredos during the seventeenth and eighteenth centuries, and is still found in many simple country churches. A painting was also sometimes used as a reredos; the Descent from the Cross seems to have been considered a particularly appropriate subject. At St Margaret Lothbury there are paintings of Moses and Aaron on either side of the altar, 'the two faithful prophets ever attendant on our altars', according to one contemporary writer. In the south aisle of the church is a very elegant font which came from St Olave Jewry. Since baptism was no longer by immersion, fonts could be much smaller, and post-Reformation fonts generally take the form of a simple bowl on a tall stem. They are sometimes wooden with a lead lined bowl. The font at St Margaret Lothbury is of stone, and its bowl is carved with reliefs showing Adam and Eve, the Baptism of Christ, Noah's Ark, and the Baptism of the Eunuch. Between the reliefs are winged heads of cherubim. The font is said by some to have been designed, if not executed, by the famous wood-carver, Grinling Gibbons, and is a perfect example of the superb quality of craftsmanship that the new churches inspired.

Despite the comfort and elegance of Wren's church interiors, outside they are usually quite plain. He considered exterior decoration to be less important since the church walls were mostly obscured by the surrounding buildings. An old engraving shows that a row of shops was actually built against the front wall of St Margaret Lothbury at one time. As the narrow streets of the city seldom allowed clear views of his churches, for Wren the focus of their exterior decoration was the spire: 'Handsome spires rising in good proportion above the neighbouring houses, may be of sufficient ornament to the town without great expense for enriching the outward walls of the church, in which plainness and duration ought principally, if not wholly, to be studied.' The spire was usually the last part of the structure to be built, and was often added years, and sometimes decades, after the rest of the church had been completed. Therefore Wren's spires represent his more mature style and have a stronger Baroque flavour than his earlier work, perhaps as a result of the increasing influence of his pupil, Nicholas Hawksmoor, who in later years became Wren's partner in all but name. With no liturgical constraints to hinder him, and few practical limitations other than expense, Wren's imagination had free rein, and the steeples of his churches show even greater variety and invention than their interiors. There were no spires in classical Greek or Roman architecture and, as yet, no Renaissance spire had been built in England. So Wren had no precedents to guide him; he was breaking new ground. As a structure, the spire is an essentially Gothic notion. In effect, what Wren did was to translate a Gothic idea into the classical language of the Renaissance. For

The steeple of St Mary-le-Bow as it is to be seen today.

instance, where crocketed pinnacles would be found on a medieval steeple, Wren might use urns supported by scroll-work or on pedestals; for a parapet he might use a classical balustrade. Some of his spires seem to have been conceived as a series of miniature classical temples stacked one on top of the other in diminishing scale. The stone steeples of St Mary-le-Bow and St Bride's, Fleet Street are two of Wren's tallest spires and are generally considered to be his best. However, comparison is difficult within such variety, and the more modest elegance of some of the simpler, lead-covered timber spires, like those of St Margaret Lothbury and St Martin, Ludgate Hill, is equally appealing.

After the Reformation, the tower, with or without a spire, continued to be considered an indispensable part of the church. Indeed the belfries were, if anything, more important. Improvements during the seventeenth century in the hanging of bells and in tuning them to a musical scale, enabled bells to be rung in sequence instead of jangling them at random. This led to the art of *change ringing*, introduced by Fabian Stedman, a Cambridge printer, in 1668 and perfected in this country alone. In each *change* every bell must be rung once and once only. On a typical ring of eight bells over forty thousand changes are possible, and to ring all the changes would take some twenty-four hours. The ringer's gallery, beneath the belfry, had its rules which were often written in rhyme on the gallery wall or on a board. A typical example reads:

'You ringers all, observe these orders well!
He pays his sixpence that o'erturns a bell;
And he that rings in either spur or hat,
Must pay his sixpence certainly for that;
And he that rings and does disturb ye peal,
Must pay his sixpence or a gun of ale.
These laws elsewhere in ev'ry church are used
That bell and ringers may not be abused.'

The work of Christopher Wren and his followers infused the horizontality of the classical style with a native feeling for Gothic verticality, exemplified by his church steeples. It gave classical form an added dynamism. On the whole however, Wren's work is too calm and calculated to be said to be Baroque in the extravagant Continental manner. It was to be his followers, John Vanbrugh, Nicholas Hawksmoor, Thomas Archer and James Gibbs, who added the missing ingredient that created an English Baroque style. 'Fancy' is how Hawksmoor described the element of movement and drama that is vital to Baroque and of which Wren had always fought shy. Writing in 1724 to defend his architectural style, Hawksmoor explained that his basic principle was to equate the 'rules of the ancients with strong reason and good fancy, joined with experience and trials, so that we are assured of the good effect of it'. Hawksmoor worked as an assistant to Christopher Wren and John Vanbrugh, and until recently his work has tended to be overshadowed by that of his masters.

Vanbrugh started out in life as a soldier before becoming a playwright who penned several very witty and very successful Res-

Above
*St Alphege's, Greenwich, London,
the first church built under the 1711
Commission for Fifty New Churches,
is mainly the work of Nicholas
Hawksmoor, the finest exponent of
the English Baroque style.*

Opposite

Above
*The west front of St Mary Woolnoth,
London, shows Hawksmoor's highly
innovatory use of the vocabulary of
Baroque architecture.*

Below
*One of three rusticated niches
from the north wall of St Mary
Woolnoth containing an aedicule in
the Ionic order.*

toration comedies. At the end of the seventeenth century, however, he suddenly developed an interest in designing buildings, provoking his contemporary, the satirist Jonathan Swift, to declare that:

> 'Van's genius, without thought or lecture,
> is hugely turn'd to architecture.'

Although Vanbrugh could express his architectural ideas clearly in accomplished freehand drawings, through lack of 'lecture' he never learned the discipline of technical draughtsmanship, and for the realisation of all his important buildings he relied on the professional expertise of Nicholas Hawksmoor. Hawksmoor was, however, far more than Vanbrugh's draughtsman; his knowledge of the antique and his practical experience gained with Wren enabled him to give order and form to Vanbrugh's theatrical imaginings. Together the two men synthesised elements of French, English and Italian taste into a particularly English version of the Baroque style.

Having no formal training was not the handicap it would be today, and Vanbrugh's imagination and influence carried him to high office. For ten years during the reign of Queen Anne he held the post of Controller of Her Majesty's Works. And when, in 1711, an Act of Parliament set up a Commission to superintend the building of 'fifty new churches in and about the City of London and Westminster and Suburbs thereof', it was only natural that Vanbrugh should be appointed as one of the Commissioners. The new churches were needed both to cope with the rapidly increasing population of the capital, which had trebled during the seventeenth century, and to

allay establishment anxiety over the growing strengths of both Protestant non-conformity and Catholicism. They were to be paid for, as Wren's city churches and St Paul's Cathedral had been, by a tax levied on all coal coming into the city. Although Vanbrugh drew up a set of guidelines which were not without influence on his fellow Commissioners, the actual designs he produced were never realised. In fact, the number of churches built fell far short of the fifty envisaged by the Act, and of these, half were designed by Nicholas Hawksmoor. St Mary Woolnoth in the City; St George-in-the-East; St George's, Bloomsbury; St Alphege's, Greenwich; St Anne's, Limehouse and Christchurch, Spitalfields are all his, and he had a hand in several others besides.

The first church to be built under the Act of 1711 was St Alphege's, Greenwich. The building is basically rectangular with porches to north and south, and a portico at the east end facing the main street. The tower of Hawksmoor's original design, an important feature of the exterior, was unfortunately never built, and that to be seen today is a rather less effective one added twenty-six years after the rest of the building had been completed. The Doric order of the eastern portico is carried around the outside of the building by Doric pilasters set between the windows. It has been suggested that the use of these pilasters was a refinement of Hawksmoor's design by Thomas Archer, another of the architects working for the Commission for Fifty New Churches. Archer was to be completely responsible for two of the Commission's churches, St John's, Smith Square and St Paul's, Deptford. His work has a strong Italian influence which makes it more like Continental Baroque than any of his contemporaries'. Inside, St Alphege's, Greenwich is one large room nearly twenty by thirty metres (sixty-five by ninety feet), with galleries along its sides and a shallow recess for a chancel that is painted in perspective to give the illusion of greater depth. The decoration around the recess and its illusionist painting give the impression of a proscenium arch with a stage set beyond, and the galleries ranged on either side add to the theatre-like air of the interior.

Hawksmoor's work on his own is generally more restrained than that designed in collaboration with Vanbrugh. But that restraint did not limit the scope of his imagination and, if anything, it strengthened his originality. The church which illustrates both these qualities most clearly is St Mary Woolnoth, the smallest and arguably the most successful of Hawksmoor's churches. The medieval church on the site had been only damaged by the Great Fire and had been repaired by Wren. But in 1716 the decision was taken to demolish and rebuild the church. The site was obscured by houses to the east and south, so Hawksmoor concentrated his efforts on the west and north sides. The north wall has a series of three identical, window-like niches, each set with a pair of miniature Ionic columns standing on pedestals and supporting a curved entablature. Columns and an entablature or pediment used in this way to frame a niche, window or doorway, are sometimes referred to as an *aedicule*. A boldly projecting sill beneath is supported by scroll-work brackets, and the niche is surrounded by heavy *rustication* – blocks of stone set with deeply recessed joints to give them particular emphasis. Each niche forms a powerful architectural composition, and together they provide a dramatically sculptured façade which shows the English Baroque style at its best in parochial architecture. The treatment of the west front is highly original: a pair of square turrets and the artful placing of columns against a massive rectangular tower, beautifully proportioned in the Ionic order, contrive to give the impression of fused twin west towers. The cube-like interior of the church is designed with a logic that Christopher Wren would have applauded. A central square is marked out by three great Corinthian columns at each corner. The columns support a rich entablature above which a square clerestory with four large semi-circular windows provides the interior with strikingly effective top-lighting. Behind the columns there were originally galleries, but they were later removed. Their carved fronts, however, are still to be seen, set back against the walls.

The Baroque style of architecture was soon to attract serious criticism that was motivated as much by politics as by matters of taste. The death of Queen Anne in 1714 followed by the accession of George I of the House of Hanover, marked the eclipse of Tory power by the Whig party. Christopher Wren's apparently autocratic control over public architecture had already caused resentment in Whig circles. In 1712, the Earl of Shaftesbury, a Whig philosopher, had published an attack on Wren and his followers and the influence of the flamboyant French Baroque style on their work. He called for a style of architecture that was distinctly British and unsullied by foreign interference. An attempt to answer that call was made by a Scottish architect called Colen Campbell. Campbell had come to London around 1711, but despite his ability as a self-publicist had failed to secure himself a position on the Commission for Fifty New Churches. In 1715 he published the first volume of his *Vitruvius Britannicus*, which included guidelines for a new national style and plates of suitable designs. Campbell scorned the recent work of Wren's followers and advocated a return to the fundamental principles of the ancients as they had been expounded by Andrea Palladio. He wanted to turn the clock back and pick up where his Palladian hero, Inigo Jones, the 'British Vitruvius' of the book's title, had left off. In the same year the first English translation of Palladio's *Quattro Libri dell'Architettura* was published, and the stage was set for a Palladian revival. Campbell's success was due in large part to astute political timing and the support of the third Earl of Burlington, an architect himself who was to become the chief patron of English Palladianism.

Although Hawksmoor despised the Palladian school, whose influence succeeded in losing him and Wren their royal posts, the Palladian elements of his architectural vocabulary became more strongly emphasised in his later work. At Christchurch, Spitalfields, for instance, Hawksmoor had intended to build a flat west front with a rather plain rectangular tower topped by an octagonal lantern. But when the time came to build the tower, around 1723, he changed his mind and decided to build a grand portico instead with a tower and spire above. In the east end of the church he had already used a large Venetian window – an important hallmark of the Palladian style that had first been used in England by Inigo Jones in the Queen's Chapel at St James' Palace. Hawksmoor now translated this pattern of a semi-

Christchurch, Spitalfields, London, one of Hawksmoor's later churches, shows the influence of Palladio in its bold interpretation of the Venetian window motif for both portico and tower.

circular headed opening flanked by two shorter, square-headed openings to the west front of his church, and designed its portico as a massive statement of the Venetian window motif, boldly repeating it in the tower above on the same scale but in slightly more disguised form. The overall effect is monumental.

James Gibbs was another of the architects who worked on the Commission for Fifty New Churches, his contribution being the elegant St Mary-le-Strand. Like Colen Campbell, he was a Scot, but there the similarity ended for the two men were rivals for most of their careers, Campbell deliberately making no mention of Gibbs' work in his *Vitruvius Britannicus*. In the political climate after 1715, Gibbs was something of an outsider. A Tory who had been raised as a Catholic, he was precluded from much public building and forced to rely mainly on private Tory patronage. Gibbs was unique among his contemporary architects in having actually studied architecture in Rome. On his return to England, he became a great admirer of the buildings of Christopher Wren, and his own work, being less overtly

Above
*St Martin-in-the-Fields, London,
designed by James Gibbs.*

Above right
*A plate showing suggested designs for
steeples from James Gibbs' 'A Book
of Architecture', one of the growing
number of architectural pattern books.*

Baroque than that of Hawksmoor and Vanbrugh, shows much
affinity with Wren's. His best known work is the impressive church
of St Martin-in-the-Fields. The exterior of this famous London
landmark is dominated by a huge Corinthian portico and a tall
Renaissance spire much in the manner of Wren. Although Gibbs'
influence on his immediate contemporaries was probably slight, his
designs were to make their impact further afield in the depths of the
countryside and across the sea in the new American Colonies. In 1728
he published 'A Book of Architecture' which was, in effect, a pattern
book of one hundred and fifty plates showing architectural designs
for everything from chimney-pieces to steeples. The book was highly
successful, making him a good deal of money and spawning Gibbs-
style steeples on both sides of the Atlantic. The steeple of St Martin-
in-the-Fields proved a particularly popular model. Unlike Wren's
steeples, which invariably rise from the ground, Gibbs' steeples sit
astride the pitched roofs of his churches. Although this created a
rather uncomfortable 'join' between roof and steeple, it restored an

Above
St Lawrence's, Mereworth, Kent, whose steeple, like many here and in America, was modelled by the local builder on that of Gibbs' St Martin-in-the-Fields.

Above right
St Nicholas', Hardenhuish, Wiltshire, built by John Wood the Younger, shows the provincial Palladian style at its most charming.

absolute symmetry to the main elevation which brought it more into line with Palladian thinking. Gibbs' work is in some ways a compromise between the Baroque and Palladian schools.

The City churches gave a lead which the provincial towns and country parishes followed as their means afforded. The eighteenth century was one of slow but steady rebuilding. The conflict between Baroque and Palladian was never completely resolved, and up and down the country churches were built in either style or somewhere between the two. The church of St Nicholas at Hardenhuish near Chippenham in Wiltshire, for instance, is a perfect little Palladian building sitting on a grassy hill like an ornamental temple in a landscaped garden. The church was built in 1779 by John Wood the Younger of Bath, and typifies the rather tranquil classical style that provincial architects produced throughout the Georgian period. By contrast, the church of St Peter at Gayhurst in Buckinghamshire, built some fifty years earlier by an unknown architect, carries the Baroque atmosphere and sophisticated charm of a City church into

St Peter's, Gayhurst, Buckingham-shire, the Baroque sophistication of a City church brought into the country-side. The monument on the right is by the famous French sculptor, Roubiliac.

the country. The interior, with its elegant plaster-work and splendid monument to Speaker Wright and his son, is completely unspoiled. The monument is the first English commission of Lois François Roubiliac, the Frenchman who was to become perhaps the finest sculptor of eighteenth-century England, famous especially for his monumental sculpture.

Gayhurst church, like many others in the country stands beside the local manor house, and was rebuilt in the latest fashion by the lord of the manor. The introduction of the classical style had brought with it a gradual but irrevocable change in the organisation of church building. The expertise which had been invested over generations in the medieval system that revolved around the master mason became redundant. The classical style had been developed by the new professional architects, and the local master masons, whose roots lay in the traditional Gothic style, were no longer able to design churches to suit fashionable taste. In the country, the onus shifted to the patron, usually the local squire or lord of the manor, to provide the designs from which his masons could work. If he were wealthy or influential enough, the squire might manage to secure the services of one of the leading architects of the day to design his new church, as Walter Chetwynd did at St Mary's Church, Ingestre in Staffordshire. Chetwynd was a friend of Dr. Robert Plot who was the Secretary of the Royal Society, and who used his influence to persuade the Society's President, none other than Christopher Wren, to prepare the designs for the new church. Unfortunately this happened rarely, and there was always a gap between the many patrons wanting to rebuild their churches and the few professional architects available to carry out commissions. This gap was bridged by the growing number of architectural pattern books like James Gibbs' 'A Book of Architecture' whose preface clearly states its intention to 'be of use to such gentlemen as might be concerned in building, especially in remote parts of the country, where little or no assistance for designs can be procured'. An aesthetic appreciation of classical architecture, but not a working knowledge, was now considered to be an essential part of the education of any young gentleman. Anyone who wished to be considered cultured undertook a grand tour of Italy as a matter of course, though many had entertainment more in mind than edification. So it is not surprising that the country gentry made a greater contribution to the architectural style of churches during the eighteenth century than at any other time. This was the heyday of the amateur architect. Here and there, local squires, their heads full of ideas picked up on the Grand Tour and their arms full of pattern books, were enthusiastically dabbling in local architecture. Such eclecticism was not always a recipe for success, and many of the churches built must have been sadly accurate reflections of the squire's taste and ability.

Occasionally, however, as at Great Packington in Warwickshire, the result was something quite fresh and unexpected. St James' Church was built on the Great Packington estate of the fourth Earl of Aylesford in 1789–90 by the Italian-born architect, Joseph Bonomi, who had come to England some twenty years earlier. From the outside the building is quite unlike any traditional idea of a church. It is a symmetrically planned square, with identical squat pepper-pot

At Great Packington, Warwick-shire, the church of St James is totally unlike any other in the country and appears quite alien across the emphatically English great park of Packington Hall.

towers topped by lead-covered domes at the corners. A simple entablature runs around the tops of the walls, rising to a broken pediment in the middle of each. Otherwise the starkness of the exterior is relieved only by severe semi-circular windows punched through the walls. The use of red brick and pinkish sandstone contrasting with the leaden grey of the tower domes, adds to the rather exotic feel of the church. The effect of this unusual building set in the familiar surroundings of a great park is altogether extraordinary. Inside, the church is equally striking. A totally plain groined vault thrown across the interior gives a cave-like impression and bears down heavily on the four stocky Greek columns of the Doric order which support it. The columns are given a rude strength by block-like entablatures and a pronounced *entasis* – the normally slight swelling given to a column to counteract an optical illusion which makes a perfectly straight column appear thinner in the middle.

Great Packington Church is unique in England. It is also quite different from the rest of Bonomi's work, especially in its use of the Greek columns, which leads to speculation that the Earl himself played an unusually important part in its design. It seems likely that Lord Aylesford had travelled with Bonomi to Italy in 1783, and it is known that he had already been keenly interested in architecture for at least ten years, because drawings and notes made by the Earl during a longer visit in the early 1770s survive at Packington Hall. Among the Earl's collection of drawings one has a particular relevance to his church. The drawing is of the interior of the Diocletian Baths in Rome, as they were before being converted to the Church of St Mary of the Angels. It was probably based on an illustration from some published work on Roman antiquities since the Baths could no longer be drawn in their original state from observation. What is immediately apparent about the Earl's drawing is its anticipation of the main structural feature of Great Packington Church, the massive groined vault supported on freestanding columns. The columns of Diocletian's Baths were, naturally, of a Roman order, but others of his drawings show Lord Aylesford experimenting with the Greek orders. Another convincing similarity is the use of the very unusual

Above
*The interior of St James', Great
Packington, is severe and monumental. Evidence suggests that its
design was as much the inspiration of
the patron, Lord Aylesford, as of the
architect, Joseph Bonomi.*

Below
*A drawing of the Diocletian Baths in
Rome by Lord Aylesford has striking parallels with St James', in particular the groined vault on freestanding
columns and the distinctive tripartite
semi-circular windows, and may well
have served as the model for his
unusual church.*

semi-circular windows divided into three parts. So it appears that the stern and monumental character of the church was the inspiration of Lord Aylesford himself, and that, while credit must be given to Joseph Bonomi for translating his ideas into practical reality, the Earl must be considered to have been the guiding hand behind the design of this exceptional church.

The scholasticism shown by Lord Aylesford in his church was rare; the average lord of the manor preferred his architecture less academic and more grandiose. After all, building a new church was an expensive business, and the patron wanted something to show for

his money. So churches sometimes became swamped in ostentatious ornament. Like Great Packington Church, St Michael's at Great Witley in Hereford and Worcester is an estate church, standing beside the ruined shell of Witley Court. Though the great house is derelict, the grandeur of its owners, the Lords Foley, lives on in the church. It was built in 1735 by the widow of the first Lord Foley, and then completely redecorated inside by the second Lord Foley in 1747. It is the very antithesis of Great Packington – a riotous Baroque interior whose walls and ceiling are encrusted with gilded stucco. The lavish relief decoration may be the work of Pietro Bagutti, who had been brought to England specially by James Gibbs to decorate the interior of St Martin-in-the-Fields. The embossed panels and scroll-work of the ceiling form an elaborate setting for three paintings attributed to the Venetian painter, Antonio Belluci. These paintings, together with ten painted glass windows, were brought by Lord Foley from the Duke of Chandos when his palatial home at Canons, near Little Stanmore in north London, was dismantled and its contents sold.

The sale of his estate at Canons had been forced upon the second Duke of Chandos by his reckless spending; within a few years of his father's death he had squandered the family fortune. The estate and the fortune had been built up, virtually from nothing, by the first Duke, James Brydges. Unlike his son, the first Duke of Chandos was an astute man, blessed with the ability not only to make money, but to enjoy it too. He built an exceptionally grand house for himself where he lived in great style which became notorious for its ostentation even in his own day. He even maintained his own private orchestra of thirty-three players, and for several years George Frederic Handel was master of the Duke's music. In 1715, James Brydges decided to demolish all but the tower of the old parish church standing on his estate, St Lawrence,

St Lawrence's, Little Stanmore, Middlesex, where the lavish decoration seems more a monument to ostentation than to piety.

Little Stanmore, and to rebuild it in more prestigious fashion to suit his new-found eminence. As soon as the actual building, designed by John James, was finished he concentrated on making it a treasure house of a church. He gathered together the best artists and craftsmen he could afford, as patrons of the church had done in centuries gone by. But unlike in medieval times, the result was not a glorious expression of the civic pride of the parish, but rather a show of the wealth and self-esteem of one man. Nearly every inch of the church is carved or painted. On the north and south walls, the *trompe l'oeil* painting, probably by Francesco Sleter assisted by Gaetano Brunnetti, just fails in its attempt to trick the eye into seeing niches set with statues of the three Christian graces – Faith, Hope and Charity – the Evangelists, and St Peter and St Paul. In panels on the ceiling are scenes of the miracles and teaching of Christ, painted by the French artist, Louis Laguerre. The east end of the church is dominated by two wooden Corinthian columns supporting a broken segmental pediment, which together form a stage-like setting behind the altar. Two large paintings on either side show the 'Adoration of the Shepherds' and the 'Descent from the Cross' by Antonio Belluci. On the 'stage' behind the altar is an organ on which the composer Handel is said to have played while under the Duke of Chandos' patronage. The beautiful craftsmanship of the carved organ case is one of the most attractive features of the church. Beside the organ, two more large canvasses crowd on to the stage, both by Antonio Verrio. All this adds up to an extravagant interior gently mocked at the time by the poet Alexander Pope:

'On painted ceiling you devoutly stare,
Where sprawl the saints of Verrio and Laguerre.'

Right
St Mary's, Whitby, North York-
shire, a medieval church crammed
full with galleries and box pews to
make it suitable for eighteenth-
century worship.

Opposite
A more successful adaptation.
Above, the deceptive fourteenth-
century exterior of All Saints',
Cottesbrooke, Northamptonshire,
and below, the elegant Georgian
interior, complete with three decker
pulpit and family pew for the lord of
the manor.

Unfortunately the impressive effect remains just that – an effect. Like the *trompe l'oeil* painting it tries hard but in the end fails to be totally convincing. There is a feel of insincerity about the interior, and when the eye looks too closely it sees something uncomfortably like stage scenery. The Duke, however, kept up the image until the end. When he died the most grandiose of monuments was set in the mausoleum that adjoins the church, with an inscription that, rather ironically, praises the Duke's modesty and dislike of ostentation.

Few lords of the manor could have afforded the extravagance of the Duke of Chandos, and most local squires and their parishes had to be content to adapt existing churches to suit the new fashion. St Mary's Church at Whitby in North Yorkshire, for instance, was crammed with box pews and galleries to accommodate the congregation that crowded in to hear the ever-popular sermon. There the galleries themselves seem to push and jostle for the best view of the pulpit, and the effect is altogether disorganised. In some of the smaller of the country churches, however, the 'Georgianising' of a medieval structure produced ordered interiors of considerable charm and dignity.

From the outside, the church of All Saints at Cottesbrooke in Northamptonshire, is a typical Gothic country church, built, according to the evidence of its window tracery, at the turn of the fourteenth century. But inside it is quite different. Virtually nothing is left of the original, medieval arrangement of the Church. The wall paintings are gone, so is the chancel screen, which is known only from records, and the open timber roof has been given a flat ceiling with coved edges painted to simulate fashionable plasterwork. The whole interior was rearranged to suit eighteenth-century worship. Box pews were fitted along both sides of the nave. In towns, a pew rent was charged, but in the country they were generally free, each household being allocated its pew. Most families would have lived in houses owned by the local lord of the manor, and a place in church went with the house. All the

pews face the pulpit, which is a particularly elegant example of a *three decker pulpit*. The three decker pulpit was peculiar to the eighteenth century. Its lowest level was the desk from which the clerk led the congregation in their responses. Above that was the parson's desk from which he read his way through the service. When the time came, he left his desk and climbed the stairs to the top deck from which commanding position the all important sermon was preached. The three decker pulpit with its sleepy clerk and bewigged parson provided the sharp caricaturists of the day with an easy target for ridicule.

Cottesbrooke church was originally cruciform in plan, but the north transept, which lay beyond the pulpit, apparently had no use in the new arrangement and was demolished at some unknown date. The pointed archway which had led from the nave to the transept was simply blocked in half way up, and the rest of the opening was glazed to form a large and rather ungainly window. The south transept was retained but with some interesting alterations. In what might be called the new theatre of the Church, which replaced the old ritual,

the parson shared the stage with the lord of the manor, who often made for himself a place in church hardly less prominent, and usually more comfortable, than the pulpit. At Cottesbrooke, the lords of the manor were the Langhams, and by raising the floor of the south transept of the church they provided themselves with a mausoleum underneath and a family pew, suitably elevated, on top. Being directly opposite the pulpit, the Langham pew has the best view in the church; the best place to see, and the best place to be seen. Today the pew serves as a make-shift organ loft, but in the eighteenth century it would have been carpeted, lined with coloured baize and set with elegant seats for the squire and his family. For their especial comfort the pew was also fitted with its own fireplace, which can still be seen today. By some standards, the Langham family pew was a very modest one. At the Duke of Chandos' church, St Lawrence, Little Stanmore, his family pew stretches across the west end and has the air of a royal box at the opera, its domed ceiling painted with a copy of Raphael's 'Transfiguration'. The family pew of Sir John Kederminster at St Mary's Church in Langley Marish, Buckinghamshire, is perhaps the most élite of all. Lattice-work screens shielded the Kederminster family from the common gaze of the rest of the congregation during the church service, and the pew even had a small library attached for the use of the clergy.

The seating arrangements of the eighteenth-century country church spelt out the social hierarchy of the village, just as the Anglican Church reinforced the values and confirmed the privileges of the Establishment. The squire and parson were often related since it was a common practice for the squire, as patron, to appoint a younger son of the manor to the living of the church. Improvements in agriculture had increased the value of tithes and therefore of country livings, so the parson might now expect to receive a respectable income. This gave him a measure of independence which was probably second only to that of the squire himself, and enabled the clergy to produce some of the finest scholars of the time, like Gilbert White, the famous naturalist who was rector of St Mary's Church at Selborne in Hampshire. Other parsons spent their energies less profitably in gaming and riding with the hunt. The eighteenth century bristled with eccentrics and the clergy seems to have had more than its share. The hunting rector of Berkeswell Church in Warwickshire, one Thomas Cattell, found that his ideas flowed more freely in the saddle and so had a special wooden stool made for him with a padded top which he sat astride to preach his sermon!

Life was cushioned for many of the clergy, especially those who had family ties with the gentry, and parsons fulfilled their duties as their consciences directed. Though many were attentive to their parochial flocks, others were not. Pluralism, whereby one clergyman accepted the livings of several parishes in order to boost his income, was as rife as it had been in the late Middle Ages. Some clerics spent their stipends on high living and hired underpaid curates to do their ecclesiastical chores for them, or just neglected their parishes altogether. On the positive side, the good education and comparative leisure of the clergy, and the fact that since the Reformation they had been allowed to marry, meant that their children were born and raised in

John Wesley, the evangelist who founded Methodism.

an atmosphere of learning. Rectories and vicarages up and down the country became the nurseries of eighteenth- and nineteenth-century culture, providing major literary figures like Samuel Johnson and Jane Austen whose novels reflect much of her vicarage upbringing. Through the pen of another child of the rectory, Joseph Addison, we gain an amusing insight into the relationship of squire and parson. Together with Richard Steele, Addison wrote a periodical called 'The Spectator' which purported to be published by a small club of gentlemen including one Sir Roger de Coverley, an affectionate parody of a country squire. 'Sir Roger,' we are told, 'desired a particular friend of his at the university to find him out a clergyman rather of plain sense than much learning, of a good aspect, a clear voice, a sociable temper, and if possible, a man that understood a little of backgammon.' When a suitable parson had been found, Sir Roger presented him with volumes of the best published sermons, requiring him to deliver one each week.

Although people went to church every Sunday, it was still rare for them to receive Holy Communion more than two or three times a year, and weekly attendances for many had become more a matter of duty than an expression of Christian zeal. Horace Walpole, whose letters provide a graphic description of Georgian England, went to church merely to set an example to the servants. 'A good moral sermon may instruct and benefit them,' he said. The Anglican religion was not one of fear, but of common sense and, above all, tolerance. Anything that smacked of 'enthusiasm' presented an uneasy memory of the fanaticism that had torn the country's religious life apart during the two centuries following the Reformation. Extremes were to be avoided or ignored, and the Established Church settled down into a comfortable middle way.

During the hundred years since the Restoration, there had been a revolution in scientific and technical thought that had completely shaken off the shackles of the medieval world. Now that intellectual revolution was being turned to practical ends and the first distant rumblings of the Industrial Revolution began to be heard. The economic basis of the nation started to shift irrevocably from agriculture and the countryside to the new manufacturing industries of the towns. There the growing commercial class keenly adopted the Established Church as part of the trappings of its success, but in the country the Church slipped further into quiescence. The easy-going mould into which English church life had settled robbed the Church of religious fervour, and left it unable to meet the growing challenge of non-conformity. Workers poured into the rapidly expanding towns making them fertile recruiting ground for non-conformists. John Wesley, who had left the Anglican Church with regret, and others like him were gathering growing armies of Christian soldiers as social change began to leave the Established Church stranded. Parish churches in many places fell into disrepair, either from sheer neglect, or from the declining fortunes of their patrons, or from both. Much of the power of the squirarchy was eclipsed, and the curtain began to fall on the cosy partnership of squire and parson.

8: Suburban Dreams

THE PRESENT REVIVAL OF CHRISTIAN ARCHITECTURE. SEE REFERENCES

The new Gothic dawn, as it was dreamt of by A W N Pugin in his 'Apology for the Revival of Christian Architecture'.

Within a hundred years of its first rumblings, the Industrial Revolution had almost entirely restructured the fabric of English society. The rural population gravitated not only to existing towns and cities, but also to the new urban areas rising on the coal seams of the Midlands and the North. The coal-devouring steam engine gathered up workers who had hitherto been spread thinly throughout the countryside and packed them into factories built around the pit-heads or within easy reach of raw materials by way of the new canals and railways. At the beginning of the nineteenth century, London was the only city with a population over 100,000; by the end of the century, there were more than fifty such cities. The industrial moguls of these new cities were mostly self-made men. Independence and hard cash became the touchstones of a growing class of *nouveau riche*, who were anxious to acquire culture and respectability. They founded institutions and set up charities; they championed organised religion and democracy, in politics but not in industry; they defended the values of the family and sexual morality; and above all they were fiercely patriotic. English influence abroad was at a peak, and the pink blush of the British Empire was spreading steadily across the atlas. On this wave of national self-confidence the Gothic style of architecture was to be revived and carried high.

Previous page
To church on Sunday in the nineteenth century.

234

But while missionaries and colonialists carried the Faith and the 'British way of life' to the four corners of the world, at home all was not well. The grimy suburbs thrown up by the Industrial Revolution were fast becoming strongholds of non-conformism and even atheism. During the late eighteenth and early nineteenth centuries there had been little church building, partly because of the Napoleonic War and partly because of the low ebb of the Established Church itself. So many large industrial communities were without Anglican churches. In an attempt to stem the rising tide of dissent in these areas, a surge of church building was launched, backed by a million pound grant from Parliament. The Church Building Act of 1818 provided for the building of well over two hundred churches in the industrial Midlands and North as well as in the suburbs of the capital. This was the beginning of the busiest period of church building since the century following the Norman Conquest; of the parish churches still in use today, nearly half date from after 1815. Since the needs of country parishes were more than adequately met already, the story of nineteenth-century church architecture is largely that of urban and suburban England. The Established Church was at last rousing itself from the torpor of the eighteenth century to face the challenges of the nineteenth, and in the blackened streets of back-to-back houses it planted great churches – suburban dreams of a new Jerusalem among the 'dark satanic mills'.

The 'Commissioners' Churches' built under the Act of 1818 could be either Classical or Gothic in style – the Commissioners' main concern was that they should be large and inviting, and as economically built as possible. The Classical churches were mostly in the Greek style which had superseded the Italian style of Palladio and was at the height of its popularity between 1810 and 1830. The architect John Nash was one of the Commissioners and his elegant church of All Souls at Langham Place is one of the best Greek Revival churches in London. John Nash's career was very favourably influenced by the Prince Regent, who later became George IV, under whose patronage he was responsible for the development of Regent's Park and Regent's Street in London, and the enlargement of Buckingham Palace. Like any other well-bred gentleman, the Prince Regent had an interest in architecture and the arts, but his partiality for Nash's work may have been mainly due to his enthusiasm for Nash's wife, Mary Anne, who was commonly believed at the time to have been the Prince's mistress. Nash's apparently privileged position and the Classical style in general, which came to be seen as the architectural style of a decadent *ancien régime*, attracted growing criticism. In 1824, George Cruikshank caricatured '*Nash*ional taste' by showing John Nash impaled on the spire of All Souls' Church, and commenting:

> 'Providence sends meat, the Devil sends cooks –
> Parliament sends funds – but who sends the Architects?'

Not all of the Commissioners' Churches were built in classical style – some were Gothic like St Peter's Church at Brighton in West Sussex, built by Charles Barry; St Luke's, Chelsea, in London, by James Savage; and St Peter's, Preston in Lancashire, by Thomas Rickman,

NASHIONAL TASTE !!!

Above
The classical style in general,
and Nashional taste in particular, satirised by George Cruikshank
in a cartoon of 1824 'dedicated
without permission to the
Church Commissioners'.

Right
The Greek Revival style represented
at its best by All Souls', Langham
Place, London, designed by
John Nash.

St Luke's, Chelsea, London,
designed by James Savage, is one of
the few Commissioners' Churches
built in the Gothic style.

the writer on Gothic architecture. But although these churches are Gothic in their ornament and use of the pointed arch, in their general composition they still have the calm and restraint of Georgian architecture, rather than the vitality of the later Victorian Gothic churches. In fact, Gothic architecture had never been completely ousted by Classical. The occasional country church had still been raised in the unfashionable medieval style. But the Gothic Revival was not built on survival. It was the result of the timely bringing together of taste and scholarship, political reform and religious enthusiasm, in a way that led inevitably to a re-awakening of the Gothic style.

The origins of the Gothic Revival lay in the eighteenth-century Romantic Movement in art and literature, which was in itself perhaps a reaction against the creeping tide of mechanisation. The movement had two faces: nostalgia and mystery. The first is typified by the works of writers like Horace Walpole, Thomas Peacock and Thomas Gray, and the second by the dark, forbidding atmosphere of 'Nightmare', painted by Henry Fuseli in 1782. The words 'abbey' and 'castle' became synonymous with romance and mystery. A taste for the picturesque developed, and a folly built to imitate a ruined abbey in an otherwise classically landscaped park, provided a *frisson* of excitement like Mary Shelley's 'Frankenstein', the epitome of the fashionable horror novel, read by the secure fireside of an elegant drawing-room. A fascination grew for all things 'Gothick'. As early as 1750, Horace Walpole had begun decking out his villa at Strawberry Hill in Twickenham with Gothic ornament to transform it into his very own Gothic castle. But the transformation he achieved was only skin-deep. Since the villa was Georgian in structure, the extravagant Gothic details of its interior were applied to rooms of inappropriately classical proportions and give the impression of stage scenery leaning against the walls. Strawberry Hill was, however, the first attempt to revive a medieval style for a complete, functional building and was, therefore, the first architectural milestone on the road to the Gothic Revival.

The second milestone was Fonthill Abbey, designed towards the end of the eighteenth century by James Wyatt for the wealthy eccentric, William Beckford. It was originally intended to be a particularly grand folly in the form of a partly ruined abbey, but Beckford soon decided that he wanted a building in which he could actually live and act out a medieval dream-world, complete with footmen dressed as monks! The big difference between Strawberry Hill and Fonthill Abbey is that Wyatt was not content to create a

The library of Horace Walpole's 'Gothick' villa at Strawberry Hill, Middlesex.

Gothic impression by grafting on the appropriate ornamental detail. He tried instead to construct the building itself in Gothic fashion. The symmetry of classicism was carefully avoided, and the architectural masses of the building were grouped in a Romantic manner around a central octagonal tower which soared over ninety metres (276 feet) into the air. It was a brave attempt to produce a more completely Gothic building, and as such formed the main link between Strawberry Hill 'Gothick' and the churches of the Gothic Revival proper, when the structural basis of the Gothic style became more fully understood. Sadly, Fonthill Abbey is now a missing link. Built too quickly and too insubstantially, it soon tumbled down. On his death bed the master mason confessed to having cut corners on the foundations, and today Fonthill Abbey is known to us only from illustrations and a very small surviving fragment.

Architecture since the Reformation had been going through a series of revivals of one sort or another. So the nineteenth century inherited a stylistic eclecticism – a catalogue of architectural styles from which its architects might choose. As well as Gothic and Roman Classical, there was now Greek Classical, Chinese as used by William Chambers for the Pagoda at Kew Gardens, and, by 1821, there was even the exotic Indian fantasy of the Royal Pavilion at Brighton designed by John Nash. Architects were spoilt for choice. Now that style had been divorced from both time and place, what were the

Fonthill Abbey, Wiltshire, built by James Wyatt as a Gothic dream-world for the wealthy eccentric, William Beckford.

criteria by which the style for any particular building could be decided? The answer came that the chief criterion should be its function. The question was asked and answered by Agustus Welby Northmore Pugin, the son of a French refugee who had worked as a draughtsman for John Nash. Pugin believed that a building should be designed to suit its function, and that decoration should be subordinate to structure. As far as churches were concerned, the very fact that they functioned as Christian buildings ruled out the Classical style which he saw as being intrinsically pagan. Classical churches, like the then recently built parish church of St Pancras, Euston Road in London, whose porches were copied from the caryatid porch of the Erechtheion on the Acropolis in Athens, were simply a contradiction in terms, and, furthermore an affront to Christianity. A Christian building, Pugin argued, must have a Christian style and a Christian architect. The greatest buildings had been achieved when all held the Catholic faith during the Middle Ages, therefore the only conceivable style for Christian architecture was Gothic. In 1836, Pugin published his first book, called, 'Contrasts: or a parallel between the noble edifices of the fourteenth and fifteenth centuries and similar buildings of the present day, showing the present decay of taste, accompanied by an appropriate text'. In the book he illustrates

Above right
*The north porch of St Pancras',
Euston Road, designed by
W and H W Inwood in the Greek
Revival style.*

Above
*The caryatid porch of the Erechtheion
on the Acropolis, on which the porches
at St Pancras' were closely modelled.*

Right
*Augustus Welby Northmore Pugin,
the pioneer of the Gothic Revival who
condemned as 'pagan' the classical
style of churches like St Pancras', and
considered Gothic the only style fit for
Christian architecture. (Painting by
J R Herbert.)*

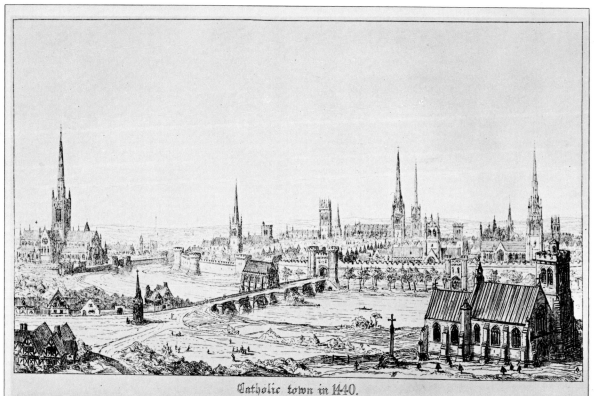

Catholic town in 1440.

1. St. Michaels on the Hill. 2. Queens Crofs. 3. St. Thomas's Chapel. 4. St. Maries Abbey. 5. All Saints. 6. St. Johns. 7. St. Peters. 8. St. Alkmunds. 9. St. Maries. 10. St. Edmunds. 11. Grey Friars. 12. St. Cuthberts. 13. Guild hall. 14. Trinity. 15. St. Olaves. 16. St. Botolphs.

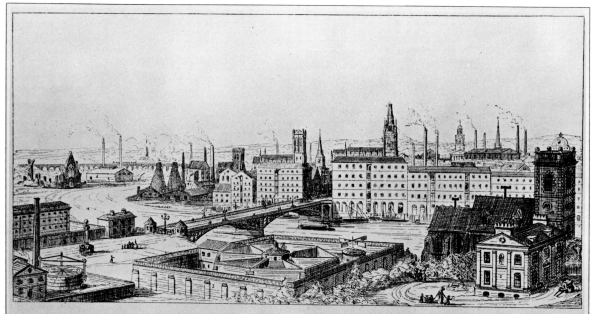

THE SAME TOWN IN 1840.

1. St. Michaels Tower, rebuilt in 1750. 2. New Parsonage House & Pleasure Grounds. 3. The New Jail. 4. Gas Works. 5. Lunatic Asylum. 6. Iron Works & Ruins of St. Maries Abbey. 7. Mt. Evans Chapel. 8. Baptist Chapel. 9. Unitarian Chapel. 10. New Church. 11. New Town Hall & Concert Room. 12. Wesleyan Centenary Chapel. 13. New Christian Society. 14. Quakers Meeting. 15. Socialist Hall of Science.

Above
The frontispiece of 'Contrasts', a book of Gothic propaganda by Pugin which used pairs of plates to compare the medieval world to that of the nineteenth century, much to the detriment of the latter.

Left
One of Pugin's contrasts: above, *the fifteenth-century town filled with churches whose steeples stretch up into the clear sky and,* below, *the same town in the nineteenth century now dominated by factories and institutions, its churches in ruins, and its skyline pierced by smoking chimneys.*

his theory that good men build good architecture by pairs of drawings comparing the medieval world with his own. The Catholic town of the fifteenth century, resplendent with its churches and abbeys, is contrasted with the same town in the nineteenth century, dominated by factories, the prison and the lunatic asylum, and its churches run down or ruined. The contrasts are sometimes witty and often exaggerated, but, despite their naivety, they made their point and things were never quite the same afterwards.

Pugin had been raised as a Non-conformist, but had been converted to the Roman Catholic Church. It is interesting to speculate whether or not the Gothic Revival would have succeeded had it not been for the legislation of the 1820s which provided for the emancipation of Catholics. Since 1791, when Catholics had been granted freedom of worship, the Catholic Church had won a steady trickle of converts, and this doubtless contributed to an atmosphere in which what we today would call 'high church' practices became more generally acceptable. The new respectability of Catholicism also made it possible to express an interest in and enthusiasm for medieval culture without cries of 'Popery!'. It is questionable whether Pugin's Catholic voice would have had the effect it did, had not his views been endorsed by the opinions of Anglican groups like the Tractarian or Oxford Movement and the Cambridge Camden Society, later known as the Ecclesiological Society. Together they provided an ecclesiastical and intellectual backing that transformed Pugin's romantic views into a vision of the Gothic world which permeated every church in the land.

The Tractarian Movement emerged in 1835 at Oxford, where a group of young priests who were appalled by the spiritually impoverished religious life of preceding years, sought to bring back the character of Catholic doctrine and, eventually, ritual to the Anglican Church. The Cambridge Camden Society was formed a few years later by an enthusiastic group of undergraduates with the expressed aim of restoring the architecture, arrangement and ritual of medieval times to English churches. The influence of the Cambridge Camden Society was responsible among other things for the introduction of the surpliced choir in their now familiar position in the stalls of the chancel, and for moving the organ from its gallery to the chancel or a nearby chapel so as to be close to the choir – a move that was not usually an improvement as far as the look of the church was concerned. The Society published an influential magazine called the 'Ecclesiologist', and *ecclesiology* became the new watchword of the day. The term had been coined by these enthusiasts and was defined by one of the Camden Society's founders as 'the science of worship carried out in all its material development'.

At the heart of ecclesiology was the firm assertion that Christian architecture was Gothic architecture. Furthermore, it was argued that Gothic architecture had reached its spiritual peak in the early fourteenth century with the Decorated style – or Middle Pointed as the ecclesiologists themselves referred to it. The preceding Early English style was considered immature, and the succeeding Perpendicular style decadent. But it was not enough to build churches that were just copies of medieval buildings – the job of the Victorian

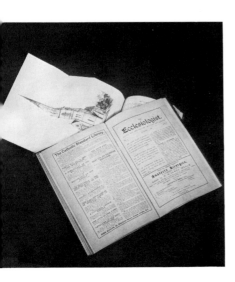

Above
*A bound volume of 'Ecclesiologist'
magazines, the mouthpiece of the
Cambridge Camden Society.*

Opposite
*An illustration from 'The Builder'
magazine showing William Butterfield's design for All Saints',
Margaret Street, London, the first
church to epitomise the new
ecclesiology. (See also page 247)*

architects as the Camden Society saw it, was to pick up where the
Middle Pointed had left off, to relearn its architectural vocabulary and
develop a progressive Gothic style fit for their own time. The
followers of the Camden Society became vigilantes guarding against
'incorrectness' in church architecture, and their magazine, the 'Ecclesiologist', publicly condemned those architects who fell short of
the mark.

The 'correct' style went hand in hand with correct arrangement
and planning of the church. Auditory churches were anathema to
the ecclesiologists. Box pews were to be removed since they prevented the congregation from seeing the altar, the true focus of the
church, and because, being rented not free, they were a symbol of
class distinction. In their place, open benches were to be set all facing
to the east. The altar itself was to be raised above the level of the
nave, and the lesson read from a lectern in the nave opposite the
pulpit. Three decker pulpits, like the box pews, were to be discarded.
Precise attention to the arrangement of the church was important
because, as the ecclesiologists saw it, all the features of the church had
had symbolic significance to the medieval congregation, and by
bringing them together in the correct way a kind of spiritual synthesis
could be achieved.

The first church to embody fully the ecclesiologists' ideals was
All Saints' Church, Margaret Street in London. It was completed in
1859 and was the work of William Butterfield who was just the kind
of Christian architect of whom Pugin had dreamed. Butterfield's own
life-style was austere and ascetic, and his employees were subject to
the pious discipline that was thought to have characterised the
building of a medieval church, but was in fact a romantic product of
Victorian imagination. There were no lunch breaks in his office, and
on the building site work was accompanied by prayer and the rule of
silence. Butterfield was a meticulous man and paid scrupulous attention to the details of his building whether or not they would in the
end be seen. Colour is used liberally throughout All Saints', Margaret
Street, not only as surface decoration but as an integral part of the
structure – 'constructional polychromy' as Butterfield himself called
it. The revival of polychromy was one of the most exciting aspects of
many of the Neo-Gothic churches. Multi-coloured tiles and brick are
set like semi-precious stones with marbles and granites to echo the
frescoes of the Middle Ages in the hard, shiny materials of the
Industrial Revolution. The result is an impressive interior in which
each element of pattern and each patch of colour is choreographed
into a moving evocation of medieval Christianity. It is not surprising
that William Butterfield was the darling of the Camden Society.

The Gothic Revival was accompanied by a revitalisation of
craftsmanship. Craftsmen slowly became accustomed to working
instinctively in the Gothic style, and the work they produced sometimes rivalled that of medieval times. Rattee and Kett of Cambridge
were noted for their fine woodwork; Skidmore and Company for
their metalwork; Hardman and Company for both metalwork and
stained glass; John Keith and Son for church plate; and Clayton and
Bell, and later William Morris, proved that Victorian stained glass
could be as good as any.

In the second half of the century, 'correctness' was relaxed, and thereafter churches were built in a wider range of Gothic styles. Even Romanesque architecture enjoyed a sporadic revival, one of the most striking examples being the church of All Saints at Petersham in Surrey, built in red brick and red terracotta by John Kelly at the beginning of this century.

During the nineteenth century, almost every architect of any standing built churches. Perhaps the most typical architect of the Gothic Revival, and certainly the most prolific, was George Gilbert Scott. Scott was born in 1811 into the family of the Reverend Thomas Scott, the fourth of thirteen children. The parson was something of an amateur architect himself and recognising his son's talent for drawing, he guided him towards a career in architecture. By the 1830s Scott was working in partnership with William Moffat, an association that lasted eleven years before ending rather sourly. Scott had a long and varied career during which he produced many designs of which

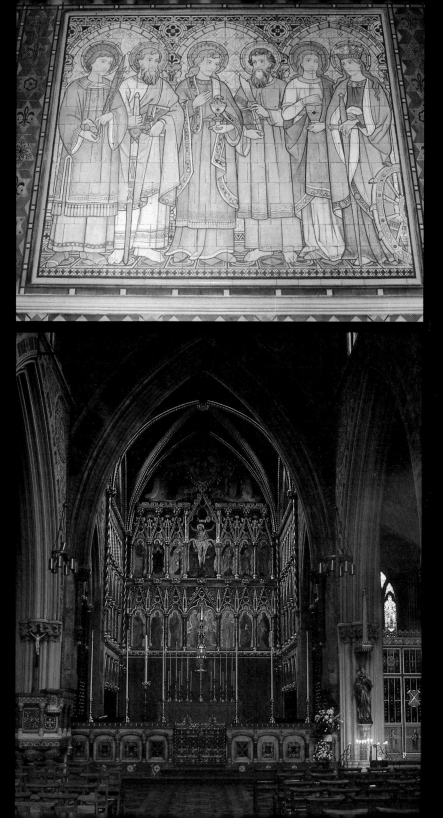

Left
The rich and colourful chancel of the Catholic church of St Giles, Cheadle, Staffordshire, one of the churches where Pugin attempted to put his theories into practice.

Right
George Gilbert Scott, the most prolific architect of the Gothic Revival. Appropriately like a medieval church builder, this photograph shows him holding his compass, the ancient symbol of the architect.

the St Pancras Hotel and the Albert Memorial in Kensington Gardens, both astounding by anyone's standards, are most famous. In many ways the Albert Memorial represented the high spot of Scott's life. It earned him a knighthood, and was, he said, 'the building by which he would have himself judged as a architect'.

As far as his churches are concerned, Scott carried out the principles of the ecclesiologists with a degree of flexibility. He saw himself as an interpreter of the Gothic Revival to the ordinary man in the street. Scott was rather low church in his own religious tastes by contemporary standards, and he felt that some architects had been too rarified and scholarly for many people. He was not a perfectionist like William Butterfield, and his churches are of slightly uneven quality, which is perhaps to be expected when it is realised that he was responsible for the building or restoration of over seven hundred churches. It is difficult to select examples from such a vast and varied output, but it is safe to say that the church of All Souls, Haley Hill, in

Edward Akroyd, the wealthy mill owner who was the generous benefactor of All Souls', Haley Hill, Halifax, West Yorkshire (right), *the finest of George Gilbert Scott's Parish churches.*

Halifax is very worthy of attention, not only because Scott considered it to be 'on the whole my best church', but also for the interesting glimpse its building gives us of the society of the day.

The patron of All Souls' Church was not a member of the gentry but a wealthy mill owner, one Colonel Edward Akroyd. Since the Land Act of 1822 had taken away the traditional rights of the lord of the manor, the nobility seemed less interested in spending their money on church building, and patronage was passing more and more into the hands of the rich industrialists. Like Scott, Edward Akroyd was a self-made man. He had done very well for himself and so Scott's design for All Souls' benefited not only from the architect's own experience, but also from what seemed an inexhaustible supply of cash. The church was to be the centrepiece of Akroydon, a self-contained community built by Edward Akroyd for his workers. The mill-owner himself lived in a rather grand house built in the style of an Italian villa. The story is told that Akroyd chose the site of his new church in such a way that from the windows of his house, it would

Part of one of Scott's own drawings for All Souls', Haley Hill, showing the west door and great west window.

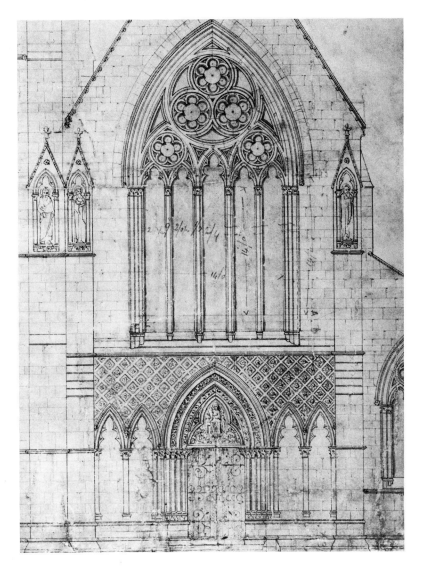

completely overshadow the Congregationalist church that was being built in the centre of Halifax by a rival family of mill-owners – the Crossleys.

All Souls' was commissioned when Gilbert Scott was forty-four years old and reaching the peak of his career. The assured handling of the Gothic style here shows the confidence he had acquired. Decoration is always in proportion, always an integrated part of the structural design; though exuberant, it never seems superfluous. The most impressive view of the church is provided by the west front. A wide flight of steps leads up to the west door which is set in a blind arcade of sharply-pointed arches. Above, a great window with Geometrical tracery is flanked by two tall buttresses, the top sections of which are hollowed out to form niches for statues. Altogether there are twenty-seven almost life-sized figures to be found on the outside of the church. Between the west window and the doorway beneath, the wall surface is decorated with a rich diaper pattern. To the north of the west front, the tower and spire lead the eye along an elegantly carved

path to the sky. Rising to almost seventy-three metres (236 feet), All Souls' has the second tallest spire in Yorkshire, beating the spire of Akroyd's rival's church by just one foot!

Scott's church at Haley Hill won immediate acclaim from the 'Ecclesiologist' magazine. In 1860 it devoted four and a half pages to an enthusiastic account of the church, and later in the year affirmed that 'in plan and style this building is the legitimate descendant of the old English Pointed parish churches' – the ultimate accolade for a Gothic Revival church.

But today Gilbert Scott's masterpiece, like many other churches, is in trouble. The building has become structurally unsound and its parish can no longer afford to maintain it, so there it stands, locked and redundant, and slowly crumbling. Paradoxically, the extravagant use of several different building stones in one church, made possible by the mobility created by the railways, has been the downfall of All Souls'. For the exterior facing Scott used stone from two different parts of the country, a magnesium limestone and a local sandstone. Unfortunately, every time it rains the limestone turns the rain-water into a dilute acid which erodes the sandstone. So the church sits on Haley Hill literally eating itself away until the half-million pounds or so it would take to restore it can be found.

Were it not for the restoration of ancient parish churches carried out, albeit too drastically on occasion, by the architects of the nineteenth century, we would have precious few churches of interest left today. surely we owe it to those architects to preserve the best products of their own minds and hands. Their churches, after all, present a unique and irreplaceable expression of their time, and of that radiant Victorian dream of a medieval world that never was.

Epilogue

The story of the English parish church did not end with the Neo-Gothic churches of the nineteenth century, but never again were churches built in such number or with such confidence. Despite the ardour of the Victorians, the revival of medieval architecture failed to engender a popular revival of medieval faith. It was not possible to turn the clock back. The Church had lost most of its economic and political power during the sixteenth and seventeenth centuries, and by the twentieth much of its social and philanthropic influence had been taken over by the government and charitable institutions. Only its spiritual role is left. And in that it holds no monopoly. Today, less than one third of church-goers in the United Kingdom belong to the Established Church. Its claim to being the national church now rests on history rather than patronage, and the parish church has to compete for its congregation not only with other Christian denominations, but with other religions as well – Muslims in this country outnumber Baptists by nearly two to one. And even of those who style themselves 'C of E', many appear from the record of their attendance at church to believe its chief function to be that of a picturesque backdrop to Saturday afternoon weddings.

Organised religion plays no major part in most people's lives any more. The twentieth century has inherited more churches than it needs or can afford to maintain. The parish church is no longer the focus of every community. A few redundant churches are demolished, others are elbowed into the backstreets as old towns are replanned to suit the modern demands of property speculators and motor cars. In the country, villages are usually still dominated, architecturally at least, by their parish churches. But the legacy of their medieval heyday is often far too large for village requirements, and their upkeep grows more expensive every year. Many churches attract more sight-seers during the week than worshippers on Sunday, and parochial church councils sometimes resent spending a considerable part of their small budgets on maintaining a building for the benefit of visitors who stay ten minutes and leave without a prayer. A few pence in the wall safe eases the conscience, but is not enough to prevent a church from falling into decay.

But how many of our churches are worth saving anyway? The Church, we are told, is not its buildings but its members, and some clergymen have begun to see their old churches as burdens not only financially but spiritually too. A medieval church, it is argued, presents a romantic image of religion that is outmoded and counter-

A carved corbel among the rubble of St John's, Kilburn, London.

productive. The Church must be relevant to today. And in its drive to be so it chases the coat-tails of social change like the 'ton-up' vicars of the 1960s on their motorbikes. But what architecture, if any, does such relevance lead to, and does it strengthen or weaken people's need for religion? In the past the Church provided a refuge, if only an illusory one, from the real world. In aligning itself to the ways of modern society it gives tacit approval to the values of that society. Perhaps instead it should again provide an alternative, a restatement, in the face of the bewildering pace of technological progress, of underlying and unchanging human values. But when life grows increasingly comfortable for more and more people, what call is there for an alternative?

Lack of interest among the laity seems to be matched by a loss of confidence among the clergy, and the Church appears unwilling to exert what authority it still retains. In a recent, widely-publicised High Court case, the law against blasphemy was invoked for the first time for more than half a century. Here if anywhere was an issue on which the Church's voice should have been heard, but it remained silent. In its anxiety not to give offence the Church has become bland and uninspiring. The new prayer book, the 'Alternative Service Book' published in 1980, is one of soft options. It offers choices and alternatives to suit all tastes, and contentious passages may be omitted altogether. The impression is one of seeking popular approval, of a Church not leading, but wanting to be led. 'The Church as it now is no human power can save,' said Thomas Arnold, the famous head-master of Rugby School, at a time when many believed that the Established Church would not survive in the nineteenth century. He was wrong. So perhaps pessimism is short-sighted. But in our age of uncertainty and contradiction it is not easy for the Church to find a definitive role, and it may even take some turn in the course of history to create one. When it does, then perhaps church architecture too will find a new and positive form.

In the meantime our national heritage of historic churches must be protected. But where will the money come from? Who are the modern patrons of the Church – the equivalents of the nineteenth-century industrialists, the lords of the manor, the wool merchants and the Norman barons? It will not be possible to preserve all our ancient churches, and in the end uneasy choices will inevitably have to be made between one church and another. Let us hope that they are wise ones. For if we leave the best of our parish churches to decay into dust, our great-grandchildren may look back on us as contemptible vandals. Future generations cannot be denied the pleasure we have in discovering English churches.

1001 Parish Churches

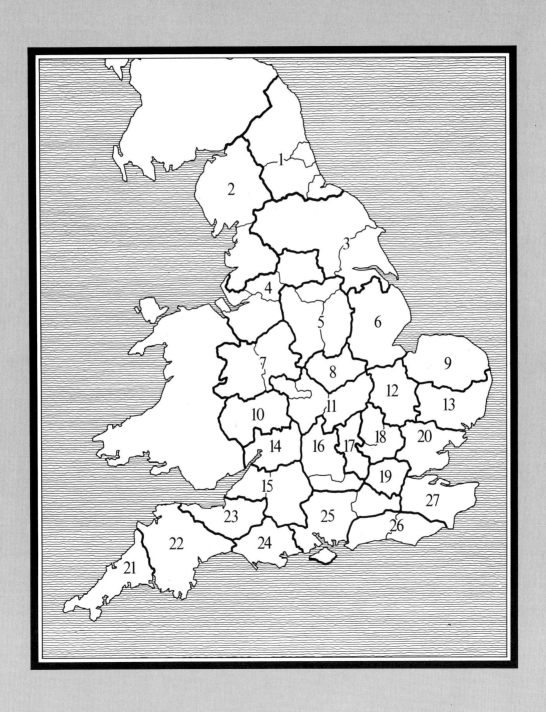

Making any kind of selection from England's thousands of ancient parish churches is of necessity an invidious exercise; every church has something to offer the visitor. The number of churches mentioned in this book has been kept to a minimum in order to illustrate the features and the ideas discussed without interrupting the flow of the text. To redress the balance, the following list sets out 1001 parish churches which are well worth a detour to visit. For the purposes of this list, the country has been divided into twenty seven areas from north to south (see previous page). Italics indicate those churches which are generally agreed to be of outstanding interest and should not be missed.

Area One

CLEVELAND

Billingham	St Cuthbert
Hartlepool	*St Hilda*
Kirkleathem	St Cuthbert

DURHAM

Brancepeth	*St Brandon*
Chester-le-Street	St Mary and St Cuthbert
Darlington	St Cuthbert
Escomb	*St John the Evangelist*
Gibside Chapel	No dedication
Haughton-le-Skerne	St Andrew
Lanchester	All Saints
Pittington	St Lawrence
Seaham	St Mary
Sedgefield	*St Edmund*
Staindrop	St Mary
Stockton-on-Tees	St Thomas

NORTHUMBERLAND

Alnwick	St Michael
Bamburgh	St Aidan
Blanchland	Abbey Church of St Mary the Virgin
Bolam	St Andrew
Hexham	*Abbey Church of St Andrew*
Kirknewton	St Gregory the Great
Morpeth	St Mary the Virgin
Norham	St Cuthbert
Ovingham	St Mary the Virgin
Ponteland	St Mary the Virgin
Seaton Delaval	Our Lady
Warkworth	St Lawrence

TYNE AND WEAR

Jarrow	St Paul
Monkwearmouth	*St Peter*
Newcastle upon Tyne	*All Saints, Gosforth*
	St Andrew, Newgate Street
	Cathedral Church of St Nicholas
	St Anne
Roker	*St Andrew*
Tynemouth	Christ Church

Area Two

CUMBRIA

Abbey Town	Holm Cultram Abbey
Armathwaite	Chapel of Christ and St Mary
Beckermet	St John the Baptist
Bewcastle	St Cuthbert
Bolton	All Saints
Brougham	St Ninian
Cartmel	*Priory Church of St Mary and St Michael*
Crosthwaite	St Kentigern
Grasmere	St Oswald
Greystoke	St Andrew
Isel	St Michael
Kirkby Lonsdale	St Mary the Virgin
Kirkby Stephen	Dedication unknown
Lanercost	*Priory Church of St Mary Magdalene*
Millom	*Holy Trinity*
Nether Wasdale	Dedication unknown
Ormside	St James
Over Denton	No dedication and privately owned
St Bees	Priory Church of St Mary and St Bega
Torpenhow	St Michael
Ulpha	Chapel of St John the Baptist
Witherslack	St Paul

LANCASHIRE

Halsall	*St Cuthbert*
Heysham	St Peter
Lancaster	Priory Church of St Mary
Ormskirk	St Peter and St Paul
Poulton-le-Fylde	St Chad
Rufford	St Mary the Virgin
Slaidburn	St Andrew
Up Holland	Priory Church of St Thomas the Martyr
Whalley	*St Mary and All Saints*
Woodplumpton	St Anne

Area Three

HUMBERSIDE

Adlingfleet	All Saints
Barton-upon-Humber	*St Mary*
Beverley	*Minster Church of St John the Evangelist*
	St Mary
Bottesford	St Peter
Boynton	St Andrew
Bridlington	Priory Church of St Mary
Eastrington	St Michael
Flamborough	St Oswald
Great Coates	St Nicholas
Great Driffield	All Saints
Hedon	*St Augustine*

Holme-upon-Spalding Moor	*All Saints*
Howden	*Minster Church of St Peter and St Paul*
Kingston-upon-Hull	Holy Trinity
Lockington	St Mary the Virgin
North Newbald	St Nicholas
Patrington	*St Patrick*

NORTH YORKSHIRE

Alne	St Mary the Virgin
Bedale	St Gregory
Birkin	St Mary the Virgin
Bolton Percy	All Saints
Bossall	St Botolph
Coxwold	St Michael
Easby	St Agatha
Hemingborough	*St Mary*
Lastingham	*St Mary*
Nun Monkton	St Mary
Old Malton	*Priory Church of St Mary*
Pickering	St Peter and St Paul
Scarborough	St Mary
Selby	Abbey Church of Our Lord, St Mary and St Germain
Skelton (near York)	*St Giles*
Studley Royal	St Mary the Virgin
Thirsk	*St Mary*
Wensley	*Holy Trinity*
Whitby	*St Mary*
York	*All Saints, North Street*
	All Saints, Pavement
	St Denys, Walmgate
	Holy Trinity, Goodramgate
	Holy Trinity, Micklegate
	St Martin-cum-Gregory
	St Mary, Castlegate
	St Michael-le-Belfry
	St Olave, Marygate

Area Four

CHESHIRE

Acton	*St Mary*
Astbury	*St Mary*
Baddiley	St Michael
Bunbury	*St Boniface*

Chester	St John the Baptist
Congleton	St Peter
Gawsworth	St James
Great Budworth	*St Mary and All Saints*
Lower Peover	St Oswald
Malpas	*St Oswald*
Mobberley	St Wilfred
Nantwich	*St Mary*
Nether Alderley	St Mary
Over Peover	St Lawrence
Shotwick	St Michael
Winwick	St Oswald
Wrenbury	St Margaret

GREATER MANCHESTER

Manchester	St Anne
	St Thomas, Ardwick Green
	St Luke, Cheetham
	St James, Didsbury
	St Leonard, Middleton
Salford	Sacred Trinity

MERSEYSIDE

Billinge	St Aidan
Liverpool	All Hallows, Allerton
	All Saints, Childwall
	St Agnes, Virgin and Martyr, Sefton Park
	Holy Trinity, Wavertree
Sefton	*St Helen*

WEST YORKSHIRE

Adel	St John the Baptist
Almondbury	All Hallows
Darrington	St Luke and All Saints
Halifax	St John the Baptist
Horbury	St Peter and St Leonard
Leeds	Holy Trinity
	St Bartholomew, Armley
	St John the Evangelist, Briggate
	St Michael, Headingley
Wakefield	Cathedral Church of All Saints

Area Five

DERBYSHIRE

Ashbourne	*St Oswald*
Chesterfield	*St Mary and All Saints*
Dale Abbey	All Saints
Derby	Cathedral Church of All Saints
Eckington	St Peter and St Paul
Melbourne	*St Michael and St Mary*
Morley	*St Matthew*
Norbury	*St Mary and St Barlok*
Repton	St Wystan
Sandiacre	*St Giles*
Steetley	Chapel of All Saints
Tideswell	St John the Baptist
Tissington	St Mary
Trusley	All Saints
Whitwell	St Lawrence
Wirksworth	St Mary the Virgin
Youlgreave	All Saints

NOTTINGHAMSHIRE

Blyth	*St Mary and St Martin*
East Markham	St John the Baptist
Egmanton	St Mary
Hawton	*All Saints*
Holme	St Giles
Newark	*St Mary Magdalene*
Normanton-on-Trent	*St Matthew*
Nottingham	*St Mary the Virgin*
Teversal	St Katherine
Willoughby-on-the-Wolds	St Mary and All Saints
Worksop	Priory Church of Our Lady and St Cuthbert

SOUTH YORKSHIRE

Ecclesfield	*St Mary the Virgin*
Fishlake	*St Cuthbert*
Hatfield	St Lawrence
Rotherham	All Saints
Sheffield	Cathedral Church of St Peter and St Paul
Sprotborough	St Mary
Tickhill	*St Mary the Virgin*

Algarkirk	St Peter and St Paul
Bicker	St Swithin
Boston	*St Botolph*
Brant Broughton	St Helen
Burgh Le Marsh	St Peter and St Paul
Caistor	St Peter and St Paul
Coates-by-Stow	St Edith
Croft	All Saints
Crowland	Abbey Church of St Mary with St Guthlac and St Bartholomew
Croxby	All Saints
Ewerby	*St Andrew*
Folkingham	St Andrew
Gainsborough	All Saints
Gedney	*St Mary Magdalene*
Grantham	*St Wulfrum*
Great Ponton	Holy Cross
Halton Holgate	St Andrew
Heckington	*St Andrew*
Ingoldmells	St Peter and St Paul
Irnham	St Andrew
Kingerby	St Peter
Kirkstead	*St Leonard*
Langton-by-Spilsby	St Peter and St Paul
Leadenham	St Swithin
Lincoln	*St Benedict*
Long Sutton	*St Mary*
Louth	*St James*
Moulton	All Saints
Northorpe	St John the Baptist
Rothwell	St Mary
Saltfleetby	All Saints
Sausthorpe	St Andrew
Silk Willoughby	*St Denys*
Skirbeck	St Nicholas
Sleaford	St Denys
Spalding	*St Mary and St Nicholas*
Stamford	*All Saints*
	St Mary
Stow	*St Mary*
Swaton	St Michael
Sutterton	St Mary the Virgin
Tattershall	*Collegiate Church of the Holy Trinity*
Theddlethorpe	St Helen
Threekingham	St Peter in Chains
Uffington	St Michael and All Angels
Westborough	All Saints
Weston	St Mary
Whaplode	St Mary
Winthorpe	St Mary
Wrangle	*St Mary the Virgin and St Nicholas*

Acton Burnell	St Michael
Bromfield	Priory Church of St Mary the Virgin
Kinlet	St John the Baptist
Langley Chapel	Dedication unknown
Ludlow	*St Lawrence*
Lydbury North	St Michael and All Angels
Melverley	St Peter
Onibury	St Michael
Richard's Castle	St Bartholomew
St Martin's	St Martin
Shifnal	St Andrew
Shrewsbury	*St Chad*
	Collegiate Church of St Mary the Virgin
Stottesdon	St Mary
Tong	Collegiate Church of St Bartholomew
Whitchurch	St Alkmund

Alrewas	All Saints
Blymhill	St Mary
Burton-on-Trent	St Chad
Checkley	St Mary and All Saints
Clifton Campville	*St Andrew*
Eccleshall	Holy Trinity
Enville	St Mary the Blessed Virgin
Gnosall	St Lawrence
Hamstall Ridware	St Michael and All Angels
Hoar Cross	*Holy Angels*
Ingestre	*St Mary the Virgin*
Mayfield	St John the Baptist
Norbury	St Peter
Penkridge	St Michael and All Angels
Sandon	All Saints
Stafford	St Mary
	St Chad
Tamworth	Collegiate Church of St Editha
Tutbury	Priory Church of St Mary the Virgin

Appleby Magna	St Michael
Bottesford	*St Mary the Virgin*
Breedon-on-the-Hill	*St Mary and St Hardulph*
Brooke	St Peter
Church Langton	St Peter
Claybrooke	St Peter
Clipsham	*St Mary*
Empingham	*St Peter*
Gaddesby	St Luke
Ketton	*St Mary the Virgin*
King's Norton	St John the Baptist
Langham	*St Peter and St Paul*
Leicester	St Margaret
	Cathedral Church of St Martin
	Collegiate Church of St Mary de Castro
Lyddington	*St Andrew*
Melton Mowbray	*St Mary the Virgin*
Oakham	*All Saints*
Peatling Magna	All Saints
Ryhall	*St John the Evangelist*
Stapleford	St Mary Magdalene
Staunton Harold	*Holy Trinity*
Stoke Dry	*St Andrew*
Stoke Golding	*St Margaret*
Teigh	Holy Trinity
Thornton	St Peter
Tickencote	*St Peter*
Tixover	St Luke
Twycross	St James the Great
Whissendine	*St Andrew*

Attleborough	*St Mary*
Beeston-next-Mileham	St Mary
Binham	*Priory Church of St Mary and the Holy Cross*
Blakeney	*St Nicholas*
Bressingham	St John the Baptist
Brisley	St Bartholomew
Cawston	*St Agnes*
Cley-next-the-Sea	*St Margaret*
East Dereham	*St Nicholas*

East Harling	St Peter and St Paul
Emneth	St Edmund
Gooderstone	St George
Great Walsingham	St Peter
Great Yarmouth	*St Nicholas*
Gunton	St Andrew
Hales	St Margaret
Ingham	*Holy Trinity*
King's Lynn	*Priory Church of St Margaret*
	Chapel of St Nicholas
Knapton	St Peter and St Paul
Little Walsingham	St Mary
Ludham	St Katherine
North Creake	St Mary the Virgin
North Elmham	*St Mary*
North Runcton	*All Saints*
Norwich	*St Peter Mancroft*
	St George, Tombland
Pulham	St Mary the Virgin
Ranworth	*St Helen*
Salle	St Peter and St Paul
Shelton	St Mary
Snettisham	St Mary
South Creake	Our Lady St Mary
Stody	St Mary
Swaffham	*St Peter and St Paul*
Terrington St Clement	St Clement
Thorpe Market	St Margaret
Tilney All Saints	All Saints
Trunch	*St Botolph*
Tunstead	St Mary the Virgin
Upwell	St Peter
Walpole St Peter	*St Peter*
Walsoken	All Saints
West Walton	*St Mary the Virgin*
The Wiggenhalls	St German
	St Mary Magdalene
	St Mary the Virgin
Wiveton	St Mary the Virgin
Worstead	St Mary
Wymondham	Abbey Church of St Mary and St Thomas of Canterbury

Area Ten

HEREFORD AND WORCESTER

Abbey Dore	*Abbey Church of the Holy Trinity and St Mary*

Aymestrey	St John the Baptist and St Alkmund
Bacton	St Faith
Bishopstone	St Lawrence
Bredon	*St Giles*
Brinsop	St George
Broadway	*St Eadburgha*
Brockhampton	All Saints
Castle Frome	*St Michael*
Chaddesley Corbett	*St Cassian*
Clodock	St Clydawg
Croft	St Michael and All Angels
Croome d'Abitot	*St Mary Magdalene*
Eardisley	*St Mary Magdalene*
Eastnor	St John the Baptist
Eaton Bishop	*St Michael and All Angels*
Elmley Castle	St Mary the Virgin
Fownhope	St Mary
Garway	St Michael and All Angels
Great Witley	*St Michael and All Angels*
Hereford	*All Saints*
Hoarwithy	St Katherine
Holt	St Martin
Kilpeck	*St Mary and St David*
Ledbury	*St Michael and All Angels*
Leominster	*Priory Church of St Peter and St Paul*
Little Malvern	Priory Church of St Mary, St Giles and St John the Evangelist
Madley	*The Nativity of the Blessed Virgin Mary*
Malvern	*Priory Church of St Mary the Virgin and St Michael*
Martley	St Peter
Monnington-on-Wye	St Mary
Much Cowarne	St Mary the Virgin
Newland	St Leonard
Ombersley	St Andrew
Overbury	St Faith
Pembridge	*St Mary the Virgin*
Pershore	*Abbey Church of the Holy Cross with St Eadburgha*
Rowlstone	St Peter
St Margaret's	*St Margaret*
Shobdon	*St John the Evangelist*
Strensham	St John the Baptist
Stretton Sugwas	St Mary Magdalene

Tyberton	St Mary
Warndon	St Nicholas
Weobley	*St Peter and St Paul*
Wickhamford	St John the Baptist
Worcester	*All Saints*
	St Swithin

Area Eleven

NORTHAMPTONSHIRE

Aldwincle	All Saints
Aynho	St Michael
Barnack	*St John the Baptist*
Brixworth	*All Saints*
Castor	*St Kyneburgha*
Daventry	Holy Cross
Earls Barton	*All Saints*
Finedon	*St Mary the Virgin*
Fotheringhay	*St Mary the Virgin and All Saints*
Geddington	St Mary Magdalene
Higham Ferrers	*St Mary the Virgin*
Kettering	*St Peter and St Paul*
King's Sutton	*St Peter*
Lowick	*St Peter*
Northampton	*All Saints*
	Holy Sepulchre
	St Peter, Weston Favell
Oundle	*St Peter*
Passenham	St Guthlac
Raunds	St Peter
Rothwell	Holy Trinity
Stanford-on-Avon	St Nicholas
Stow-Nine-Churches	St Peter and St Paul
Tichmarsh	*St Mary the Virgin*
Warmington	St Mary the Virgin
Wellingborough	St Mary the Virgin
Whiston	*St Mary the Virgin*

WARWICKSHIRE

Astley	*St Mary*
Brailes	*St George*
Coleshill	*St Peter and St Paul*
Compton Wynyates	St Mary Magdalene
Great Packington	St James
Lapworth	St Mary the Virgin
Merevale	St Mary the Virgin
Over Whiteacre	St Leonard
Preston-on-Stour	The Blessed Virgin Mary
Stratford-on-Avon	*Holy Trinity*

Tredington	St Gregory
Warwick	*Collegiate Church of St Mary*
Wootton Wawen	*St Peter*

WEST MIDLANDS

Berkswell	St John the Baptist
Binley	St Bartholomew
Birmingham	Cathedral Church of St Philip
	St Peter and St Paul Aston
	St Agatha, Sparkbrook
Castle Bromwich	*St Mary and St Margaret*
Knowle	St John the Baptist, St Lawrence and St Anne
Wolverhampton	*Collegiate Church of St Peter*
	St John the Evangelist

Area Twelve

CAMBRIDGESHIRE

Alconbury	St Peter and St Paul
Babraham	St Peter
Bartlow	St Mary
Bottisham	*Holy Trinity*
Buckden	St Mary
Burwell	*St Mary the Blessed Virgin*
Cherry Hinton	St Andrew
Chesterton	St Michael
Glatton	St Nicholas
Great Paxton	Holy Trinity
Haslingfield	All Saints
Ickleton	St Mary Magdalene
Isleham	*St Andrew*
Landwade	Chapel of St Nicholas
Leighton Bromswold	*St Mary*
Leverington	*St Leonard*
Little Gidding	*St John the Evangelist*
March	*St Wendreda*
Over	St Mary the Virgin
St Neots	*St Mary the Virgin*
Soham	St Andrew
Sutton	St Andrew
Tilbrook	All Saints
Trumpington	St Mary and St Michael
Westley Waterless	St Mary the Less

Whittlesey	*St Mary the Virgin*
Wimpole	St Andrew
Wisbech	St Peter and St Paul
Wittering	All Saints
Yaxley	*St Peter*

Area Thirteen

SUFFOLK

Aldeburgh	St Peter and St Paul
Bacton	St Mary
Badingham	St John the Baptist
Barningham	St Andrew
Beccles	St Michael
Bildeston	St Mary Magdalene
Blythburgh	*Holy Trinity*
Bramfield	*St Andrew*
Bungay	Holy Trinity
Bury St Edmunds	St Mary
Clare	St Peter and St Paul
Combs	St Mary
Cotton	St Andrew
Cretingham	St Peter
Dalham	St Mary
Dennington	*St Mary*
Denston	*St Nicholas*
Earl Stonham	St Mary the Virgin
East Bergholt	St Mary the Virgin
Euston	St Genevieve
Eye	*St Peter and St Paul*
Framlingham	*St Michael*
Fressingfield	*St Peter and St Paul*
Gislingham	St Mary
Kedington	St Peter and St Paul
Lakenheath	St Mary the Virgin
Lavenham	*St Peter and St Paul*
Long Melford	*Holy Trinity*
Mildenhall	*St Mary*
Mutford	St Andrew
Needham Market	St John the Baptist
Rougham	St Mary
Rushbrooke	St Nicholas
Southwold	*St Edmund*
Stoke-by-Nayland	*St Mary the Virgin*
Sudbury	*St Gregory*
Thornham Parva	St Mary
Ufford	*The Assumption of Our Lady*
Walsham-Le-Willows	St Mary
Wenhaston	St Peter
Westhall	St Andrew
Wingfield	St Andrew

Wissington	St Mary the Virgin
Woodbridge	*St Mary the Virgin*
Woolpit	*The Nativity of the Blessed Virgin Mary*

Area Fourteen

GLOUCESTERSHIRE

Bagendon	St Margaret
Baunton	St Mary Magdalene
Berkeley	St Mary the Virgin
Bibury	*St Mary*
Bishop's Cleeve	St Michael and All Angels
Bledington	St Leonard
Buckland	St Michael
Chedworth	St Andrew
Cheltenham	St Paul
Chipping Campden	*St James the Great*
Chipping Sodbury	St John the Baptist
Cirencester	*St John the Baptist*
Daglingworth	*Holy Rood*
Deerhurst	*St Mary*
Down Ampney	All Saints
Duntisbourne Rous	*St Michael*
Eastleach Turville	St Andrew
Elkstone	*St John the Evangelist*
Fairford	*St Mary the Virgin*
Hailes	Dedication unknown
Kempley	*St Mary*
Kempsford	St Mary the Virgin
Leonard Stanley	St Swithin
Minchinhampton	Holy Trinity
Newland	All Saints
North Cerney	*All Saints*
Northleach	*St Peter and St Paul*
Oddington	St Nicholas
Painswick	St Mary the Virgin
Quenington	St Swithin
Rendcomb	St Peter
Tetbury	*St Mary the Virgin*
Tewkesbury	*Abbey Church of St Mary the Virgin*
Winchcombe	*St Peter*

Area Fifteen

AVON

Backwell	St Andrew
Banwell	St Andrew
Bath	Abbey Church of St Peter and St Paul

Bristol	All Saints
	St John the Baptist
	St Mark, The Lord Mayor's Chapel
	St Mary Redcliffe
Great Badminton	St Michael and All Angels
Iron Acton	St James the Less
Redland	*No dedication*
Westbury-on-Trym	Holy Trinity, Our Lady, St Peter and St Paul
Weston-super-Mare	All Saints
Wrington	*All Saints*
Yate	*St Mary*
Yatton	*St Mary the Virgin*

WILTSHIRE

Amesbury	Abbey Church of St Mary and St Melor
Bishops Cannings	*St Mary the Virgin*
Bishopstone	*St John the Baptist*
Bradford-on-Avon	Holy Trinity *St Lawrence*
Bromham	St Nicholas
Cricklade	*St Sampson*
Devizes	St John the Baptist
Edington	*Priory Church of St Mary, St Katherine and All Saints*
Farley	All Saints
Great Chalfield	All Saints
Hardenhuish	St Nicholas
Heytesbury	St Peter and St Paul
Inglesham	St John the Baptist
Lacock	St Cyriac
Lydiard Tregoz	*St Mary*
Malmesbury	*Abbey Church of St Peter and St Paul*
Mere	St Michael the Archangel
Mildenhall	St John the Baptist
Potterne	*St Mary the Virgin*
Purton	St Mary
Salisbury	*St Thomas of Canterbury*
Steeple Ashton	*St Mary the Virgin*
Stratford Tony	St Mary the Virgin
Tisbury	St John the Baptist
Urchfont	St Michael and All Angels
Wanborough	St Andrew
Westwood	St Mary the Virgin
Wilton	St Mary and St Nicholas

Winterbourne Bassett	St Katherine and St Peter

Area Sixteen

BERKSHIRE

Aldworth	St Mary
Avington	*St Mark and St Luke*
Hampstead Marshall	St Mary
Lambourn	St Michael and All Angels
Padworth	St John the Baptist
Shottesbrooke	*St John the Baptist*
Theale	Holy Trinity
Wickham	St Swithin

OXFORDSHIRE

Abingdon	St Helen
Adderbury	*St Mary the Virgin*
Bloxham	*St Mary*
Burford	*St John the Baptist*
Chislehampton	St Katherine
Church Handborough	St Peter and St Paul
Churchill	All Saints
Compton Beauchamp	St Swithin
Dorchester	*Abbey Church of St Peter and St Paul*
Ducklington	St Bartholomew
East Hagbourne	St Andrew
Ewelme	*St Mary the Virgin*
Faringdon	All Saints
Iffley	*St Mary the Virgin*
Kidlington	St Mary the Virgin
Langford	St Matthew
North Moreton	All Saints
Nuneham Courtenay	All Saints
Oxford	All Saints
	St Mary the Virgin
Rycote	Chapel of St Michael and All Angels
Sparsholt	Holy Rood
Stanton Harcourt	*St Michael*
Sutton Courtenay	All Saints
Swinbrook	St Mary the Blessed Virgin
Thame	St Mary
Uffington	*St Mary*

Witney	*St Mary*
Yarnton	St Bartholomew

Area Seventeen

BUCKINGHAMSHIRE

Aylesbury	St Mary
Bledlow	Holy Trinity
Chenies	St Michael
Chetwode	St Mary and St Nicholas
Clifton Reynes	St Mary the Virgin
Dinton	*St Peter and St Paul*
Dorney	St James
Edlesborough	St Mary the Virgin
Great Kimble	St Nicholas
Hillesden	*All Saints*
Little Kimble	All Saints
Little Missenden	St John the Baptist
Maids Moreton	St Edmund
North Marston	*St Mary*
Penn	Holy Trinity
Pitstone	St Mary
Quainton	Holy Cross and St Mary
Stewkley	*St Michael and All Angels*
Stoke Poges	St Giles
Stowe	The Assumption of the Blessed Virgin Mary
Tattenhoe	St Giles
Weston Turville	St Mary the Virgin
West Wycombe	*St Lawrence*
Willen	*St Mary Magdalene*
Wing	*All Saints*

Area Eighteen

BEDFORDSHIRE

Bedford	St Paul
Chalgrave	All Saints
Dean	All Saints
Dunstable	*Priory Church of St Peter*
Eaton Bray	*St Mary the Virgin*
Elstow	*Abbey Church of St Mary and St Helena*
Felmersham	*St Mary the Virgin*
Houghton Conquest	All Saints
Leighton Buzzard	*All Saints*
Luton	St Mary
Marston Morteyne	*St Mary the Virgin*

Odell	All Saints
Shillington	All Saints
Toddington	St George
Wymington	St Lawrence

HERTFORDSHIRE

Anstey	*St George*
Ashwell	*St Mary the Virgin*
Ayot St Lawrence	St Lawrence
Bishop's Stortford	St Michael
Great Gaddesden	St John the Baptist
Harpenden	St John the Baptist
Hemel Hempstead	*St Mary*
Hitchin	St Mary the Virgin
St Paul's Walden	All Saints
Stanstead Abbots	St James
Ware	St Mary
Watford	St Mary
Wheathampstead	*St Helen*

Area Nineteen

CITY OF LONDON

All Hallows, London Wall
St Anne and St Agnes, Aldersgate
St Bartholomew the Great, Smithfield
St Benet, Paul's Wharf
St Bride, Fleet Street
St Katherine Cree
St Dunstan-in-the-West
St James, Garlickhythe
St Lawrence, Jewry
St Magnus the Martyr, London Bridge
St Margaret, Lothbury
St Margaret Pattens
St Martin-within-Ludgate
St Mary Abchurch
St Mary Aldermary
St Mary-at-Hill
St Mary-le-Bow
St Mary Somerset
St Mary Woolnoth
St Michael, Paternoster Royal
St Peter, Cornhill
St Stephen, Walbrook
St Vedast, Foster Lane

LONDON AND SUBURBS

Beddington	St Mary the Virgin
Camberwell	St George
Carshalton	All Saints
Chelsea	*Holy Trinity, Sloane Street*
	St Luke, Sydney Pl.

Clerkenwell	St James
Cranford	St Dunstan
Croydon	St Michael and All Angels
Harefield	St Mary the Virgin
Harrow-on-the-Hill	St Mary
Kensington	Holy Trinity, Kensington Gore
Lambeth	St Peter, Vauxhall
Northolt	St Mary the Virgin
Paddington	*St Augustine*
	St Mary Magdalene
Petersham	St Peter
Marylebone	*All Saints, Margaret Street*
	All Souls, Langham Place
	St Cyprian, Clarence Gate
	St Peter, Vere Street
	St Michael, Camden Town
St Pancras	*St Pancras, New Church*
South Mimms	St Giles
Stepney	*St Anne, Limehouse*
	Christ Church, Spitalfields
	St George-in-the-East
Stoke Newington	St Matthias
Twickenham	St Mary the Virgin
Wanstead	St Mary the Virgin
Westminster	*St James, Piccadilly*
	St John, Smith Square
	St Martin-in-the-Fields
	St Mary-le-Strand
	St Paul, Covent Garden
Whitchurch	St Lawrence, Little Stanmore

Area Twenty

ESSEX

Blackmore	*Priory Church of St Lawrence*
Bradwell-on-Sea	*Chapel of St Peter-on-the-Wall*
Brightlingsea	All Saints
Castle Hedingham	*St Nicholas*
Chrishall	Holy Trinity
Clavering	St Mary and St Clement

Copford	St Michael and All Angels
Dedham	*St Mary the Virgin*
East Horndon	All Saints
Finchingfield	St John the Baptist
Great Bardfield	*St Mary the Virgin*
Great Bromley	*St George*
Great Warley	St Mary the Virgin
Greensted	*St Andrew*
Hatfield Broad Oak	St Mary the Virgin
Ingatestone	*St Edmund and St Mary*
Layer Marney	*St Mary the Virgin*
Little Dunmow	St Mary the Virgin
Little Maplestead	*St John the Baptist*
Margaretting	St Margaret
Navestock	St Thomas the Apostle
Newport	St Mary the Virgin
Rivenhall	St Mary and All Saints
Saffron Walden	*St Mary the Virgin*
St Osyth	St Peter and St Paul
Sandon	*St Andrew*
Shenfield	St Mary the Virgin
Stebbing	*St Mary the Virgin*
Stock	All Saints
Thaxted	*St John the Baptist, Our Lady and St Lawrence*
Tilty	*St Mary the Virgin*
Waltham Abbey	*Abbey Church of Holy Cross and St Lawrence*
Wendens Ambo	St Mary the Virgin

Area Twenty-one

CORNWALL

Altarnun	*St Nonna*
Blisland	*St Protus and St Hyacinth*
Chacewater	St Paul
Kilkhampton	*St James*
Laneast	*St Sidwell*
Lanlivery	St Dunstan
Lanteglos-by-Fowey	St Wyllow
Launcells	*St Swithin*
Launceston	*St Mary Magdalene*
Lostwithiel	St Bartholomew
Mullion	St Melina
North Hill	St Torney
Probus	St Probus
St Austell	Holy Trinity

St Buryan	St Borian
St Clement	St Clement
St Endellion	St Endellienta
St Ives	St Ia
St Keverne	St Keverne
St Neot	*St Neot*
St Winnow	St Winnow

Area Twenty-two

Ashcombe	St Nectan
Ashton	St John the Baptist
Atherington	St Mary
Branscombe	St Winifred
Braunton	St Brannock
Brentor	St Michael
Bridford	St Thomas à Becket
Buckland-in-the-Moor	St Peter
Chittlehampton	St Hieritha
Coldridge	St Matthew
Crediton	*Holy Cross*
Cruwys Morchard	Holy Cross
Cullompton	*St Andrew*
Dartmouth	St Petrock
Exeter	St Mary Arches
Harberton	*St Andrew*
Hartland	*St Nectan*
High Bickington	St Mary
Honeychurch	St Mary
Horwood	St Michael
Kentisbeare	St Mary
Kenton	*All Saints*
Lapford	St Thomas of Canterbury
Molland	St Mary
Ottery St Mary	*St Mary*
Parracombe	St Petrock
Plymtree	St John the Baptist
Sampford Courtenay	St Andrew
Swimbridge	St James
Tawstock	St Peter
Torbryan	Holy Trinity
Widecombe-in-the-Moor	St Pancras

Area Twenty-three

Axbridge	*St John the Baptist*
Batcombe	*St Mary the Virgin*
Bishop's Lydeard	St Mary the Virgin
Broomfield	All Saints
Bruton	*St Mary*
Chewton Mendip	*St Mary Magdalene*
Crewkerne	St Bartholomew
Croscombe	*St Mary the Virgin*
Dunster	St George
East Brent	St Mary
Evercreech	St Peter
Glastonbury	*St John the Baptist*
High Ham	St Andrew
Huish Episcopi	*St Mary the Virgin*
Ilminster	*Minster Church of the Blessed Virgin Mary*
Isle Abbotts	*St Mary the Virgin*
Kingsbury Episcopi	St Martin
Leigh-on-Mendip	St Giles
Long Sutton	Holy Trinity
Martock	*All Saints*
Mells	*St Andrew*
North Cadbury	St Michael
North Curry	St Peter and St Paul
North Petherton	*St Mary*
Norton-Sub-Hamdon	St Mary the Virgin
Selworthy	All Saints
Shepton Mallet	St Peter and St Paul
Staple Fitzpaine	St Peter
Stogursey	St Andrew
Stoke-Sub-Hamdon	St Mary the Virgin
Swell	St Katherine
Taunton	*St Mary Magdalene*
Trull	*All Saints*
Watchet	St Decuman
Wedmore	St Mary the Virgin
Wells	*St Cuthbert*
Westonzoyland	*St Mary the Virgin*
West Pennard	St Nicholas

Area Twenty-four

Affpuddle	St Lawrence
Bere Regis	*St John the Baptist*
Blandford Forum	St Peter and St Paul
Cattistock	St Peter and St Paul
Cerne Abbas	St Mary
Chalbury	Dedication unknown
Charlton Marshall	St Mary the Virgin
Charminster	St Mary
Christchurch	*Priory Church of the Holy Trinity*
Hazelbury Bryan	St Mary and St James
Hilton	All Saints
Kingston	St James
Lyme Regis	St Michael the Archangel
Piddletrenthide	All Saints
Puddletown	St Mary the Virgin
Sherborne	*Abbey Church of St Mary*
Studland	*St Nicholas*
Trent	St Andrew
Wareham	St Martin
Whitchurch Canonicorum	*St Candida and Holy Cross*
Wimborne Minster	*Minster Church of St Cuthburga*
Wimborne St Giles	St Giles
Winterborne Tomson	St Andrew
Worth Matravers	St Nicholas
Yetminster	St Andrew

Area Twenty-five

Avington	St Mary
Basing	St Mary
Beaulieu	Abbey Church of the Blessed Virgin and Holy Child
Bramley	St James
Breamore	*St Mary*
Crondall	All Saints
East Meon	*All Saints*
Minstead	All Saints
Odiham	All Saints
Pamber	Priory Church of the Holy Trinity, St Mary the Virgin and St John the Baptist
Portchester	Priory Church of St Mary
Romsey	*Abbey Church of St Mary and St Ethelflaeda*
Silchester	St Mary the Virgin
Southampton	Church of the Ascension, Bitterne Park
Stoke Charity	St Mary and St Michael
Winchester	*St Cross*
	St John the Baptist
Winchfield	St Mary

Arreton	St George
Carisbrooke	St Mary the Virgin
Godshill	*All Saints*
Mottistone	St Peter and St Paul
Shorwell	*St Peter*

SURREY

Betchworth	St Michael
Burstow	St Bartholomew
Chaldon	St Peter and St Paul
Chipstead	*St Margaret*
Compton	St Nicholas
Esher	St George
Godalming	St Peter and St Paul
Great Bookham	St Nicholas
Guildford	St Mary
Holmbury St Mary	St Mary
Lingfield	St Peter and St Paul
Ockham	*All Saints*
Shere	*St James*
Stoke d' Abernon	*St Mary*
Wotton	St John the Evangelist

Area Twenty-six

EAST SUSSEX

Alfriston	St Andrew
Ashburnham	*St Peter*
Brighton	St Bartholomew, Ann Street
	St Martin, Lewes Road
	St Peter
Eastbourne	St Mary
Etchingham	St Mary and St Nicholas
Glynde	St Mary the Virgin
Penhurst	St Michael the Archangel
Pevensey	St Nicholas
Playden	St Michael
Rotherfield	St Denys
Rye	St Mary the Virgin
Winchelsea	*St Thomas the Martyr*

WEST SUSSEX

Amberley	St Michael
Arundel	St Nicholas
Bosham	Holy Trinity
Boxgrove	Priory Church of St Mary and St Blaise
Findon	St John the Baptist
Hardham	St Botolph
Lowfield Heath	St Michael and All Angels
New Shoreham	*St Mary de Haura*
Old Shoreham	St Nicholas
Sompting	*St Mary*
South Harting	St Mary and St Gabriel
Steyning	St Andrew
Trotton	St George
Warminghurst	Holy Sepulchre
West Burton	Dedication unknown
West Chiltington	St Mary
West Grinstead	St George
Worth	St Nicholas

Area Twenty-seven

KENT

Badlesmere	St Leonard
Barfreston	*St Nicholas*
Brookland	St Augustine
Chartham	*St Mary the Virgin*
Chilham	St Mary
Cliffe	St Helen
Cobham	St Mary Magdalene
Cranbrook	St Dunstan
Elham	St Mary the Virgin
Graveney	All Saints
High Halden	St Mary the Virgin
Hythe	St Leonard
Ivychurch	St George
Lullingstone	St Botolph
Lydd	All Saints
Mereworth	*St Lawrence*
Minster-in-Thanet	St Mary the Virgin
New Romney	*St Nicholas*
Patrixbourne	*St Mary*
Rainham	St Margaret of Antioch
St Margaret's at Cliffe	St Margaret
Stone	*St Mary the Virgin*
Tenterden	St Mildred
Tunbridge Wells	King Charles the Martyr
Upper Hardres	St Peter and St Paul
Westwell	St Mary
Wingham	St Mary the Virgin
Woodchurch	All Saints
Wrotham	St George
Wye	St Gregory and St Martin

It is a sad fact of life that many of our churches have to be kept locked to protect them from theft and vandalism. The determined visitor can often find the key close at hand, hidden on top of a ledge or under a bench. But if the key cannot be found in the church porch, the best course is to knock on the vicarage door, or to call at the nearest cottage or the local post office who usually know where the key is kept.

Please remember that, although to you, the visitor, each church is a free museum and art gallery, to the local parishioners it is a cherished part of their local heritage and one that is expensive to maintain. A generous donation in the church's collecting box is a practical expression of your appreciation.

Glossary of Architectural and Ecclesiastical Terms

Periods of Architecture

The historical periods into which church architecture is commonly divided are seldom clearly defined. Occasionally some political event or major liturgical change separates one period from another quite distinctly; more often the slower changes of taste and technical development account for the new styles of building, and sometimes the dividing line is the quite arbitrary change of reigning monarch. So allowance must be made for much overlapping of periods and styles when using any general guide.

Romanesque

Saxon or Pre-Conquest	600–1066
Norman	1066–1160
Transitional	1160–1200

Gothic

Early English	1200–1300
Decorated	1300–1350
Perpendicular	1350–1530

Tudor	1485–1603
Stuart	1603–1714
Georgian	1714–1830
Victorian	1830–1910

Detail from medieval manuscript showing stone masons at work

Development of the Church Plan

This series of plans of a fictitious parish church illustrates the typical development of a church founded, as most of our churches were, during the years after the Norman Conquest.

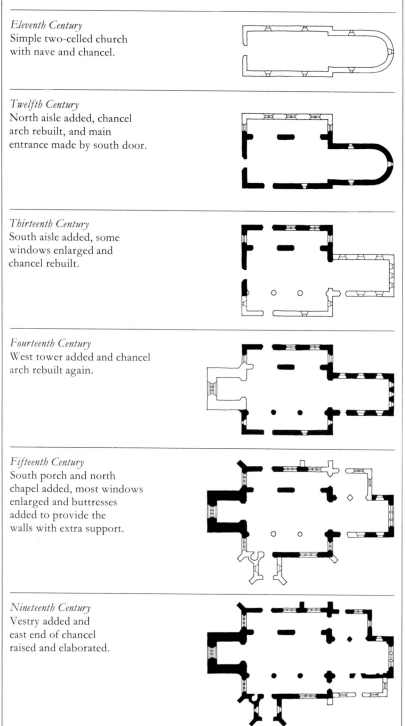

Eleventh Century
Simple two-celled church with nave and chancel.

Twelfth Century
North aisle added, chancel arch rebuilt, and main entrance made by south door.

Thirteenth Century
South aisle added, some windows enlarged and chancel rebuilt.

Fourteenth Century
West tower added and chancel arch rebuilt again.

Fifteenth Century
South porch and north chapel added, most windows enlarged and buttresses added to provide the walls with extra support.

Nineteenth Century
Vestry added and east end of chancel raised and elaborated.

Typical Gothic Parish Church

1	Tower	10	Rood
2	Battlemented	11	Chancel
	parapet	12	Altar
3	Clerestory	13	Piscina
4	Nave arcade	14	Sedilia
5	Pier	15	Vestry
6	Parclose	16	Sanctuary
	screen	17	Transept
7	Pulpit	18	Porch
8	Nave	19	Font
9	Rood loft	20	Aisle

Abacus
Flat slab of stone that forms the top part of a capital. It takes the thrust at the springing point of an arch, or supports an architrave. (See *Capital*.)

Abbey
Ecclesiastical establishment occupied by nuns or monks under an abbess or abbot, or a church that once belonged to such an establishment.

Acanthus
Stylised leaf-form, based on the broad scalloped leaf of the acanthus, which originally appeared as a decorative feature in Greek architecture, especially on capitals of the Corinthian order.

Alms Box
Box for collecting offerings of money for charitable purposes. Medieval boxes were usually carved from a solid piece of oak, bound with iron bands and secured by several locks.

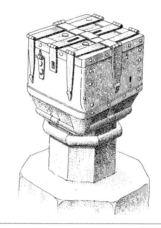

Altar
Flat-topped table of stone or wood for the celebration of the Mass (ie the Eucharist), and on which the cross and other objects of religious significance may be placed. The altar is usually at the east end of the chancel, although nowadays it is often placed away from the east wall so that the priest can officiate facing the congregation from behind the altar. A stone altar is generally incised with five consecration crosses – one at each corner and one in the centre. The front of the altar is usually covered with a richly patterned cloth called the *Altar Frontal*. The colour of the altar frontal varies according to the liturgical season of the Church's year.

Altar Rails
(See *Communion* and *Laudian Rails*.)

Ambulatory
Aisle or processional way behind the high altar; also sometimes used to describe a cloister or other place for walking round.

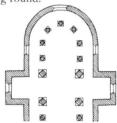

Anchorite Cell
Small dwelling for the solitary confinement of a pious recluse, often built against the north wall of the church. An opening in the wall, called a *Squint*, enabled the anchorite to see Mass celebrated at the high altar.

Annulet
Narrow ring of stone or metal, which encircles a column or shaft.

Apron
Raised panel beneath a window sill, sometimes decoratively carved.

Apse
Semi-circular or polygonal end to the chancel, or sometimes a transept. Usually vaulted or dome-roofed.

Arcade
Series of columns or pillars supporting arches. They may be open, like the arcade that separates the aisle of a church from its nave; or they may be 'blind', used simply as a form of relief decoration, in which case the term *Arcading* is often used.

Arch
Curved supporting structure made up of wedge-shaped sections. The style of its arches gives a good clue to the architectural period of a church. (See right.)

Architrave
In classical architecture, the main beam resting on the *Abacus* of a column (see *Column*), or the moulded frame around a window or doorway.

Armature
Framework made of iron which holds the pieces of glass together in windows without stone tracery.

Ashlar
Comparatively thin, squared stone blocks with a smooth surface, used to face a rubble or brick wall.

Atlantes
Sculptured male figures which serve as pillars.

Auditory Plan
Type of church plan, beginning in the seventeenth century, in which the congregation and the clergy are housed in a single, undivided interior. The pulpit is prominent and the seating arranged in such a way that all can see and hear clearly.

Aumbry
Small cupboard or recess, in a wall near the altar, to house the sacred vessels used at Mass or Communion.

Ball-flower
One of the favourite motifs of the Decorated Gothic period. A small ball is enclosed by three petals to form a globular flower. They were set in rows on a concave moulding.

SOME TYPES OF ARCH

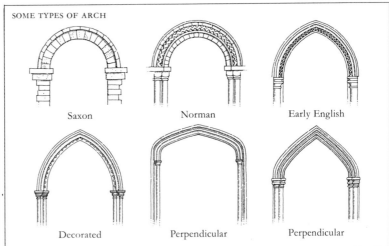

Saxon   Norman   Early English

Decorated   Perpendicular   Perpendicular

Baluster
Short column, usually slender at top and bottom and pear-shaped between. A set of balusters supporting a rail forms a *Balustrade*.

Baptistry
Part of the church used for Holy Baptism and containing the *Font*, usually at the west end.

Barrel Vault or Wagon Vault
(See *Vault*.)

Base
Bottom section of a column, between the shaft and the floor. (See *Column*.)

Bas-relief
Sculpture carved in low relief, usually against a flat background.

Batter
Inclination of a wall away from the vertical.

Battlement
Parapet cut with regular, square indentations. Originally designed for defensive purposes, but used on most churches for decorative effect. The spaces in the battlements are called *Embrasures* and the raised sections, which are sometimes pierced, are called *Merlons*.

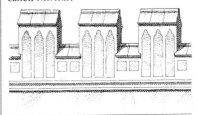

Bay
Space between two adjacent columns in an arcade.

Beakhead
Form of decoration common in Norman architecture. The stylised head of a bird or animal with a long beak is used as a repeated sculptural motif to achieve a rich effect round doorways or arches.

Belfry
Part of the church tower containing the bells.

Bench end
Vertical sections at each end of a bench. Medieval ones are often richly carved with scenes from the Bible, animals both real and fantastic, portraits, representations of the seven deadly sins, and many other flights of the carpenter's fancy.

Church of
St Mary
Great Snoring
Norfolk

Church of
St Andrew
Little Snoring
Norfolk

Billet
Chequer-board decoration of raised rectangles, popular in the Norman period.

Boss
Ornamental projection at the point where the ribs of a vault or roof meet. They are usually carved with foliage or faces, but may take more complex forms.

Box Pew
Seating surrounded by a panelled wooden enclosure with a door. The inside was often lined with coloured baize, and some of the grander pews even had their own fireplaces.

Church of All Saints, Shorthampton, Oxon

Broach
Elongated half-pyramid of stone or timber set at the corner of a square tower to effect the transition to an octagonal spire. A spire so formed is called a *Broach Spire*.

Buttress
Mass of masonry built against a wall to give extra stability or to counteract the outward thrust of an arch or vault behind the wall. When two such buttresses meet at right angles on a corner of a building, they are called *Angle Buttresses*. (See *Flying Buttress*.)

Cable Moulding
Decorative moulding resembling a thick rope or intertwined string.

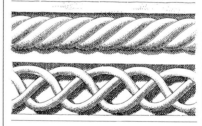

Caen Stone
Fine-grained limestone from Normandy introduced after the Conquest; one of the best stones used by early medieval builders.

Camber
Upward curve or rise in an otherwise horizontal member, such as a beam.

Campanile
Bell tower standing separately from the rest of the church.

Capital
Topmost part of a column or pillar, often richly carved. The style of its capitals provides another clue to the date of a church.

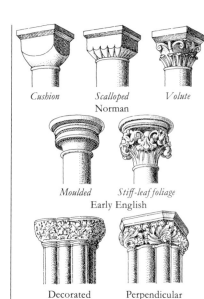

Cushion *Scalloped* *Volute*
Norman

Moulded *Stiff-leaf foliage*
Early English

Decorated *Perpendicular*

Cartouche
Tablet bearing an inscription or device in a frame carved with scrolls.

Caryatid
Sculptured female figure which serves as a pillar.

Church of St Pancras, London

Castellated
Decorated with battlements.

Ceilure or Cellure
Area of the roof over the altar or the *Rood* which is particularly well adorned to call attention to the features beneath.

Chamfer
Pared-down edge of a corner.

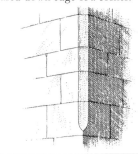

Chancel Arch
Single arch across the east end of the nave which opens into the chancel. (See below.) There is often a *Doom* over the arch. (See *Doom*.)

Chancel or Rood Screen
Screen that divided the chancel from the nave of a church, usually wooden, sometimes stone. The chancel screen, especially its dado, was a high point for decoration in the medieval church. It often incorporated elaborate tracery work and panels richly painted with devotional figures of saints, kings or angels.

Church of St Andrew, Bramfield, Suffolk

Chancel Arch: *Church of St Mary, Great Canfield, Essex*

Chantry Chapel
Chapel within or attached to a church, endowed by an individual or sometimes a group, for the saying of Masses for their souls after death. The chantry usually contained the tomb of its benefactor.

Charnel House
Crypt or vault in which bones were piled when removed from graves in the churchyard.

Chevron
Most ubiquitous of the Norman mouldings. This one takes the form of a continuous zigzag pattern.

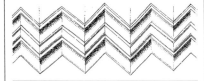

Ciborium
Canopy over an altar or shrine, sometimes used to mean the whole canopied shrine. The term is also used to describe the receptacle for the reservation of the consecrated elements of the Mass.

Church of St Ledger, Ashby Northamptonshire

Cinquefoil
Five-cusped ornament in a circle or at the head of an arch.

Clerestory
Upper storey of the nave walls rising above the roofs of the aisles and pierced by windows to light the nave. (See also *Triforium*.)

Cloister
Covered walk around a quadrangle with a wall on the outside and an arcade on the inside.

Coffering
Sunken square or polygonal panels used to decorate ceilings.

Church of St Stephen, Walbrook, London

Colonnade
Row of columns.

Column
Cylindrical pillar, usually supporting an arch.

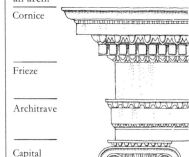

Cornice

Frieze

Architrave

Capital

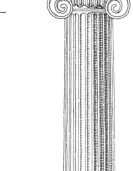

Shaft

Base

Pedestal

Plinth

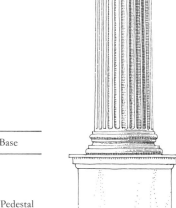

Communion Rails
Low wooden or iron palings enclosing the altar, introduced to mark off the area of the *Sanctuary* and provide a kneeling place for communicants. (See also *Laudian Rails*.)

Communion Table
In Elizabethan and Jacobean times the medieval altar was replaced by a wooden table. The table was originally placed in the centre of the chancel, away from the east wall, and was often handsomely carved.

Consecration Cross
A set of crosses, usually twelve, was marked on the inside and outside walls to be blessed by the bishop and anointed with holy oil during the consecration of the church.

Coping
Top course of masonry on an exterior wall or buttress, usually sloping to throw off rain-water.

Corbel
Supporting block of stone bonded into a wall. Usually carved decoratively, sometimes as an angel or other figure.

Church of St Mary, Sompting, West Sussex

Cornice
Uppermost and most prominent moulding on a wall or above a column. (See *Column*.)

Credence
Small shelf or table for the elements of the Mass before consecration, sometimes built into a wall to form part of a *Piscina*.

Crockets
Ornaments in the form of buds or curled leaves used at regular intervals on the sloping sides of spires, gables, canopies and pinnacles. They were especially popular during the Decorated Gothic period, when one might be forgiven for thinking that some churches were about to burst into leaf all over! Crockets also served the practical purpose of providing footholds for the masons.

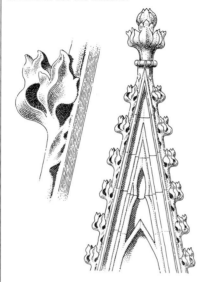

Cruciform Plan
Church planned in the shape of a cross, usually with a central tower above the intersection of the nave and transepts.

Crypt
Underground chamber or vault, usually beneath the chancel.

Cupola
Small, domed or polygonal turret crowning a roof.

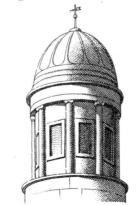

Cusp
A projecting point between the *Foils* in Gothic arches and tracery. They are sometimes foliated.

Decalogue
The Ten Commandments, usually found together with the Lord's Prayer and the Creed on panels behind a communion table.

Devil's Door
Doorway in the north wall of a church which was left open during a baptism to let out any evil spirits in the child. Evil and ignorance of the Gospel were thought to come from the north, so the *Gargoyles* facing that way were particularly fierce and only people who died in shady circumstances were buried on the north side of the church. Most of the Devil's doors were blocked up as the customs associated with them fell out of use in less superstitious times.

Diaper
Uniform pattern made up of squares or diamond-shaped motifs, carved in low relief or painted on a plain wall surface.

Dissolution
Used to describe the disbanding of the monasteries and appropriation of their lands by Henry VIII.

Dogtooth

Form of decoration used during the Early English period. It is made up of a succession of raised tooth-like motifs in pairs or groups of four, set diagonally in a moulding.

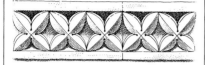

Dole Cupboard, Dole Table

Cupboard for storing bread for travellers or the poor. The table was a stone ledge, generally in the south porch, for the distribution of alms.

Church of All Saints, Milton Ernest, Beds

Doom

Dramatic representation of the Last Judgement usually painted above the chancel arch. Its layout followed a strict plan. At the top, Christ appears in Majesty to judge the quick and the dead. Beneath him the souls of the departed rise from their graves to be weighed in the balance by St Michael. Those found wanting are herded by demons into the gaping jaws of Hell to the right. On the left the souls of the blessed are guided by angels to Heaven. (See right.)

Dormer

Upright window projecting from a sloping roof.

Dripstone

The stone moulding above a doorway, window or arch intended to throw off rain-water. It is also called a *Hood Mould*, or *Label* if it is rectangular.

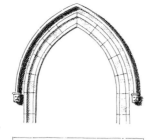

Easter Sepulchre

Recess in chancel wall used to house the consecrated host from Maundy Thursday until Easter morning, symbolic of Christ's entombment.

Embrasure

Space between the projecting parts of a battlement.

Encaustic Tiles

Glazed clay tiles of various colours, earth-red being the most common, which were much loved by the Victorians for flooring churches old and new.

Entablature

Part of an *Order* above the column which includes cornice, frieze and architrave. (See *Column*.)

Fan Vaulting

The most spectacular form of Gothic vaulting. (See *Vault*.)

Finial

Ornamental termination to a pinnacle, gable, bench-end or canopy, usually carved like a leaf.

Doom: *Church of St Thomas of Canterbury, Salisbury, Wiltshire*

Flushwork
Flint cut and set into dressed stonework to form a decorative pattern. Its use is common in East Anglia.

Church of St Mary, Woodbridge, Suffolk

Fluting
Grooved or bevelled surface of a column, arch or pilaster.

Flying Buttress
Buttress in the form of an open half-arch which directs the thrust of a high wall across the roof of an aisle to a main buttress on the outer wall.

Foil
Space between the projecting cusps of a traceried opening. (See *Cusp*.)

Foliated
Carved with leaf shapes. Capitals, crockets and finials are frequently foliated.

SOME TYPES OF FONT

Norman

Norman

Early English

Decorated

Perpendicular

Post-Reformation

Font
Receptacle for the holy water used in baptism. Its style reflects the architectural features of the period to which it belongs. Most fonts are of stone; lead ones survive here and there; occasionally they are made of metal, wood or brick; and there is a particularly interesting group of seven made of blue-black marble from the quarries of Tournai in Belgium. Fonts usually have a cover, taking the form of a flat lid or pinnacled wooden canopy.

Four-leafed Flower
Ornamental form typical of the Decorated period. The repeated motif consists of a small ball set in the centre of four joined leaves.

Freestone
Fine-grained limestone or sandstone so called because it can be cut or sawn in any direction.

Fresco
Decoration painted on a wall or ceiling before the plaster is dry, though the word is often used loosely to describe any wall painting.

Frieze
In classical architecture flat section of the entablature, between the cornice and the architrave, sometimes carved or painted decoratively. (See *Column*.)

Funerary Hatchment or Escutcheon
A diamond-shaped board or canvas painted with the arms of a deceased person and hung in the church after being displayed at the funeral.

Gable
The triangular upper section of an exterior wall at the end of a roof, often topped by a *Gable Cross*.

Galilee
Small porch or chapel built against the west entrance of a church.

Gargoyle
A stone water-shoot draining a gutter and generally carved as a grotesque face or animal.

*Church of St Mary the Virgin
Over, Cambridgeshire*

Grisaille
A type of stained glass, greyish-white in colour, with decoration or figure work painted in neutral grey or brown enamel.

Groined Vault or Cross Vault
(See *Vault*.)

Hagioscope or Squint
An oblique opening in a wall or pillar that affords a view of the high altar from a transept or aisle.

Hammer Beam
Beam projecting from a wall at right angles to give support to the vertical and arch-braced members of a timber roof. (See also *Roof*.)

Herringbone
Masonry with stones laid diagonally, each row inclining alternately to left and right to produce a zigzag effect.

*Church of All Saints, Markham Clinton
Nottinghamshire*

Hog Back Tombstone: *Durham Cathedral*

Hog Back Tombstone
Carved, Saxon gravestone. Its name refers to the arch-shaped top. The patterns carved on them often show Scandinavian influence. (See below.)

Hood Mould
(See *Dripstone*.)

Impost
Point from which an arch springs, usually indicated by a moulded band.

Jamb
The straight sides of a doorway or window.

Keystone
Middle stone in an arch, sometimes more prominent than the rest, particularly in Baroque architecture.

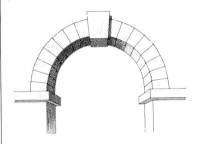

Label
Rectangular dripstone, often ending in a carved head or animal called a *Label Stop*. (See *Dripstone*.)

Lady Chapel
Chapel dedicated to the Blessed Virgin Mary, often to the east of the high altar in larger churches.

Lancet
Tall, narrow and pointed window of the Early English period. Sometimes set together in groups of three or five, and occasionally seven. (See *Window*.)

Lantern Tower
Central tower pierced by windows, above the level of the surrounding roofs, for lighting the crossing beneath.

Lattice Window
Window made up of diamond-shaped panes set in diagonal lead strips.

Laudian Rails
Low wooden or iron railings placed around altar tables in the seventeenth century and named after Archbishop William Laud who ordered them to be set up. They were invented to prevent dogs from entering the Sanctuary and provided communicants with a place to kneel.

Lectern
Reading stand which supports the Bible, usually made of wood or brass and often in the shape of an eagle with spread wings.

Church of St Peter, Oundle Northamptonshire. (Medieval replica of lectern in the Duomo, Urbino, Italy)

Ledger
Large flat stone covering a grave, often let into the church floor.

Light
Window opening, or division within a window created by the *Mullions*.

Lintel
Horizontal timber or stone beam across a doorway or window opening.

Long and Short Work
Characteristic feature of Saxon construction used to strengthen the corners of a building.

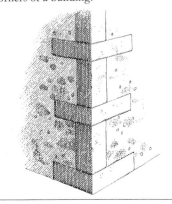

Lucarne
Vertical, unglazed opening in the sloping surface of a spire, usually gabled and traceried.

Lychgate
Roofed gateway into the churchyard to shelter the coffin until the arrival of the priest. It originally provided shelter for shrouded bodies at a time when coffins were not common and takes its name from the Old English 'lych' meaning corpse.

Church of St Peter, Boughton Monchelsea, Kent

Mason's Mark
Distinguishing device incised on a piece of stonework as a 'signature' to identify the craftsman who worked it. Some of the more complex marks illustrated the pedigree of the mason, others were simple identifications for the purposes of the wages clerk. They are not to be confused with position marks which indicated the order in which the stones were to be set.

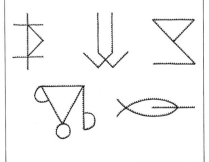

Mass Dial
Sundial with radiating lines to indicate the times of church services, scratched or carved on a door jamb or buttress on the south side of the church.

Church of St Mary the Virgin, Fairfield, Glos.

Merlon
Raised part of a battlement which may be decoratively pierced or carved. (See *Battlement*.)

Misericord
Bracket on the underside of a hinged seat in the choir stalls, often enriched with lively carvings of subjects both sacred and profane.

Church of St George, Anstey, Hertfordshire

Moulding
Projecting band of carved ornament which provides visual emphasis, especially around doors and windows.

Mullions
Vertical stone bars which divide a window into lights and from which the tracery springs.

Tracery

Mullions

Musicians' Gallery
Between the late seventeenth and early nineteenth centuries a gallery was sometimes built above an aisle or at the west end of a church to house the village musicians who provided church music during this period.

Nailhead
Another Norman decorative moulding. This one is made up of a string of raised pyramid shapes reminiscent of nail heads.

Narthex
Single-storied western vestibule, typical of Saxon churches but also used by some Victorian architects.

Niche
Recess designed to hold a statue.

Ogee
Shape formed by a pair of double curves with the convex part of the curves below, and the concave parts above meeting in a point.

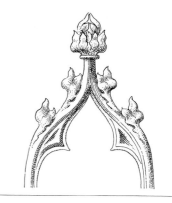

Order
In classical architecture all the parts of a column and its entablature are referred to collectively as an order. There are five classical orders, three Greek and two Roman, each having its own particular design. They are Doric, Ionic, Corinthian, Tuscan and Composite. (See right.)

Parapet
Section of a wall rising above the level and eaves of a roof to disguise the roof-line. It may be solid, pierced or battlemented.

Parclose
Screen separating a chapel or aisle from the rest of the church.

Parvis
Strictly speaking, an enclosed space in front of the entrance to a church; but commonly, though incorrectly, used to describe a room over the south porch which often served as a schoolhouse or store-room.

Pedestal
Supporting base between a column and its plinth. (See *Column*.)

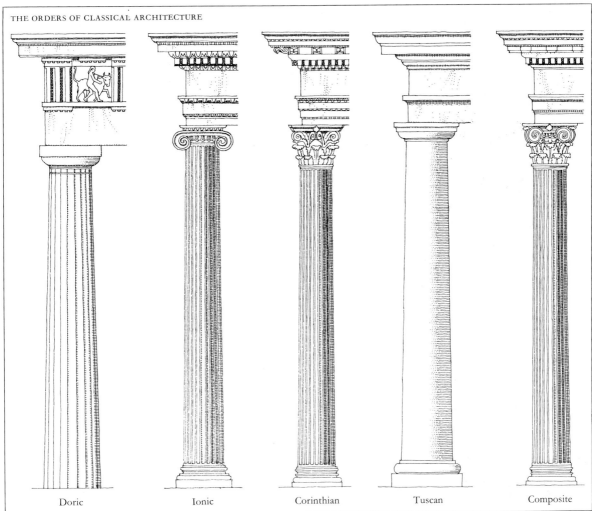

Doric   Ionic   Corinthian   Tuscan   Composite

Pediment
Low-pitched classical gable found on the front of Greek temples, supported by a *colonnade*, and introduced to England after the Renaissance as a decorative feature over windows, doorways and porticos. (See *Portico*.)

Pier
Solid free-standing masonry support for arches or vaulting. It may be round, square, rectangular, octagonal or a cluster of shafts. (See right.)

Pilaster
Shallow rectangular column attached to a wall and used for decorative rather than structural reasons.

Pillar
Free-standing support for an arch, slender and less massive than a pier.

SOME TYPES OF PIER

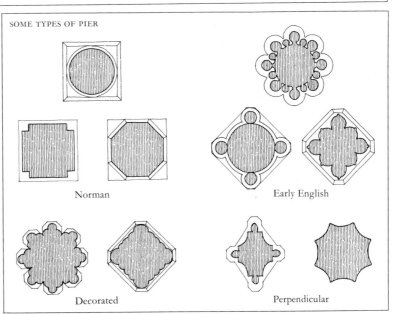

Norman   Early English

Decorated   Perpendicular

Pinnacle

Ornamental form used to crown a tower, gable or buttress. It is cone- or pyramid-shaped, usually decorated with crockets and topped by a finial.

Piscina

Niche containing a shallow stone basin, with a drain, for disposing of the holy water used by the priest to wash his hands during the Mass. It was almost invariably set in the south wall of the chancel and some have carved stone canopies above them. Sometimes a double piscina was used.

Church of St Mary and St Barloke, Norbury, Derbyshire

Plinth

The lowest projecting part of a pedestal, column or wall. (See *Column*.)

Poppyhead

Leaf-like or floral finial used to decorate the top of a bench end or choir stall.

Portico

Roof supported by columns at regular intervals, often surmounted by a pediment and forming a porch to a building.

St Martin's in the Fields, London

Pulpit

Platform from which the priest preaches, its decoration reflecting the architectural period. In the seventeenth and eighteenth centuries. *Three decker Pulpits* were used. The first level was for the use of the clerk leading the responses, the second for the reader, and the third for the preacher. The congregation of the time sat in tall box pews so the preacher had to be high up to be seen. The pulpit is usually surmounted by a *Tester* or sounding board to direct the preacher's voice down into the nave.

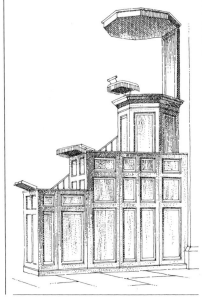

Quadripartite Vaulting

(See *Vault*.)

Quarry

Diamond-shaped piece of glass.

Quatrefoil

Analogous to *Cinquefoil*, but with four lobes instead of five.

Quoin

Large dressed stone at the corner of a building, often giving extra strength to a rubble wall.

Reredos

An ornamental screen or hanging on the wall behind the altar. It takes many forms and may be a tapestry, a painting, or made of stone or wood.

Church of All Saints, Aisholt, Somerset

Respond

Half-pillar, attached to a wall, supporting the last arch of an arcade.

Rood

Cross bearing the body of Christ, usually flanked by the figures of the Virgin and St John the Evangelist.

Church of St Philip and St James, Oxford

Rood Screen
Carved wooden or stone screen across the chancel which supported the *Rood Loft*, a gallery for the Rood, and from which the Gospel was sometimes sung during Mass.

Roof
There are many types of timber roof construction. The earliest and simplest is the *Tie-Beam Roof*; the most impressive are the *Hammer Beam* and *Double Hammer Beam Roofs*. (See right and page 107.) Medieval carpenters often combined various types of structure to solve individual problems or achieve particular effects. Chancels, aisles and porches of parish churches are sometimes roofed by stone vaulting. (See *Vault*.)

Rose Window
Circular window with tracery radiating from the centre. (See right.)

Rustication
Large blocks of stone, sometimes pitted or faceted, set with deep joints around doors, windows or corners to give an impression of greater strength. (See far right.)

SOME TYPES OF ROOF CONSTRUCTION

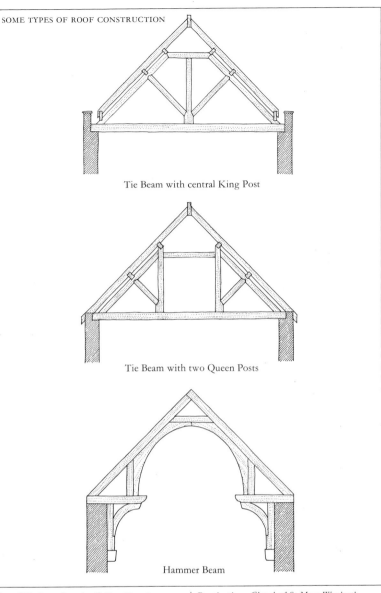

Tie Beam with central King Post

Tie Beam with two Queen Posts

Hammer Beam

Rose Window: *Lancing College Chapel, Lancing, Sussex*

Rustication: *Church of St Mary Woolnoth Lombard Street, London*

Saddleback Roof
Roof of a tower built like a short, gabled roof.

Church of All Saints, Tinwell, Leicestershire

Sanctuary
The area of the chancel containing the altar.

Sanctus Bell
Small bell usually hung above the roof of the church where the nave and chancel meet. It is rung at the elevation of the host, a custom which originated in the early church when the sacrament was consecrated behind curtains drawn around the altar. The ringing of a bell told the congregation that the miracle of the Mass had been achieved.

Scratch Dial
(See *Mass Dial*.)

Sedilia
Recessed seats, usually three in number, for priests in the south wall of the chancel. They are generally built of stone and canopied, and sometimes combined with a piscina. (See right above.)

Shaft
Small slender column, or the part of a column between the base and capital.

Spandrel
Area between two arches or the triangle-shaped space formed by a square hood mould, or label, surrounding an arch.

Sedilia: *Church of St Helen, Cliffe, Kent*

Church of St Peter and St Paul, Salle, Norfolk

Spire
Tall, tapering structure built on top of a tower.

Squinches
Arches built across the inside angles of a square tower to support an octagonal structure on top.

Squint
(See *Hagioscope*.)

Steeple
The whole structure made up of tower and spire.

Stiff-leaf
Stylised foliage decoration, with stiff stems and lobed leaves, commonly found on capitals of the Early English period. (See *Capital*.)

String Course
Moulding or projecting band of masonry that runs horizontally round the walls of a church, or divides the stages of a tower.

Stucco
Ornamental plasterwork.

Tester
Canopy over a pulpit.

Tracery
Intersecting decorative ribwork in the upper parts of Gothic windows, or screens, vaults, panelling, etc. Several distinctive forms of tracery evolved during the three main periods of the Gothic style, and they provide a useful key to dating. (See *Window*.)

Transom
Horizontal bar across a window.

Trefoil
Three-cusped ornament in a circle or arch.

Triforium
Arcaded wall passage, or blank arcading between the nave arcade of a church and the clerestory above. (See right.)

Tympanum
Area between the lintel of a doorway and the arch above it, often filled with sculpture.

Church of St Mary and St David, Kilpeck, Hereford and Worcester

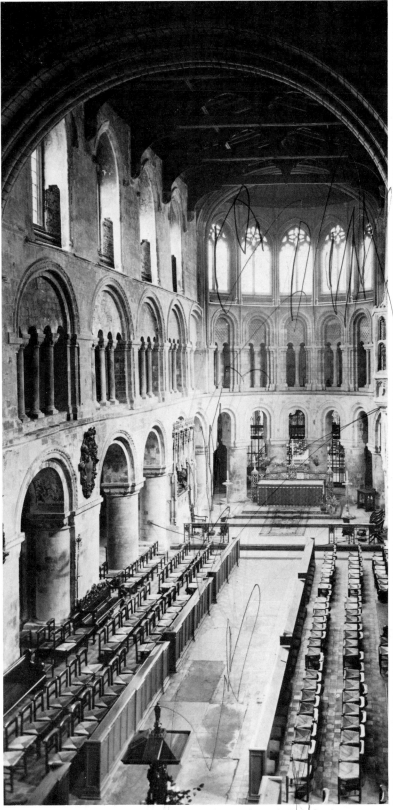

Nave Arcade, Triforium and Clerestory: *Church of St Bartholomew the Great, London*

Vault

An arched roof or ceiling built of stone, brick or timber. The *Barrel* or *Tunnel Vault* has a semicircular cross section and is the simplest type of vault. A *Groined Vault* is formed by the intersection of two barrel vaults at right angles. It takes its name from the lines of intersection which are called *Groins*. In Gothic architecture groins became replaced by *Ribs*, used to support and decorate the vault. A *Quadripartite Vault* is divided by two diagonal ribs into four equal sections. A *Sexpartite Vault* is formed when the vault is divided again by a transverse rib into six unequal sections. Vaulting is often further elaborated by the addition of *Tierceron Ribs* which run from a main springer generally to a point on the ridge rib and provide extra support, and by *Lierne Ribs* which do not spring from one of the main springers or the central boss but are used as decorative links between the main ribs and the tiercerons. The most spectacular form of vaulting, perfected during the Perpendicular period is the *Fan Vault*. Numerous ribs of the same length and curvature radiate from one springer at equal angles to form a fan-like pattern over an inverted cone of masonry. (See right.)

Voussoir

One of the wedge-shaped stones that fit together to make an arch. The central stone, the *Keystone*, is sometimes the most prominent.

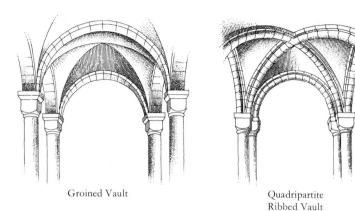

Groined Vault

Quadripartite
Ribbed Vault

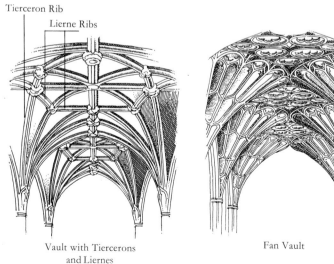

Sexpartite Vault

Tierceron Rib

Lierne Ribs

Vault with Tiercerons
and Liernes

Fan Vault

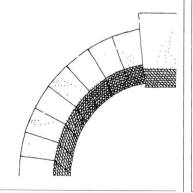

Weepers

Small carved figures set in niches round the sides of a tomb. Not to be confused with representations of the deceased's children who also sometimes appear in miniature.

Church of St Mary, Tong, Salop

Window

Early windows were small as glass was expensive, but the technical developments of the Gothic era made possible larger windows with glass set in a network of stone *tracery*. Though of infinite variety, tracery design evolved through several phases: *plate tracery, geometrical, reticulated, curvilinear* and *perpendicular*. Later, tracery was abandoned in favour of the plain, round-headed windows of Georgian architecture.

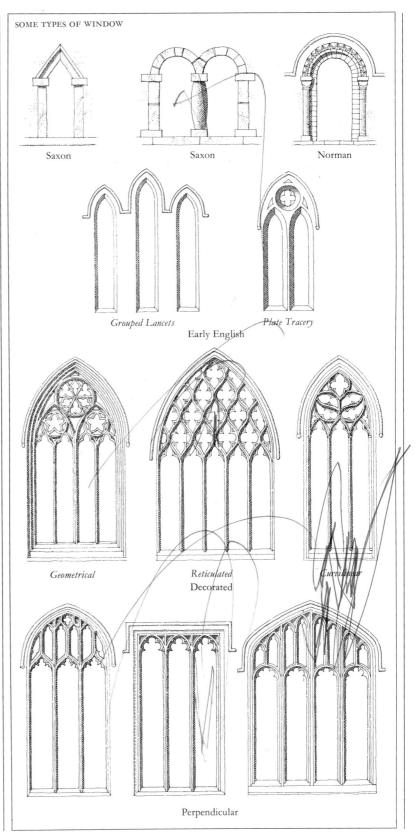

Saxon   Saxon   Norman

Grouped Lancets   *Plate Tracery*

Early English

Geometrical   *Reticulated*   *Curvilinear*
                        Decorated

Perpendicular

Index

Acknowledgements

Acknowledgement is due to the following for permission to reproduce illustrations:

BLACK AND WHITE page 9 BBC; p. 10 BOARD OF TRINITY COLLEGE, DUBLIN Alban 734U; p. 11 above CORINIUM MUSEUM, CIRENCESTER, below BARBER INSTITUTE; p. 12 TRUSTEES OF THE BRITISH MUSEUM; p. 13 BRITISH MUSEUM; p. 14 top THE ROYAL LIBRARY, COPENHAGEN, above BBC HULTON PICTURE LIBRARY; p. 15 above CAMBRIDGE UNIVERSITY COLLECTION copyright reserved, right, TRINITY COLLEGE, DUBLIN; p. 16 BARNABY'S PICTURE LIBRARY; p. 17 above JANET & COLIN BORD, left ROYAL COMMISSION ON THE ANCIENT MONUMENTS OF SCOTLAND, right JOSEPH P. ZIOLO (André Held); p. 18 BBC HULTON PICTURE LIBRARY; p. 19 above A. F. KERSTING, right BRITISH LIBRARY detail from Utrecht Psalter Ms Harl 603; p. 20 BRITISH LIBRARY from Luttrell Psalter Add 42130 fol. 58; p. 21 NATIONAL MONUMENTS RECORD; p. 22 left BRITISH FILM INSTITUTE, centre and right NATIONAL MONUMENTS RECORD; p. 23 above DERBYSHIRE TIMES, below NATIONAL MONUMENTS RECORD; p. 24 EDWIN SMITH; p. 25 PITKIN PICTORIALS LTD (Sydney W. Newbery); p. 26 above JACK HILL, right A. F. KERSTING; p. 27 A. F. KERSTING; p. 28 above BBC HULTON PICTURE LIBRARY, right NATIONAL MONUMENTS RECORD; p. 29 BARNABY'S PICTURE LIBRARY (W. F. Meadows); p. 30 WINCHESTER EXCAVATIONS COMMITTEE; p. 31 above A. F. KERSTING, right EDWIN SMITH, far right NATIONAL MONUMENTS RECORD; p. 32 both RICHARD FOSTER; p. 33 NATIONAL MONUMENTS RECORD; p. 34 A. F. KERSTING; p. 35 BRITISH LIBRARY Royal Ms 14C VII, fol. 8v; p. 36 BBC; p. 37 NATIONAL MONUMENTS RECORD; p. 38 MAURICE H. RIDGWAY & FRED H. CROSSLEY; p. 39 TRUSTEES OF THE PIERPOINT MORGAN LIBRARY Old Test Fr. Ms 638, fol. 3R; p. 40 BBC HULTON PICTURE LIBRARY; p. 41 NATIONAL MONUMENTS RECORD; p. 42 EDWIN SMITH; p. 43 MANSELL COLLECTION; p. 44 AEROFILMS LTD; p. 45 above NATIONAL MONUMENTS RECORD, below A. F. KERSTING; p. 46 NATIONAL MONUMENTS RECORD; p. 47 EDWIN SMITH; p. 48 NATIONAL MONUMENTS RECORD; p. 49 above NATIONAL MONUMENTS RECORD, right REECE WINSTONE; p. 50 EDWIN SMITH; p. 51 top NATIONAL MONUMENTS RECORD, above RICHARD FOSTER; p. 52 EDWIN SMITH; p. 53 above B. T. BATSFORD LTD, right NATIONAL MONUMENTS RECORD; p. 54 top EDWIN SMITH, bottom NATIONAL MONUMENTS RECORD; p. 55 top RICHARD FOSTER, bottom NATIONAL MONUMENTS RECORD; p. 56 EDWIN SMITH; p. 58 above NATIONAL MONUMENTS RECORD, below EDWIN SMITH; p. 59 NATIONAL MONUMENTS RECORD; p. 60 BRITISH LIBRARY Add 39843 fol. 6v; p. 61 NATIONAL MONUMENTS RECORD; p. 63 BRITISH LIBRARY Ms Royal 18D 11, fol. 148; p. 64 BIBLIOTHEQUE NATIONALE, PARIS Ms Français 4276 fol. 6; p. 65 above BRITISH LIBRARY Ms Roy 2A XXII fol. 220, top NATIONAL MONUMENTS RECORD; p. 66 AUSTRIAN NATIONAL LIBRARY Cod. 609 fol. 4r; p. 67 both NATIONAL MONUMENTS RECORD; p. 68 RICHARD FOSTER; p. 71 both BBC HULTON PICTURE LIBRARY; pp. 72–74 EDWIN SMITH; p. 75 BBC; p. 76 PHOTOGRAPHIE GIRAUDON, Bibliotheque des Arts Decorative; from Miracles de Notre-Dame; p. 78 BRITISH LIBRARY Ms Cotton Nero Dl fol. 23v; p. 79 DEAN & CHAPTER OF WESTMINSTER ABBEY; p. 80 BIBLIOTHEQUE NATIONALE, PARIS Ms Fr 19093; p. 81 left PHOTOGRAPHIE GIRAUDON, facsimile from B.N., Ms Fr. 19093, fol. 10, pl. XIX, right SCHOOL OF FINE ARTS, UNIVERSITY OF EAST ANGLIA; p. 82 BRITISH LIBRARY Add 35313, fol. 34r; p. 84 BIBLIOTHEQUE NATIONALE, PARIS Ms Fr. 19093 fol. 20; p. 85 BRITISH LIBRARY Ms Roy. 15 E 11, fol. 265; p. 88 NATIONAL MONUMENTS RECORD; p. 90 JENNIFER FRY; p. 92 BIBLIOTHEQUE NATIONALE, PARIS Ms Fr. 19093, fol. 32; p. 94 NATIONAL MONUMENTS RECORD; pp. 95 & 96 EDWIN SMITH; p. 97 both NATIONAL MONUMENTS RECORD; p. 98 EDWIN SMITH; p. 99 NATIONAL MONUMENTS RECORD; p. 100 above MAURICE H. RIDGWAY and FRED H. CROSSLEY, below BARNABY'S PICTURE LIBRARY (Mustograph); p. 101 NATIONAL MONUMENTS RECORD; p. 102 left DR HENRY TEED, centre JACK HILL, right EDWIN SMITH; p. 103 left JUDY MOORE, centre and right NATIONAL MONUMENTS RECORD; p. 108 NATIONAL MONUMENTS RECORD; p. 109 above BARNABY'S PICTURE LIBRARY (I. Griffiths), right SCHOOL OF FINE ARTS, UNIVERSITY OF EAST ANGLIA (Stella M. Shackle); p. 110 ALEXANDER RAMSAY; p. 111 left EDWIN SMITH, centre A. F. KERSTING, right MAURICE H. RIDGWAY and FRED H. CROSSLEY; p. 112 BARNABY'S PICTURE LIBRARY (W. F. Meadows); p. 113 BBC HULTON PICTURE LIBRARY; p. 114

NATIONAL GALLERY, LONDON; p. 115 MIKE WILLIAMS; p. 116 EDWIN SMITH; p. 118 MAURICE H. RIDGWAY and FRED H. CROSSLEY; p. 119 both B. T. BATSFORD; p. 120 left JOHN A. LONG, centre ALEXANDER RAMSAY, right EDWIN SMITH; p. 121 left and centre EDWIN SMITH, right A. F. KERSTING; p. 123 NATIONAL MONUMENTS RECORD; p. 124 A. F. KERSTING; p. 125 EDWIN SMITH; p. 126 above A. F. KERSTING, above right SCHOOL OF FINE ARTS, UNIVERSITY OF EAST ANGLIA, above far right EDWIN SMITH; p. 127 both PETER WALTERS; p. 128 MAURICE H. RIDGWAY and FRED H. CROSSLEY; p. 131 A. F. KERSTING; p. 132 NATIONAL MONUMENTS RECORD; p. 133 A. F. KERSTING; p. 134 BRITISH LIBRARY, Roy. Ms 16 GV, fol. 73v; p. 135 above DR HENRY TEED, below NATIONAL MONUMENTS RECORD; p. 136 NATIONAL MONUMENTS RECORD; p. 137 BRITISH LIBRARY, Ms Add 24189, fol. 16; p. 139 A. F. KERSTING; p. 145 SCHOOL OF FINE ARTS, UNIVERSITY OF EAST ANGLIA (Stella M. Shackle); p. 146 BODLEIAN LIBRARY, OXFORD, Ms Liturg 41, fol. 147r; pp. 149 & 150 NATIONAL MONUMENTS RECORD; p. 151 EDWIN SMITH; p. 152 RICHARD FOSTER; pp. 154 & 155 brasses from HENRY H. TRIVICK, *The Art and Craft of Monumental Brasses*, pub. by J. Baker, 1969; p. 156 MANSELL COLLECTION; p. 157 BBC; p. 158 EDWIN SMITH; p. 160 both MAURICE H. RIDGWAY and FRED H. CROSSLEY; p. 161 above JOHN A. LONG, above right HOPE STUART; p. 162 EDWIN SMITH; p. 163 RICHARD FOSTER; p. 164 EDWIN SMITH; p. 165 left from HENRY H. TRIVICK, *The Art and Craft of Monumental Brasses*, right BRITISH LIBRARY, Add Ms 42130 fol. 163v; p. 166 BRIAN GAVIGAN; p. 167 NATIONAL MONUMENTS RECORD; p. 169 BBC HULTON PICTURE LIBRARY; p. 170 left B. T. BATSFORD, centre SCHOOL OF FINE ARTS, UNIVERSITY OF EAST ANGLIA (Stella M. Shackle), right NATIONAL MONUMENTS RECORD; p. 171 left EDWIN SMITH, centre DR HENRY TEED, right SCHOOL OF FINE ARTS, UNIVERSITY OF EAST ANGLIA (Stella M. Shackle); p. 172 above A. F. KERSTING, right B. T. BATSFORD LTD; p. 173 above RICHARD FOSTER, above right B. T. BATSFORD; p. 174 B. T. BATSFORD; p. 175 MAURICE H. RIDGWAY and FRED H. CROSSLEY; p. 176 EDWIN SMITH; p. 177 above NATIONAL MONUMENTS RECORD, top MAURICE H. RIDGWAY and FRED H. CROSSLEY; p. 178 above EDWIN SMITH, above right MAURICE H. RIDGWAY and FRED H. CROSSLEY; p. 179 EDWIN SMITH; p. 180 ROY NASH; p. 181 EDWIN SMITH; p. 183 RICHARD FOSTER; p. 184 A. F. KERSTING; p. 185 above EDWIN SMITH, right BARNABY'S PICTURE LIBRARY (W. F. Meadows); p. 186 OXFORDSHIRE COUNTY LIBRARIES; p. 187 J. C. D. SMITH; pp. 188 & 189 above NATIONAL PORTRAIT GALLERY, LONDON, above right SIMON WARNER; p. 191 both MANSELL COLLECTION; p. 193 BBC; p. 194 HOPE STUART; p. 195 ROYAL ACADEMY; p. 196 EDWIN SMITH; p. 197 DEVONSHIRE COLLECTION, CHATSWORTH, Reproduced by Permission of THE TRUSTEES OF THE CHATSWORTH SETTLEMENT; p. 198 Reproduced by Gracious Permission of HER MAJESTY THE QUEEN; pp. 199 & 201 above BRITISH ARCHITECTURAL LIBRARY, RIBA, LONDON, above right BARNABY'S PICTURE LIBRARY (P. D. Barkshire); p. 202 above NATIONAL PORTRAIT GALLERY, LONDON, above right TOWNLEY ART GALLERY, BURNLEY; p. 203 above BRITISH MUSEUM, above right ALEXANDER RAMSAY; p. 204 CLIO, COLCHESTER; p. 205 BBC HULTON PICTURE LIBRARY; p. 206 centre MANSELL COLLECTION, below JOHN FREEMAN LTD; p. 208 THOMAS PHOTOS, OXFORD; p. 210 above BBC HULTON PICTURE LIBRARY, above right A. F. KERSTING, p. 211 above A. F. KERSTING, above right RICHARD FOSTER, p. 212 BODLEIAN LIBRARY, OXFORD, Gough, Maps 44, fol. 31; pp. 213, 214 & 215 above A. F. KERSTING, below RICHARD FOSTER; p. 217 A. F. KERSTING; p. 218 above BARNABY'S PICTURE LIBRARY, above right BRITISH ARCHITECTURAL LIBRARY, RIBA, LONDON; p. 219 above DR HENRY TEED, above right ED BUZIAK; p. 220 EDWIN SMITH; pp. 222 & 223 above NATIONAL MONUMENTS RECORD, below THE 11TH EARL OF AYLESFORD; pp. 224–226 NATIONAL MONUMENTS RECORD; p. 227 above LINE PHOTOGRAPHY, KETTERING, below RICHARD FOSTER; p. 228 above N. V. SALT, right BBC HULTON PICTURE LIBRARY; pp. 231 & 232 BBC HULTON PICTURE LIBRARY; p. 233 BBC HULTON PICTURE LIBRARY; p. 234 RIBA; p. 236 above BBC HULTON PICTURE LIBRARY, right A. F. KERSTING; p. 237 A. F. KERSTING; p. 238 above right GOETHE MUSEUM, FRANKFURT-AM-MAINE, above BRITISH LIBRARY from Designs by Mr R. Bentley for 6 poems by Mr T. Gray, 1753; p. 239 A. F. KERSTING; p. 240 BRITISH ARCHITECTURAL LIBRARY, RIBA, LONDON; p. 241 above and above right A. F. KERSTING, right THE PALACE OF WESTMINSTER; p. 242 both BRITISH ARCHITECTURAL LIBRARY, RIBA, LONDON; p. 244 VICTORIA & ALBERT MUSEUM, LONDON; p. 246 A. F. KERSTING; p. 249 BBC HULTON PICTURE LIBRARY; p. 250 above BANKFIELD MUSEUM, HALIFAX, right LESLIE HORN; pp. 251 & 252 VICTORIA & ALBERT MUSEUM, LONDON; p. 254 RICHARD FOSTER; p. 265 RICHARD FOSTER; p. 266 BBC HULTON PICTURE LIBRARY; p. 270 left and centre NATIONAL MONUMENTS RECORD, right EDWIN SMITH; p. 271 above A. F. KERSTING, below left NATIONAL MONUMENTS RECORD, below right EDWIN SMITH; p. 272 left BARNABY'S PICTURE LIBRARY (Mustograph), right EDWIN SMITH; p. 273 BARNABY'S PICTURE LIBRARY (Mustograph); p. 274 both NATIONAL MONUMENTS RECORD; p. 275 EDWIN SMITH; p. 276 above and below left NATIONAL MONUMENTS RECORD, above right THE DEAN AND CHAPTER LIBRARY, DURHAM; p. 277 left EDWIN SMITH, right BARNABY'S PICTURE LIBRARY (Mustograph); p. 278 above J. C. D. SMITH, below EDWIN SMITH; p. 280 left MAURICE H. RIDGWAY and FRED H. CROSSLEY, centre EDWIN SMITH, right J. C. D. SMITH; p. 281 left THOMAS PHOTOS, OXFORD, centre A. F. KERSTING, right NATIONAL MONUMENTS RECORD; p. 282 all EDWIN SMITH; p. 283 BARNABY'S PICTURE LIBRARY (Mustograph); p. 285 EDWIN SMITH.

COLOUR p. 129 SONIA HALLIDAY; p. 130 AUSTRIAN NATIONAL LIBRARY, VIENNA, Cod 2554, fol. I, v; p. 147 BBC & RICHARD FOSTER; p. 148 JOHN KEELING; p. 229 CLIO, COLCHESTER; p. 230 COUNCIL FOR PLACES OF WORSHIP; p. 247 above HOPE STUART, below GEORGE ARCHBOLD; p. 248 FRANK BENNETT; Front Cover AEROFILMS LTD; Back Cover RICHARD FOSTER.

Acknowledgement is also due to:
MICHAEL ALEXANDER for extracts from his English translations of the Anglo-Saxon poems 'Dream of the Rood' and 'The Ruin'.

JOHN HARVEY for the illustration on page 93 from *Master Builders* published by Thames and Hudson.